Trojan Horse

Death of a Dark Nation

Trojan Horse

DEATH OF A DARK NATION

by Anon

TROJAN HORSE PRESS

Third Edition
First Printing: June 2009
Second Printing March 2010
Third Printing May 2011

Library of Congress Control Number: 2009926944
ISBN: 978-0-9822061-0-2
ISBN: 0-9822061-0-0

Disclaimer for resemblance to real persons

This book includes political satire and works of fiction. Names, characters, places, and incidents are either the product of the authors' imaginations or used fictitiously. Any resemblance to actual persons, living or dead, business establishments, events, or locales is entirely coincidental. The publisher does not have any control over and does not assume any responsibility for any third-party websites or their content.

Printed and bound Manufactured in the United States of America

Trojan Horse Press
PO Box 245
Hazel Crest, IL 60429

email: info@trojanhorse1.com
website: www.trojanhorse1.com

Cover Illustration by P. Evans

Dedication

To our beautiful black women, our mothers, wives, lovers, and best friends.
To our courageous black brothers, wherever you are, fighting for justice.

And a very special dedication to:

Dr. Frances Cress Welsing
Neely Fuller, Jr.
Haki R. Madhubuti
Dr. Yosef Ben-Jochannan
Chancellor Williams
Malcolm X

Acknowledgements

This book could not have been written or completed without the ground-breaking works of Neely Fuller, Jr., Dr. Frances Cress Welsing, Haki R. Madhubuti, Dr. Yosef Ben-Jochannan, John Henrik Clarke, Marcus Garvey, Chancellor Williams, Malcolm X, George Orwell, Tony Brown, Jawanza Kunjufu, Carter G. Woodson, James Baldwin, Willard Motley, and many others too numerous to mention. Naturally, we accept total responsibility for any misinterpretations of their works, and any errors that may appear in this book.

A sincere thanks to E. Wright for her editorial assistance, Nia Lizanna (The Sentencing Project), LaWanda Johnson (The Justice Policy Institute), Robert Jensen (Washington Post), and Donna Lamb and Ida Hakim (Caucasians United for Reparations and Emancipation CURE) for their invaluable help, research, and encouragement. And a very special thanks to H.H., D.H., Wendy Williams, R. Parker, J. Wickett, B. Harris, D.B., K. Richardson, D. Robinson, and all the friends, family, and mentors who shared their special insights and wisdom with us.

We only hope we do justice to all who inspired us to complete our first of many contributions to the fight for universal justice for all the people on God's planet.

Foreword to Readers Outside the US

Because the authors were born and raised in the United States of America, *Trojan Horse: Death of a Dark Nation* was written from our life experiences and perspectives. We fully acknowledge that the same racism/white supremacy dynamic that exists inside the US, also exists in other parts of the world.

Since it is impossible (and undesirable) to describe the experiences of all non-white people under the system of racism/white supremacy, we will not attempt that here.

However, throughout this book, the words "black" and "black people" are sometimes (but not always) interchangeable with "brown," "yellow," and "red" people.

Our experiences as blacks in America will strike a chord with non-white people in every part of the world. We hope our perspectives will encourage others to pursue their own truths and to use that wisdom to fight for justice in their own countries.

About the Authors

Why the authors use a pseudonym

There is nothing original about the ideas presented here. Wiser minds have come before and will certainly come long after this book was written. The authors are not falsely modest; we are acknowledging we did not invent the wheel.

The authors are not seeking fame. This is not an attempt to be mysterious or provoke curiosity. This is not a gimmick or a perverse, reverse publicity ploy. In today's media-obsessed world, there is too much focus on "show" and not enough on "substance." The authors choose not to participate.

The authors reserve the right NOT to be a distraction to the message. We are the least important part of this book. You, the reader, are more important. Even more important, is what you do with this information.

You may not agree with everything or anything written here. We have presented *our* truths to the best of our ability. If this book inspires you to seek your own truths, the book has been a success.

The Purpose of this Book

Why does this book focus almost entirely on Racism/White Supremacy? Because Racism/White Supremacy is responsible for the vast majority of human suffering on the planet, whether it is global poverty, starvation, oppression, imperialism, colonialism, slavery, man-made diseases, displacement, racism, wars, and genocide, particularly among people of color.

We believe that those individuals and groups who oppose the God-given rights of all the non-white people on earth, and who allow themselves to benefit from a system of injustice (racism/white supremacy), must be held accountable for their actions and beliefs.

At the risk of offending some readers, we will not waste any time being politically correct. However, we have done our best to be fair, to tell the truth, and be correct in what we understand and know to be true.

That being said, this book was not written to provoke racial animosity, dislike, or hatred of whites. We do not oppose the rights, dignity, or freedoms of any people. Nor was this book written to elevate blacks or to make excuses for Black America's current dilemma.

Every word in this book was designed to inform, decrease confusion, provoke discussion, and promote the kind of constructive action necessary to replace the system of Racism/White Supremacy with a system of universal justice for all the people on the planet.

We hope you will read this book with an open, inquiring mind. Thank you for allowing us to share our insights (and possible solutions) with you.

The Authors

Contents

Part I - 13 Weapons of Mass Mind Destruction

Important Note to Readers

In the interest of keeping down the cost of printing and the cost to our readers, we have included the links to the sources we used in this book on our website: www.trojanhorse1.com under "Links & Sources," by page number. Click on the link to go to the sources.

PART ONE

13 WEAPONS OF MASS MIND DESTRUCTION

Trojan Horse: Death Of A Dark Nation

"Outside the battle-weary gates of the Dark Nation sat a steed of monstrous height: the Trojan Horse. In its hollow inside, 13 Weapons of Mass Mind Destruction hide.

Then shall the War's signal be given by the battle cry, 'Come forth the Horse!' and slaughter the unsuspecting fathers, sons, mothers, and daughters of the Dark Nation."

"Do not trust the Horse, Black Trojans! Within its hollow belly hide, the number 13 lurks inside! Whatever it is, I fear our enemies bring death disguised as gifts!" - Umoja

Introduction

What is a Trojan Horse?

According to Webster's dictionary, a Trojan Horse is *"a subversive group OR device placed within enemy ranks that is designed to have destructive effects."* The story of the Trojan Horse began with Greek mythology and the clever scheme by the wily Greek hero, Odysseus, to defeat the city of Troy:

Legend of the Trojan Horse

After a ten-year war between the Trojans and the Greeks, the Greeks devised an ingenious plan to defeat the city of Troy. Odysseus instructed the Greeks to build a giant, hollow, wooden horse on a wheeled platform, and to leave it outside the well-guarded gates of the city of Troy.

The Greek army boarded their ships and pretended to sail away. The Trojans assumed that the huge horse was a parting gift from the departing Greeks, signaling that the long war was finally over.

The unsuspecting Trojans opened the gates and pulled the horse inside, unaware that hidden inside the hollow belly of the horse, were dozens of heavily-armed Greek soldiers. The Trojans celebrated their premature victory with wine, food, and song.

The Greek soldiers waited until nightfall before they slipped out of the trap door built into one side of the horse. They killed the gatekeepers, opened the city gates, and let the rest of the waiting Greek Army inside. The Greeks overpowered the drunken and unsuspecting Trojans and finally defeated the city of Troy.

How did the Greeks defeat the Trojans?

The Trojans were not defeated because the Greeks had a superior army; they were defeated for *lack of knowledge*. Because the Trojans were ***unaware*** of the armed soldiers hiding inside the "gift" of a Trojan Horse, they could not ***beware***. Had the Trojans known the ***three fundamental rules of warfare***, they would not have been so easily deceived -- or defeated:

1. An enemy never rewards their enemies; they destroy them – when the time is right.
2. An enemy (the Greeks) that announces its premature defeat will soon be celebrating victory.
3. A nation or people (Trojans) at war, that fails to heed the signs of war, will lose the war by default.

What is the Dark Nation?

The "Dark Nation" does not refer to skin color or pigmentation; it refers to the "darkened" state of mind of a people who lack knowledge of self and knowledge of their enemies.

The Dark Nation -- Like The Trojans -- Failed To Heed The Three Fundamental Rules Of Warfare

1. An enemy never rewards their enemies; they destroy them – when the time is right.
2. An enemy that announces its premature defeat will soon be celebrating victory.
3. A nation (or people) at war, that fails to heed the signs of war, will lose the war by default.

The last stages of the **Trojan War against the Dark Nation** are being fought as these words are being written. The revolution will NOT be televised, but the war's casualties can be seen on every television station in the nation. The **Dark Nation** is reeling from the deadliest Trojan War in human history, yet most of its people do not understand (or accept) one undeniable fact:

WE ARE AT WAR

The last Trojan War will not be fought with guns and bullets. It must be fought with the most powerful weapon we possess: ***information.***

Once our darkened minds are illuminated with knowledge of self, and of our enemies, the **13 WEAPONS OF MASS MIND DESTRUCTION HIDDEN INSIDE THE TROJAN HORSE WILL BE NEUTRALIZED.** The Dark Nation will cease to exist, and a New Nation will be born.

"If you know the enemy and know yourself, you need not fear the result of a hundred battles." – Sun Tzu, Art of War

"I will say then that I am not, nor ever have been in favor of bringing about in anyway the social and political equality of the white and black races - that I am not nor ever have been in favor of making voters or jurors of negroes, nor of qualifying them to hold office, nor to intermarry with white people; and I will say in addition to this, that there is a physical difference between the white and black races which I believe will forever forbid the two races living together on terms of social and political equality.

And inasmuch as they cannot so live, while they do remain together there must be the position of superior and inferior, and I as much as any other man am in favor of having the superior position assigned to the white race. I say upon this occasion I do not perceive that because the white man is to have the superior position the negro should be denied everything."

-- Abraham Lincoln
(1809 - 1865)

WEÂPON #1

RÂCISM/ WHITE SUPREMÂCY

(FOUNDÂTION)

"If you do not understand White Supremacy (Racism), what it is, and how it works, everything else that you understand, will only confuse you."

Neely Fuller, Jr. (1971)

CHAPTER ONE

WHAT IS RACISM/WHITE SUPREMACY?

"Racism is white supremacy. White supremacy is racism. There is no other form." -- Neely Fuller, Jr.

Let's Begin At The Beginning By Defining The Words:

1. **White Supremacy** -- a social, economic, and political system based on the belief that whites are superior to non-whites. (the Foundation).
2. **Racism** -- the systematic discrimination (the denial of rights and benefits) by whites against non-whites in all areas of human activity: (1) economics, (2) education, (3) entertainment, (4) labor, (5) law, (6) politics, (7) religion, (8) sex, and (9) war. (the Behavior).

Q: Why is it called "Racism/White Supremacy?"
A: Because this describes exactly WHO is practicing racism. For one group to practice racism that group must have MORE POWER than another group. Since whites control **ALL** the major areas of human activity in America -- housing, education, health, entertainment, economics, politics, law, and religion -- it is accurate to define all "**racism**" as **"white supremacy."** We must be accurate so the victims of racism do not become confused.

Q: Isn't all racism the same, regardless of who is practicing it?
A: There is only ONE kind of racism: **white supremacy**. White people are the only group in America with the POWER to discriminate (deprive or punish other ethnic groups), and the systems and institutions to maintain the imbalance of power.

For example, rich people are more powerful than poor people. Rich people have the POWER to discriminate against poor people by depriving them of income, promotions, jobs, housing, land, justice, and any other rights – if they choose to do so.

In America, whites have the POWER to discriminate against blacks (and other non-whites) by depriving them of income, promotions, jobs, housing, land, justice, and any other rights – if they choose to do so. It doesn't matter that some whites are poorer than some blacks.

In all things and in all places in America, whites are **collectively** more powerful than blacks are **collectively**. This imbalance of (white) power creates the opportunity and the ability to practice racism against non-whites.

Racism is not empty rhetoric (words) or mindless emotion. Racism is economic, political, institutional, and systematic POWER. Since whites control all the institutions and systems of power in America, only whites have the power to practice racism.

Q: Why are people referred to as "groups" instead of "races?"
A: Because there is ONLY ONE RACE: ***the white race.*** To prove this statement, let's look at the TRUE meaning of "race." In ancient civilizations tens of thousands of years ago (before Europeans inhabited the planet), the world's people identified themselves by bloodline, birthplace, and culture – but NEVER by the artificial construct (concept) of "race."

What is the "black race" in real terms? It does NOT describe the place where black people were born because there is no such place as "black land," (or red, yellow, brown, or white land). Race does not describe a person's religion because there is no such thing as a black, red, brown, yellow, or white religion.

Race does not describe a person's culture (except in false, stereotypical terms), and it does NOT define biology, ethnicity, or nationality. Race does not describe skin color because the so-called "black race" includes people whose complexions range from the palest pink to the purest blue-black. Therefore, "race" is a false, manmade concept.

Q: If "race" is a false concept, why was it created?
A: Race was created for ONLY one purpose: ***to practice race-ism (racism).*** To practice "racism," whites had to separate themselves from other groups of people by artificially creating different "races."

Q: Why was "racism/white supremacy" created?
A: Dr. Frances Cress Welsing, a black psychiatrist and the author of *'The Isis Papers: The Keys to the Colors'* (1991), states that White Supremacy is practiced by the global "white" minority on the conscious and unconscious level to ensure their genetic survival by any means necessary.

Because of their "numerical inadequacy," whites may have defensively developed *"an uncontrollable sense of hostility and aggression" towards people of color, and developed a social, political, and economic structure to give blacks and other non-whites the appearance of being inferior."*

Q: Who decides what "race" a person will be?
A: The same (white) people who created the concept of race. If the ONLY purpose of "race" is to practice racism, and whites are the only group or "race" (in a white supremacy system) that can practice racism, then it is logical to assume there is ONLY ONE RACE: ***the white race.***

Q: If the white race is the only race, what are the other 'groups' called?
A: There are three types of people in a white supremacist system:

1. Non-white people
2. White people (Racist Suspects)
3. White Supremacists (Racists)

Q: What is a "Non-White" person?
A: Anyone who is NOT classified as "white." This includes all black, red, yellow, and brown people aka "people of color."

Q: What is a "Racist Suspect?"
A: ANY white person who is CAPABLE of practicing racism against non-whites. Since all whites are able to practice racism in a white supremacy system if they choose to do so, it is correct (and logical) to use the term "racist suspects" to identify whites who do not openly function as white supremacists (racists). This is not a hateful, unjust, or racist statement, but it is a **logical statement**.

Q: What is a "White Supremacist?"
A: A white person (a racist) who practices racism against non-whites. Being a white supremacist has nothing to do with income, title, or status. It does not mean a white person belongs to the KKK, the Aryan Nation, or is covered with Nazi tattoos.

A white supremacist can be a soccer mom, a businessman, or a US Senator if they are practicing racism against non-whites. Another term for a white supremacist is "racist white man" and "racist white woman."

Q: How can a non-white person determine if a white person is a racist?
A: Non-whites cannot always determine who is a racist, and who is not, because it is impossible to monitor (or judge) all the individual actions and words of any white person at all times. To illustrate this point:

Case Of The Stolen Wallet

There are five people in a room when a wallet that belongs to a sixth person (who is not in the room) is stolen. All five are "suspects" because every person in the room had the ability and the opportunity to take the wallet. This does not mean all five are thieves NOR does it mean all five are not thieves, because any of them could have stolen something at an earlier time.

As it turns out, two of the five people in the room CONSPIRED to steal the wallet by breaking into the sixth person's locker. The other three saw it happen, did not participate in the crime, did not care that the wallet was stolen, and did and said nothing to stop it from happening.

The sixth person – the owner of the wallet -- has no idea who stole it, if anyone saw what happened, or how many participated in the theft. All he knows is has been the VICTIM of a crime because his wallet is missing.

The two people who stole the wallet are guilty of "commission" – they actually **committed the crime**. The three witnesses are guilty of "omission" since they **witnessed the crime, said nothing and did nothing to stop it, and refused to help the victim with the information they had.**

The next day the two thieves treat the three witnesses to lunch, paying for it with the money from the stolen wallet. The witnesses did not steal the wallet but are knowingly or unknowingly benefiting from the theft.

The three witnesses are not **legally liable**, but they are **morally liable,** and are correctly viewed as **"suspects" by the victim.**

Racism operates the same way. There are whites who:

- are practicing racism against non-whites at a particular moment
- are not practicing racism at that moment but have practiced it at a previous time, or will practice it at a later time
- are not practicing racism at that moment, but say and do nothing to stop those who are
- are not practicing racism at that moment, but have no problem with other whites practicing racism (don't care)
- are benefiting from the crime of racism even if they are not practicing racism at that moment
- refuse to tell WHO is practicing racism; HOW racism is being practiced; and refuse to help the victims with the information they have
- oppose racism by exposing and opposing whites who practice it

Another Example:

Mr. X, a black management trainee, is looking for an apartment closer to his new job. He calls an upscale rental complex near his office, and asks if they have any one-bedroom apartments. The rental agent, a young white male, says there are two one-bedroom apartments available, takes Mr. X's name and phone number, and asks him to stop by and fill out an application.

The next day Mr. X stops by the complex after work. A different rental agent, Mrs. W, a middle-aged white female, greets him in the reception area. She says she's sorry, but there are no apartments available.

She suggests he fill out an application so they will have his information on file, and promises Mr. X that he will be the first one she calls when a one-bedroom becomes available.

Mr. X is immediately suspicious, but he fills out an application anyway. On his way home, he replays the conversation with the rental agent. Mr. X has no way of knowing if the first rental agent made an honest mistake, or if he has just been a victim of racial discrimination. His gut tells him it was the latter.

The Crime

When Mrs. W saw Mr. X was black, she used the same line she always used with black applicants. Later, she warns the new rental agent -- who talked to Mr. X over the phone – to never rent to blacks or Hispanics.

The Victim

Like the man whose wallet was stolen, Mr. X is the victim of a crime. The problem is, Mr. X can't be sure a crime was even committed, which makes it more difficult for him to protect himself from being victimized in the future.

It is this kind of confusion that wreaks the most psychological damage on black people who run a DAILY risk of being victimized by racism – without being able to prove they were victimized.

The Criminals

Mrs. W is guilty of commission (practicing racism). The new rental agent is guilty of omission because he said and did nothing, and refused to help Mr. X with the information he had (that another white person, Mrs. W, was practicing racism).

It is the ***crime of commission AND omission*** that allows the system of racism/white supremacy to function so effectively. The system does not require all whites to practice racism at all times, but it does require that **the majority of whites say and do nothing when racism is occurring and allow themselves to benefit from the victimization of non-whites.**

Those benefits include better jobs, housing, food, medical care, education, police protection, justice, etc., than non-whites. If the majority of whites were opposed to racism/white supremacy, it would NOT be the most powerful social, economic, and political system on the planet.

It is LOGICAL to assume that the majority (or possibly all) white people have made a DELIBERATE DECISION to do one or all of the following:

- practice racism
- do nothing and say nothing to stop others from practicing racism
- deny racism is being practiced even when they know it is happening
- refuse to help the victims of racism with the information they have

That's why simple-minded thinking is useless when determining which white person is a racist and which one is not. It cannot be determined by a white person's sexual behavior. White slave owners had sexual relations with male and female slaves but they were still white supremacists (racists).

Whites have engaged in sexual relations with black people, but that doesn't mean they are not racists. Whites who have black friends, wives, husbands, or children are still "racist" if they are practicing racism against non-whites.

It cannot be determined by observing the words or the actions of a particular white person, who may or may not be practicing racism at that particular time. It cannot be determined by a random (or deliberate) act or acts of kindness toward a non-white person. Mass child-murderer John Gacy was "kind" to children when he performed in his clown costume. There were slave-owners who were "kind" to their slaves, but not kind enough to stop selling human beings.

AXIOM #1: YOU CANNOT OPPOSE SOMETHING AND KNOWINGLY BENEFIT FROM IT AT THE SAME TIME.

It is LOGICAL in a white supremacist society to assume the **majority of whites** are either practicing racism (the act of commission), or are cooperating with those who are, by saying and doing nothing to stop them, refusing to help the victims of racism with the information they have (the act of omission), and are ***benefiting*** from the practice of racism.

Q: Do non-racist whites benefit from White Supremacy?

A: ALL white people benefit from white privilege in a white supremacy system, even if they are not practicing racism at that moment. It does not matter if they rich or poor; or whether they admit there is such a thing as white privilege.

Anyone who is classified as "white" in a white supremacy system will always have advantages over someone who is not. Just as a black person in a black supremacy system (if one existed) would have advantages over someone who is not black.

Q: Aren't some white people opposed to racism?
A: Only if they are saying and doing something to oppose it. For example, John Brown, a white male, encouraged armed insurrection by slaves as a means to end slavery, and as a result, was charged with treason and hanged. However, that does not mean John Brown did not practice racism at an earlier time OR would not have practiced it at a later time had he lived.

Q: What about the white anti-racist activists who speak out against about racism? Aren't they opposed to white supremacy?
A: The self-annointed, white anti-racist activists offer little more than LIP SERVICE. They sacrifice NOTHING, take NO risks, and reap MORE financial rewards than the black activists fighting in the (real) trenches.

The white anti-racist actually creates MORE confusion by creating the FALSE illusion that the devastated black masses can be liberated from racism by sitting in an auditorium or conference room, listening to a white person making anti-racism speeches (while STILL enjoying their white privileges).

It is UNLIKELY that the same white anti-racist activists who PROFIT from writing books and giving speeches about racism -- have any real desire (or intent) to destroy the same white supremacy system that allows them to oppose it without losing a single 'white privilege. There may be whites who SINCERELY want to replace the system of white supremacy with a system of justice, but ***that number is so statistically small, it is insignificant***.

Q: When blacks mistreat whites, isn't that "racism/black supremacy?"
A: No, because black supremacy does not exist. If black people were collectively more powerful than whites collectively, blacks would have the power to practice racism. Logically speaking, that would mean the end of white supremacy.

AXIOM #2: BLACK SUPREMACY CAN EXIST ONLY IN THE TOTAL ABSENCE OF WHITE SUPREMACY. WHITE SUPREMACY CAN EXIST ONLY IN THE TOTAL ABSENCE OF BLACK SUPREMACY. THE TEXTBOOK DEFINITION OF "SUPREMACY" IS:

THE HIGHEST RANK OR AUTHORITY.

THIS MEANS ONLY ONE THING CAN BE "SUPREME" OR OCCUPY THE "HIGHEST RANK" AT A TIME.

If blacks and whites had equal power and resources, there could be no black supremacy OR white supremacy. Our ability (power) to discriminate against (mistreat) each other would be cancelled out, leaving only two options: ***coexist peacefully or destroy each other.***

Chapter Two

BLACK POWER IN A WHITE SUPREMACY SYSTEM

"What about black people who believe in 'black supremacy?' You can believe in something like a prisoner believes in being the warden, or thinks he or she is the warden, but that doesn't make it true. There's a difference between being in a position and aspiring to be in a position." -- Neely Fuller, Jr.

Q: Aren't "black supremacy" groups like the Nation of Islam racist toward white people?

A: The Nation of Islam is a religious organization, not a black supremacy group. Even if its members so desired, the Nation of Islam cannot be a "black supremacy" organization because "black supremacy" cannot exist at the same place and same time as "white supremacy."

The Nation of Islam cannot be a "racist" organization because it does NOT have the ability or a history of interfering with the rights of white people, or dictating where whites can live, work, shop, play, learn, or teach.

The Nation of Islam does not advocate harming or killing white people. To the authors' knowledge, no white person has ever been attacked, murdered, denied housing, a job, a fair trial, an education, a law license, or any rights by the Nation of Islam, or under the banner of black supremacy.

In fact, every so-called "black supremacist" organization in America was created ***in self-defense*** to white racism. To compare the KKK to any black group is the same as comparing the bully to the person being bullied, who eventually fights back, then calling BOTH of them bullies.

Q: Are you saying blacks cannot be racist toward whites?

A: That's correct. Of course, all people can be hateful or prejudiced. Those terms describe individual behaviors, not systematic power. Racism is the COLLECTIVE behaviors of a group. A white individual within a system of racism/white supremacy has the implicit or explicit support of that system IF they choose to practice racism.

If a poor man robs a rich man at gunpoint that doesn't mean the poor man is more powerful (economically and politically) than the rich man. The poor man is an individual who committed a crime of opportunity. There are no powerful institutions or systems that support his right to rob the rich man, but there are institutions and systems that allow the rich man to rob the poor man – which is why he doesn't need a gun to do it.

A black person who mistreats a white person doesn't mean black people are more powerful (economically and politically) than white people. Never confuse the actions of a black individual (or a group of black individuals) that mistreats someone white as proof that black racism exists. Their "power" is limited ONLY to what they can do as individuals. There are NO black institutions or systems that support, defend, or finance the right of blacks to mistreat whites.

There are NO black individuals or black organizations that have the power to strip whites of their collective right to live where they want, work where they want, get an education wherever they want, or control what white people do collectively in ANY area of human activity. There are NO black institutions that are more powerful than white institutions. Therefore, blacks do not have the COLLECTIVE POWER to diminish the quality of life for the white collective.

Q: What is collective power?
A: Collective power is the institutions and systems that benefit one group at the expense of another group, and allow one group to dominate another group in all areas of human activity.

For example, when a white policeman shoots an unarmed black man (50 times), his fellow officers, the police chief, internal affairs, the union, the media, the prosecutor, the judge, and the jury will support, defend, and finance that white police officer's "right" to shoot (murder) an unarmed black person. That is ***white collective power***.

It is rare for a white police officer to be punished for using excessive force against a black man, woman, or child. It is just as rare for a black police officer to use excessive force against a white person.

In fact, the authors were unable to find a single instance of a black police officer shooting or killing an unarmed white person in the history of modern law enforcement. This is not surprising but it is absolute proof that the black individual operating within a system of white supremacy cannot mistreat whites even if he or she is wearing a uniform, a badge, and carrying a gun.

Another example of white collective power is the mortgage and real estate industry, which systematically discriminates against black (and non-white) renters, homebuyers, and homeowners by:

- **Red-lining** – denying home loans to minority geographical areas.
- **Reverse red-lining** -- targeting minority areas for fraudulent sub-prime home loans that are designed to self-destruct.
- **Inflating home appraisals** in racially changing neighborhoods to defraud (overcharge) minority homebuyers.
- **Low-balling appraisals** in minority areas to reduce home equity.
- **Refusing to rent or sell** to minorities in certain geographical areas.
- **Raising property taxes in minority areas** to drive minority residents out of desirable inner-city neighborhoods. (gentrification)
- **Exclusion from special financing deals** that are not generally known to the public, and are only offered to a select group of white buyers.

Banks, real estate brokers, appraisers, and mortgage lenders represent INSTITUTIONAL RACISM (power) that is reinforced by the courts, banking, and government (systems).

This does not mean blacks are less likely to abuse power than whites if given the opportunity. It means blacks cannot abuse power that does not exist. The proof: there is no place in America where blacks are collectively practicing racism against whites collectively.

Q: Don't black politicians and corporate executives represent black power?

A: Not necessarily. Having a powerful position does not make a person powerful. For example, shortly after a female employee sued the XYZ firm for sex discrimination, Ms. X and Mrs. Y are appointed to the corporate board. They will be used as proof in the upcoming trial that the XYZ firm does not discriminate against women.

Like most token board members, Ms. X and Mrs. Y are benchwarmers; not policy makers. Their "powerful" positions are an ILLUSION designed to deceive the public and the courts. The black man or woman in a (public) position of power often serves the same purpose: to give the appearance that certain companies do not discriminate.

These blacks may be qualified for their position; however, even the "powerful" black person – regardless of title -- is still controlled by more powerful whites who limit whatever authority or power this black individual possesses.

Q: If a powerful black person mistreats a less powerful white person, isn't he or she practicing black racism?

A: A black person whose power comes from a white institution will not be allowed to mistreat whites – unless he or she is following orders from more powerful whites. In a system of white supremacy, all whites are more powerful than blacks.

A white supremacy system by its very NATURE forbids ALL non-white people – regardless of wealth, status, or position – from victimizing white people. Of course, a powerful black person can – as an individual – harm a white individual. For example, it was well known that OJ Simpson physically abused his white ex-wife, Nicole, but that abuse was limited to what he was able to do as an individual.

Powerful blacks present no danger to the white collective but they can be extremely dangerous to other blacks. They are often rewarded for victimizing black people (doing the dirty work), and are usually following orders from more powerful whites behind the scenes.

If they are not following direct orders, they will abuse other blacks: (1) for profit or career advancement; (2) out of fear of losing status or income; (3) out of fear of being lumped with the "inferior" black masses; (4) because of self-hatred issues, which they project onto other blacks; or (5) out of frustration because they have no real power (over whites).

Even the most "powerful" blacks in America cannot practice black racism because it does not exist. Nor can they be black supremacists because black supremacy cannot co-exist within a system of white supremacy. They cannot practice white racism because they are not white. They cannot be racists of any kind; but are knowingly OR unknowingly agents (extensions) of the white supremacist system. If anyone disagrees with this premise and believes that blacks can be racist, he or she should be able to answer the following question:

Name one thing that black people – *as a group* -- have stopped white people – *as a group* -- from doing that they had a RIGHT to do? For example, denying them the right to work, own a home, live in a certain area, get a fair trial, an education, or use any public facility.

Affirmative action is not a correct response. Affirmative action is NOT black racism. Black people did not create affirmative action, the terminology, or the where, when, and how it becomes a policy in Corporate America. Blacks do NOT have the power to implement any just or unjust policies at any white college or university. Whites control, name, legislate, and decide everything that happens within America's institutions of power – including black institutions.

If it can be documented (proven) that black people are COLLECTIVELY mistreating white people COLLECTIVELY in the United States, someone should write a book about it. The truth should be made public, even if it contradicts what is written here. Any corrections would be greatly appreciated in the interest of being as accurate as possible.

Q: What about rich black entertainers and athletes? They don't work for Corporate America. Isn't that "black power"?
A: All black entertainers work for Corporate America in one fashion or another. Corporate America controls everything that happens in the entertainment industry; whether it's the movie, music, television, radio, news, advertising, publishing, or sports industry.

It is impossible to be a successful black (or white) entertainer if you do not have access to movie theaters, chain music and bookstores, comedy clubs, stadiums, ballparks, cable, radio, magazine, and television.

The corporations that control the airwaves, athletic arenas, retail stores, networks, movie, and television studios, distributors, and advertisers are more powerful than all the black entertainers combined.

Money is NOT synonymous with power. Power is NOT a paycheck; even a forty-million-dollar one. The person with the most power is the one who SIGNS THE CHECK. For every black person who is paid in the millions, there are whites behind the scenes making BILLIONS.

Q: If money isn't power, what is power?
A: Power is self-evident. **Power** answers to no one other than God, himself. Power is the ability to determine the status quo and who sits at the top of the pecking order. **Power** is the ability to determine what is news and what is not.

Power is controlling the financial, political, and educational institutions so *you and your kind* benefit. **Power** is the ability to CONTROL your own images and the images of those who are less powerful than you are. **Power** is the ability to determine WHO goes to jail, for what crime, and for how long. **Power** is the ability to VOTE in an election and STILL HAVE THAT VOTE COUNTED.

Power is other people coming to you to get what they need and you deciding how much they get. Power is the ability to feed yourself without depending on others. **Power** is the ability to generate and produce what you need to survive -- which includes your own infrastructure and necessities: electricity, gasoline, water, housing, food, clothing, weapons, schools, universities, currency, banking, and hospitals – without depending on others for your survival.

Power is the ability to decide what your currency looks like; how much it is worth; and how much it buys; whether it is a gallon of milk or a gallon of gas. **Power** is the ability to determine who lives where, how many of them can live there, and how long they can stay there.

Power is the ability to move populations, and to determine what part of what city will be black and what part will be white. **Power** is the ability to own land that no one can take from you, even with eminent domain, because YOU make the laws. **Power** is the ability to punish a police officer for shooting an unarmed man 41 times. **Power** is the ability to rescue people from rooftops after a hurricane in *less than four days*, and to make sure a "Katrina" never happens in the first place.

Not ONE black politician, poet, activist, entertainer, corporate board member, CEO, businessperson, millionaire, or billionaire had the juice (power) to pick up a phone, call the White House, and get ONE black person off the roof after Katrina struck.

Power Is NOT...

...a Mercedes or a Jaguar, a dozen rental properties, a good job in a Fortune 500 corporation, a dozen college degrees, or a Pulitzer Prize. It is not being the biggest rap star or black movie star with the most crossover appeal. It is not owning the biggest house on the block when the bank still holds the mortgage; the taxing authority can seize it for unpaid taxes; and the government can take the land it sits on by declaring eminent domain. It is NOT owning a black business when the business relies on white suppliers, bankers, dealers, distributors, contracts, and advertising dollars.

This is not intended to demean or diminish the accomplishments of so many distinguished, successful, and talented black people, but it is **time to be honest about our situation.** We cannot afford to keep telling ourselves that the only color "the (powerful) white man" cares about is the color "green." **If that were true, "white supremacy" would be called "green supremacy."**

AXIOM #3: IN A SYSTEM OF WHITE SUPREMACY, SKIN COLOR ALWAYS TRIUMPHS OVER CASH (GREEN SUPREMACY).

Skin color is as fundamental to racism/white supremacy, as reading is to education. There is short-term rich and long-term wealth, and the white supremacists know the difference. They are long-range strategists who know it is wiser (and more profitable) to pay millions to a handful of blacks in sports, entertainment, and business than to allow blacks to accumulate the tools and capital to generate our own billions.

Q: If blacks are not inferior to whites, why are blacks in such an inferior position, not just in America, but all over the world?

A: There is no way to do justice to such a complex, profound question in one book NOR do the authors pretend to have all the answers. In the Resource Section of this book (page 323) is a list of authors who have written excellent books on Africa before and after European colonization. Historical documents and artifacts prove (without a doubt) that Africans were once the most powerful people on the planet, and that all intellectual human endeavors -- the arts, sciences, writing, astronomy, medicine, architecture, and the world's first universities – ***began in Africa.***

Do not mistake the present condition of African people as proof of black inferiority. What is happening on the African continent -- widespread starvation, tribal warfare, political chaos, AIDS, or crushing international debt – is the by-product of European imperialism and white supremacy.

John Perkins, author of the controversial bestseller, *Confessions of an Economic Hitman,* explained how third-world economies were deliberately undermined to gain control of their natural resources and UN votes. Perkins describes in chilling detail, the two primary objectives of an Economic Hit Man:

1. Make huge loans to third-world countries and funnel the money back to US engineering companies in exchange for construction projects that are (deliberately) never completed.
2. Without the promised infrastructures to modernize their countries, the huge international loans go into default, bankrupt their economies, forcing these third-world nations to turn over control of their natural resources and UN votes to their US "creditors."

These third-world nations were robbed of their ability to eliminate poverty, educate their people, provide a higher standard of living, and were also deliberately excluded from the technology and information-sharing that occurred freely between non-third-world nations. The conditions in third-world nations have nothing to do with inferiority, **but everything to do with skin color and white supremacy**.

What Ancient Africans And White Supremacists Have In Common

All great civilizations are destroyed from within, not from without. The seeds of destruction are built into the system of white supremacy because **the system is built on corruption, cruelty, racism, and injustice**. If the white supremacists do not learn from the history of ancient rulers who once wielded supreme power and misused it, they are doomed to repeat it.

CHAPTER THREE

WHITE PRIVILEGE

"At least I ain't a nigger!" -- Michael Richards (Seinfeld's "Kramer") taunting blacks in audience at a L.A. comedy club. (2006)

It was a revealing comment from Michael Richards, who later claimed he was not a racist. However, when Richards used his "skin color rank" as the ultimate weapon to beat down his non-white opponents, he *knew* he had something that black people (niggers) will *never* have in America – regardless of wealth, position, or title: **white privilege**.

What is "white privilege?" Let's defer to an expert on the subject: a white person

"The whole idea is to grapple with the difficult issue of racism by looking at it from a fresh viewpoint - the viewpoint of what I, as a white person, am given, unearned, simply because of the color of my skin in contrast to what other people are deprived of unfairly because of the color of theirs." – Donna Lamb, Communications Director for Caucasians United for Reparations and Emancipation (CURE), a white organization that supports reparations for descendants of slaves.

In his 1935 book, "**Black Reconstruction in America,**" W. E. B. DuBois first described the "psychological wages" of whiteness:

"It must be remembered that the white group of laborers, while they received a low wage, were compensated in part by a sort of public and psychological wage.

They were given public deference and titles of courtesy because they were white. They were admitted freely with all classes of white people to public functions, public parks, and the best schools.

The police were drawn from their ranks, and the courts, dependent on their votes, treated them with such leniency as to encourage lawlessness. Their vote selected public officials, and while this had small effect upon the economic situation, it had great effect upon their personal treatment and the deference shown them.

White schoolhouses were the best in the community, and conspicuously placed, and they cost anywhere from twice to ten times as much per capita as the colored schools. The newspapers specialized in news that flattered the poor whites and almost utterly ignored the Negro except in crime and ridicule.

74 Years Later And Not Much Has Changed

While (some) whites deny the existence of white privilege, their flimsy denials quickly evaporate whenever they are engaged in a conflict or competition with a non-white person. The belief that a white person should (always) triumph over a non-white person, usually surfaces when:

1. A black person is hired or promoted over a white person.
2. A black person is more affluent than a white person (unless the black person is an entertainer or athlete).
3. A white authority figure takes a black person's word over a white person's.
4. A black authority figure attempts to dominate them.
5. A black person beats the (white) system (OJ Simpson verdict).
6. A white person is treated (or mistreated) in a way usually reserved for black people.

Suddenly, all is not right with the (white) world. Either there's an assumption that the black person did something illegal or unethical to be in a "superior" position over a white person, or there is a blatant refusal to acknowledge the superior position of a black person.

"A white salesman rings my doorbell and asks to speak to the homeowner. I'm standing there in a pair of old shorts and house slippers. Do I look like a damn butler? I knew right then what time it was. I decided, no matter what this white man was selling, even if he was giving it away for free, he wasn't stepping one foot inside my house." – A black, fifty-something attorney from an affluent suburb of Virginia.

This is a common experience for many affluent blacks. A black person who drives a luxury car or lives in an expensive home is often perceived by (some) whites of obtaining them through immoral or illegal means, such as welfare fraud or drug dealing. The assumption is: *"How can this black person afford something that I – as a white person – cannot afford?"*

This perception is based on the fear of losing something (white privilege) that most whites deny even exists. White privilege also surfaces in the workplace whenever a white employee is told to perform a menial task that is usually reserved for black employees:

"You ain't working me like a nigger." -- A white male employee said after his supervisor told him to move some heavy boxes.

Black students attending predominantly white colleges and universities are regularly regarded with suspicion and scorn. The assumption on the part of (some)white students and faculty is: *"This unqualified black is here because of reverse discrimination policies that penalized a more qualified white applicant who really deserved this spot."*

Even when the educational or financial backgrounds of these black students is unknown (they usually aren't), the negative stereotypes persist. After graduation, the degrees of black graduates are routinely dismissed as "dumbed-down affirmative-action degrees," or "affirmative-action things."

In the minds of (some) whites, blacks have not earned whatever they have; do not deserve whatever they get; and wouldn't have anything at all had it not been for the (misguided) generosity of whites. Some have gone as far as stating that blacks should be grateful they were "rescued from the jungle" and enslaved for 400 years so they could live in the greatest country on earth.

"America has been the best country on earth for black folks. It was here that 600,000 black people, brought from Africa in slave ships, grew into a community of 40 million, were introduced to Christian salvation, and reached the greatest levels of freedom and prosperity blacks have ever known." -- Pat Buchanan: "Slavery Best Thing Ever to Happen to Blacks"

The obvious (and false) assumption is that America would still be the same great country even WITHOUT our 400 years of free labor, ingenuity, inventions (which helped to modernize the country), literature, art, music, science, and medicine. Perhaps, black people should be thanked for "rescuing" white America from an almost certain, mediocre, colorless, and less prosperous existence.

"Mr. Trump, it's not 'The Apprenti, it's 'The Apprentice.'"

In December 2005, Dr. Randall Pinkett became the first black person to win first place in Donald Trump's *"The Apprentice"* reality TV show. Dr. Pinkett was the only Rhodes Scholar 'Apprentice' in the history of the show with five degrees: a Bachelor of Science in Electrical Engineering from Rutgers; a Master of Science in Electrical Engineering from the MIT School of Engineering; a Master of Science in Computer Science from Oxford University in England as a Rhodes Scholar; a Master of Business Administration from the MIT Sloan School of Management; and a PhD from the MIT Media Laboratory, in the history of the show

Despite Pinkett's impressive credentials and masterful performance on *"The Apprentice,"* his victory was almost stolen before a live audience of millions of viewers. When Trump asked Dr. Pinkett if he was willing to share first place with the runner-up, Rebecca Jarvis (a white female), Dr. Pinkett's controversial (and correct) response was:

"Mr. Trump, I firmly believe that this is 'The Apprentice,' that there is one and only one apprentice, and if you want to hire someone tonight it should be one. It's not 'The Apprenti,' it's 'The Apprentice.'"

After Pinkett's respectful but firm refusal, Mr. Trump looked properly chastened because he had just revealed his racial bias on national television. Pinkett's self-respecting response created a firestorm of resentment from the white press and angry (white) viewers, who booed, boo-hooed, and blasted Pinkett for choosing "selfishness over selflessness."

It was illogical (and racist) to expect Dr. Randall Pinkett – a **competitor** in the most competitive reality show in television history -- to suddenly become ***non-competitive***. Certainly, selflessness is not one of the qualities that made Donald Trump one of the most admired businessmen in America.

Yet, a black man was condemned for doing exactly what Mr. Trump would have done under the same circumstances: *rightfully claim his prize*. Dr. Pinkett's real crime was not selfishness; it was his refusal to do what all black people are expected to do in a system of white supremacy: submit; be subordinate to the demands and expectations of white people; and sacrifice themselves (share his prize) to rescue a white damsel in distress.

Fair-minded viewers understood that asking the first black winner to share his prize was Trump's gaffe, not Pinkett's. Dr. Pinkett had every RIGHT (and every obligation) to resist a double standard that would have cheated him out of being the one and only winner.

The resentment from the white media and (some) white viewers can be explained with two words: white privilege. In other words: *"It ain't right for a non-white (nigger) to win over a (superior) white person, and that's why you should share your prize, Pinkett (nigger)."* In the face of this black man's victory over a white person, white privilege reared its ugly head. That is the bottom line.

Black Success And White Resentment

"Please, I'm blacker than her mother." – Meadow, teenage daughter of mobster Tony Soprano, referring to a black classmate. (HBO's Sopranos)

After "Meadow" learned of a black classmate's early acceptance into an Ivy League school, she and a white male classmate sullenly assumed skin color was the reason for the black classmate's acceptance to a prestigious college NOT academic performance. In addition, since the black classmate's mother did not fit Meadow's stereotype of what a black woman should be, Meadow decided she wasn't "authentically black."

White Perception Is More Powerful Than Black Reality

"I couldn't get over the fact that there was no difference between Sylvia's restaurant and any other restaurant in New York City. I mean, it was exactly the same, even though it's run by blacks, primarily black patronship," said radio and TV commentator Bill O'Reilly, about his trip with Al Sharpton to the famous Harlem restaurant on his nationally syndicated radio show.

"There wasn't one person in Sylvia's who was screaming, 'M-Fer, I want more iced tea.' You know, I mean, everybody was -- it was like going into an Italian restaurant in an all-white suburb in the sense of people were sitting there, and they were ordering and having fun. And there wasn't any kind of craziness at all." (September 2007)

Perhaps, O'Reilly's words were not meant to be taken literally, but the fact that he saw nothing wrong with saying them publicly speaks volumes about the power of **perception VS reality**.

It's hard to believe Mr. O'Reilly has never met any educated or sophisticated blacks in his profession. Yet he just *"couldn't get over the fact"* that the black diners at Sylvia's (a black establishment) weren't screaming, *"M-Fer, I want more iced tea!"* at their waitresses.

Certainly, there are loud and ignorant blacks, just like there are loud and ignorant whites in New York City, yet no one – including Mr. O'Reilly -- would make the mistake of thinking all whites behaved a certain way.

Much of the credit for the negative stereotypes of blacks belongs to a mainstream media that (deliberately) rewards and promotes black entertainers who portray blacks as foul-mouthed buffoons, clowns, criminals, whores, and fools, instead of the wide range of humanity we represent: store clerks, mothers, fathers, sons, daughters, doctors, lawyers, chemists, architects, educators, students, business people, cooks, clerks, firemen (and women), police officers, postal workers, and some extraordinary, but mostly average, imperfect human beings.

The OJ Simpson Verdict And White Privilege

The 1995 acquittal of OJ Simpson was not the first time a defendant was acquitted of murder, but it was the first time in American history that a black man was acquitted of allegedly murdering not one, but two whites. After the verdict was announced, many whites were shocked and outraged, while many blacks were overjoyed. The unthinkable had finally happened: a black man (a nigger) accused of murdering two whites had leveled the uneven playing field of white privilege by having enough "green privilege" to hire a dream team of the best trial lawyers money could buy.

Guilty Until Proven Guilty

The OJ Simpson "not guilty" verdict led to frantic calls from politicians, talk show pundits, law enforcement, and (white) citizens for a drastic overhaul of the criminal justice system. Some of the proposed changes:

1. Allow non-unanimous jury verdicts.
2. Create a verdict system with three possible outcomes: guilty, not guilty, and not proven.
3. Set a minimum time limit for deliberation (because the four-hour Simpson verdict upset many people).
4. Allow juries of less than 12 people (overturning the tradition of a 12-person jury).
5. Change the venue rules to create a jury that is more "racially balanced" (eliminate predominantly black juries).

6. Use professional jurors. Train and pay people to be jurors, so they will have job experience and a "big picture" view by overturning the constitutional right to a "jury of our peers."
7. ***Repeal the sixth amendment*** (eliminate juries altogether!)

Ironically, the same justice system that has railroaded thousands of black men and women into prison was suddenly called into question because it failed to convict ONE black man (a nigger) accused of murdering two whites.

A legal system that allowed a black man (a nigger) to get a taste of the best white privilege his millions could buy was more than the white collective could stomach.

Murderous Spouses And White Privilege

Charles "Chuck" Stuart -- Boston, MA

On October 23, 1989, **Charles "Chuck" Stuart** murdered his pregnant wife, Carol, then told police that a **black gunman** forced his way into their car at a stoplight, robbed them, shot Charles in the stomach, then shot Carol in the head. Carol Stuart died that night.

Their son, Christopher, died 17 days after his father discontinued his life support. Boston police searched for black suspects, abusing the civil rights, using stormtrooper tactics, and racial profiling of blacks in Boston. On December 28, Stuart picked a black man, Willie Bennett, out of a lineup.

The case against Bennett came to an abrupt close when Stuart's brother, Matthew, identified Charles Stuart as the killer. Matthew admitted he saw his brother shoot his wife and then shoot himself to support his false story.

Police discovered Charles Stuart had been involved in an affair and was having financial difficulties. On January 4, 1990, Stuart jumped from the Tobin Bridge to his death. He left no suicide note.

Susan Smith -- Columbia, SC

On October 25, 1994, **Susan Smith** murdered her two boys by driving her auto into a lake while the children slept in their car seats. The case gained worldwide attention because Smith initially reported to police that she had been carjacked by a **black man** who drove away with her sons still in the car. Nine days later, after an intensive, heavily publicized investigation and nationwide search, Smith confessed to drowning her children.

Charles Stuart and Susan Smith assumed their white skin would guarantee their innocence if they accused a black man (a nigger) of committing the crime. And they were almost right.

Ironically, if we were able to ask Charles or Susan if they used *white privilege* to try to get away with murder, both would probably deny such a thing existed.

Black VS White Justice

Those who compare these cases with blacks who have (allegedly) falsely accused whites should be reminded that the white defendants went free – regardless of the evidence – 99% of the time.

To believe blacks have the same opportunity as whites to get justice when whites control the police, the media, the courts, the appointment of judges, the laws, the district attorneys -- even the DNA analysis labs -- is illogical and ludicrous.

It is just as illogical to believe wealthy and politically powerful white families wouldn't use their influence (power) to "persuade" law enforcement officials to destroy or falsify evidence to assure a dismissal of all charges against their sons.

At the opposite end of the economic, political, and racial spectrum, there are thousands of cases where law enforcement planted or fabricated evidence against black defendants to ensure a conviction.

American Justice: Tulia, Texas-Style

In 1999, in a dusty town that boasted a population of around 5000, 40 black men and women in Tulia, TX were sent to prison by the Dallas County District Attorney's Office during a fake drug scandal. The "defendants" were pressured to plead guilty even though no large sums of money, illegal drugs, drug paraphernalia, or illegal weapons were found.

However, the trials of the first defendants by all-white juries, which resulted in long sentences despite the lack of evidence, made most of the untried defendants plead guilty in exchange for shorter sentences.

The "drugs" used to convict the black defendants were later discovered to be chalk not cocaine, a fact that the police and prosecutors were aware of. After the cases were legally challenged, most had already served several years in prison.

The recent wave of overturned convictions of falsely imprisoned black men freed after DNA evidence confirmed their innocence is ABSOLUTE PROOF that the American justice system is inherently racist and unjust.

We Can (Logically) Draw The Following Conclusions:

1) If blacks can be convicted on the basis of skin color (regardless of the evidence), it is logical to assume that whites can be acquitted or never charged on the basis of skin color (regardless of the evidence).

2) If evidence can be falsified by police and district attorneys to CONVICT black defendants, then it is logical to assume evidence can be falsified to ACQUIT white defendants.

"...there are almost 50,000 people in the FBI's database of missing persons cases. Almost 30 percent of those abducted or kidnapped are black."

Josh Mankiewicz, NBC
Dateline, correspondent

Chapter Four

THE DEAD WHITE WOMEN'S CLUB

Recognize these names?

Lacey Peterson, Natalee Holloway, JonBenet Ramsey, Anna Nicole Smith, Nicole Brown Simpson, Stacey Peterson, Polly Klaas, Chandra Levy...

For most Americans, their names and faces are permanently etched on our memories. We know the color of their hair and eyes. We know the most intimate details of their lives: where they lived; who they loved or didn't love anymore; if they were married, pregnant, or single; and how they spent the last days of their lives. We know more about them than we know about our next-door neighbors, and much more than we want to know – yet, their stories keep on coming.

While the media conveniently overlooks the activities of the most influential club in the country -- the United States Congress – it refuses to let us forget the members of the DWWC: *the Dead White Women's Club.*

Their disembodied spirits and images haunt the most prominent news organizations in the nation: CNN, FOX-TV, MSNBC, ABC, CBS, NBC, People Magazine, Time, Newsweek, New York Times, Chicago Tribune, Los Angeles Times, The Washington Post, radio, cable, and television stations, websites, blogs, and forums throughout the nation.

DWWC members are immortalized in national magazines, best-selling books, talk shows, and made-for-TV movies. Years after their deaths or disappearances, DWWC members are regularly exhumed, resurrected, and exploited for national consumption.

The nation respectfully holds prayer vigils and candlelight memorials, as hundreds of volunteers scour rivers and countrysides, searching for clues to a member's untimely demise. New laws, such as "Megan's Law" and "Amber Alert," are created to reduce (but not eliminate) the number of new members.

In death, the members of the DWWC have accomplished something most did not achieve in life: ***fame***. They are not famous for being rich, for curing AIDS, or for bringing peace to the Middle East. They are famous for only one thing: being ***the victims of tragic circumstances.***

With the media's blessing and donated air time, the DWWC members define for all of us – whether we are white, black, red, brown, or yellow -- what the most precious resource is in this multi-cultural, multi-ethnic land we call the United States of America: **WHITE LIFE.** However, there is a darker side to this macabre tribute: the barely disguised delight in retelling and detailing the deaths and mysterious disappearances of so many young white females.

DWWC Membership Requirements

The process for selecting members has never been made public until now since no members have ever voluntarily applied for membership. Regardless, the unwritten rules state that the candidate must be:

- White
- Female
- Under 40
- Middle class or above
- Attractive (i.e., not overweight)
- Sexually appealing (to someone, including pedophiles)
- Missing or dead (with a few exceptions)

Women Of Color Are Not Eligible For DWWC Membership

For obvious reasons, non-white female victims are NOT eligible for DWWC membership. Nor are males of any age, race, or economic background. They all belong to a little known club -- the ***NNC (No Name Club)*** -- that exists among the shadows of American society. The NNC club has no membership requirements. Anyone – male, female, black, red, brown, yellow, or white -- can join, which explains why their membership dwarfs that of the DWWC.

There are no fringe benefits for the NNC's members. Little or no press coverage. No prayer vigils. No memorials or candlelight services. No "angel pins" are worn on jacket lapels. No new laws have ever been named after a single NNC member. Their only tribute is the heartbreak of a handful of family members, friends, and neighbors who gave a damn.

Recognize the names of these NNC (No Name Club) members? (chances are you won't)

Nailah Franklin (black woman murdered by ex-boyfriend)
Adji Desir (7-yr-old black boy still missing)
Anibal Cruz, 11, Daniel Agosto, 6, and Jesstin Pagan, 5, (three Hispanic boys missing two days, found dead in trunk of abandoned car in 2005)
Donnisha Hill (13 yr. old black girl murdered by 57 yr. old man)
Tierra Adams (pregnant young black woman still missing)
Diamond and Tionda Bradley (black sisters still missing)
Elijah Eely (9-yr-old black boy still missing)
Megan Williams (black female kidnapped, tortured and raped by six whites)
Matthew Grendel (white male college student still missing)
Denise McNair, Cynthia Wesley, Carole Robertson, and Addie Mae Collins (four black girls killed in 1963 in the 16TH church bombing by the KKK)
Clark Toshiro Handa (3-yr-old Japanese boy abducted/still missing)

Unfortunately, most missing NNC members are never found, mainly because law enforcement and the mainstream media expend very little time, money, and energy searching for NNC members or their kidnappers/killers.

The Purpose Of The DWWC

Contrary to popular opinion, neither the families nor the public chooses the DWWC members. The news media nominates the members by deciding what is news and what is NOT. The public has never demanded 24 hours, 7 days-a-week coverage on anyone or anything, including OJ Simpson or Anna Nicole Smith.

Short of turning the TV or radio off, the public has little choice BUT to be force-fed a constant diet of manufactured news by the media. In the case of the DWWC, the two main purposes are DISTRACTION from more important issues, and PROGRAMMING the public with the following subliminal messages:

1. White life is more valuable than non-white life.
2. The white female – if she meets certain criteria – is symbolic of white innocence, purity, and deserves universal empathy and protection.
3. The non-white male population should regard the white female as superior to non-white females.
4. Non-white females do not deserve the same protection and empathy that is given to white females.

By elevating the white female (if she meets certain criteria), the white male also elevates himself since he is a product of a white female (womb). By "rescuing" the white female -- the eternal damsel-in-distress -- the white male is also establishing himself as a hero and a protector (a real man). This fine, "manly" tradition can be traced back to early film days:

> *European fairy tales frequently feature damsels in distress, a young, nubile woman placed in a dire predicament by a villain or a monster and rescued by a hero. The damsel-in-distress is a mainstay of TV and film, from Fay Wray in the 1933 movie King Kong, Lois Lane in Superman, to more recent movies starring black "heroes" (mammy men) rescuing white "females-in-distress."*

The DWWC members represent the ULTIMATE white damsels in distress; the fragile Fay Wrays in a world full of savage King Kongs. They are the sacrificial white lambs used to focus all care and concern in the white collective's direction, and to ensure the DEHUMANIZATION of anyone who is not white.

Make no mistake; the white female is neither cherished nor is she placed on a pedestal. If she was truly cherished, she would be honored, not slaughtered. The white female is a tool that is used to promote the most successful product in the world: ***white supremacy.***

In contrast, the black female (the nappy-headed ho who is unworthy of protection and respect) is used to demonize the black collective. After all, if the black female is inferior; then the fruit of her womb -- the black male -- MUST be inferior as well.

The racist portrayal of the black female as "hostile and aggressive" by the mainstream media sends the message that she neither wants, needs, nor deserves to be rescued, and any attempts by anyone -- including the black male -- will be met with resistance and resentment, mainly from *her*.

The white female image is clearly being used by the white elite to promote white supremacy, with the racist white female's consent. However, both the black and white female imagery, whether in mock sympathy or blatant degradation, also points to a pervasive problem in America: ***misogyny – the hatred of all women***.

The Wrong Business

Stephanie, 25, worked as a news assistant for a television station in a mid-sized city. Three years after earning a bachelor's in journalism, she was still pulling news off the wire services and Xeroxing scripts; a far cry from her dreams of becoming a prime-time TV anchor.

On top of that, the pay sucked. Her $27,000-a-year salary was barely enough to pay her student loans and her car note. Thank God, she lived with her parents and didn't have to pay any rent.

Speaking of scripts, Stephanie couldn't stop thinking about the story that had just come across the wire. A young black woman was raped and tortured by several white men and women who held her captive for a week. Stephanie just didn't understand how any woman could rape another woman!

The budding news anchor inside her was aching to grab the mike and voice her outrage in the professionally modulated voice she practiced at home in front of the mirror. At she neared the end of her 10-hour shift, she was surprised that none of the news anchors had mentioned the rape but had found time to gossip about Britney Spears!

Stephanie was slipping on her coat when the news tip phone started ringing. Her relief hadn't showed up yet, so she tramped back to her desk and snatched the phone.

"WXYZ hotline," she said with a false brightness.

"I want to know why y'all didn't say nothing about that black girl who was raped," an angry female voice demanded.

"I don't—"

"If some black people had kidnapped and raped a white girl, it would be all over the news."

"I–" Stephanie stammered, intimidated by the accusatory tone.

"They wouldn't be out on bail, they'd be *under* the jail."

"Ma'am," Stephanie pleaded, at a loss for words.

"You white?"

"Uh...yes." Why did it feel like she had just confessed to a crime?

"I hope you ain't fat."

"Excuse me?" Stephanie yanked the phone away and stared at it before placing it against her ear. She was not fat! She was big-boned, like her mother.

"If you fat, you might as well be black."

"Ma'am, if you'd like to write to the—" Stephanie began, but the dial tone was already buzzing in her ear. She had to admit she sort of agreed with the caller. Every crime story they ran that involved a black, the black person was always the criminal, never the victim.

Just a few weeks ago, Stephanie had asked Juliet, the AM news director, why they never ran any stories about the black kids who were killed on a weekly basis in the city.

Either Juliet didn't like Stephanie's tone, or the question itself, because her narrow face turned a bright red. "I hope you're not suggesting race is a factor in deciding which stories we run." Juliet's voice was tight, angry. "We do the kinds of stories that are important to our core audience. We certainly can't broadcast every crime in the city. If you don't understand that, maybe you're in the wrong business."

Stephanie understood, all right. Stay in her place and keep her mouth shut. The next day Stephanie was told to report to the news tip-line desk until further notice. Stephanie was outraged. She was paying back $30,000 in student loans for the privilege of answering phones? Juliet was right. Maybe she was in the wrong business.

THE END

"You know, it's not the world that was my oppressor, because what the world does to you, if the world does it to you long enough and effectively enough, you begin to do to yourself."

James A. Baldwin

Chapter Five

HOW WHITE SUPREMACY DAMAGES BLACK PEOPLE

Given our painful 500-year history of white oppression, do blacks hate whites?

A better question: can blacks -- who depend on white institutions and systems for survival -- afford to hate whites? It would be less confusing if all whites were openly racist, but that is not the case.

Black Paranoia Is A Natural By-Product Of Racism/White Supremacy

Whenever we are denied a job, a promotion, are stopped by the police, followed by store security, denied a loan, told there are no apartments available, or are seated at a table near a swinging kitchen door, it is difficult to tell if race was a factor. Today's racism is more refined and more subtle, which makes it more psychologically and financially devastating because the victims become confused.

If we attempt to be reasonable, we wonder if we have been the victim of discrimination or if we just had an unpleasant encounter with a disagreeable human being who just happened to be white.

If we are angry, bitter, and tired – an understandable reaction to living black in a white supremacist society -- we may feel that *everything* is about race, and that every white person who denies us something we want or says something we don't like is a racist.

This is why our focus MUST BE on understanding how the system of white supremacy works, and all the different faces it wears. If we judge racism solely on our pleasant or unpleasant interactions with whites, or by individual whites we like (or love), we will confuse ourselves and draw faulty conclusions.

For example, we might assume that a white person who is nice to us can't be a racist (untrue), and a white person who is not nice must be practicing racism (untrue).

It is the collective AND individual behaviors of white people who function as racists AND racist suspects that results in systemic racism/white supremacy.

The answer to the question – do blacks hate whites – is no. Do blacks fear, resent, and distrust whites? Absolutely -- whether we admit it or not. It is natural to distrust a member of a group that has a history of mistreating your group.

It is natural to fear someone who has the power to abuse you and get away with it. It is natural to resent someone who benefits from your mistreatment, knows you are being abused, but says and does nothing to stop the abuse.

This is NOT the definition of "hate;" this is the law of physics. *For every action, there is a reaction.*

To accuse blacks of being "as racist as whites" -- when whites, collectively, have the power and a 500-year history of practicing racism against blacks – makes as much sense as comparing the schoolyard bully to a bullied child who now fears and dislikes the bully because of the way the bully has treated him.

"I am quite certain that there will never be healing between blacks and whites in this country until whites face up to the crime we as a people committed against people of African descent and begin to set it right. That's the only way Blacks will ever be able to genuinely respect us.

And, odd as it may seem, it's the only way we'll ever be able to respect them, because no one can feel clean, at ease with and respectful with someone they've robbed and brutalized and then felt they got away with it.

Working toward mutual respect is the only way to bring about true racial harmony. Anything else is divisive." -- Donna Lamb, C.U.R.E. (Caucasians United for Reparations and Emancipation).

AXIOM #4: IN A SYSTEM OF WHITE SUPREMACY, IT IS NATURAL FOR BLACK PEOPLE COLLECTIVELY TO FEAR AND RESENT WHITE PEOPLE COLLECTIVELY.

The consequences of speaking openly and honestly about racism can be severe, so many blacks remain silent. Out of fear and confusion, we allow ourselves to be drawn deeper into a false and dangerous sense of security, forgetting there is NO security for black people within a black-hating society.

To survive (and advance) in a predominantly white workplace, blacks often feel they must wear a compliant mask in the presence of whites for the same reason an employee hides his feelings from a boss he does not like or trust.

"I keep my voice even and low in meetings because if I raise it, the white people get scared," said one black male Hollywood insider, who preferred to remain anonymous. "I can't afford to be perceived as an 'angry black man,' but the truth is, I'm angry most of the time. People think my job is glamorous but they have no idea how racist this business is."

If You Can't Beat Them, Join Them: The Black Appeasers

"An appeaser is one who feeds a crocodile, hoping it will eat him last."
-- Prime Minister Winston Churchill

This is the unspoken mantra of blacks who deliberately seek out white friendships, relationships, and environments to the exclusion of black friendships, relationships, and environments. They may send their children to all-white schools, attend white churches, and religiously mimic the tastes and lifestyles of the whites they wish to emulate.

Some blacks may go as far as to avoid associating with other blacks (except for family) for fear of being perceived as "too black" in a black-hating society. Some blacks are so self-hating they go out of their way to degrade other blacks in the presence of whites – hoping to separate themselves from the despised black masses. Other blacks are so disconnected from their own racial heritage (and reality) that they are unable to identify with it at all:

At a highly publicized 2006 Cape Cod murder trial of a black male accused of the rape and murder of a white female, the sole black male juror told a white female juror that all his brothers' wives were white, that he had always been around white people, and that he did not like blacks because, "look at what they are capable of."

Whites should not make the mistake of taking these smiling, fawning, agreeable, submissive, self-hating, or assimilated (lost) blacks as a compliment. It is little more than a SURRENDER by a black person who fears being a target of white supremacy to such a degree that they align themselves with whites, because whites are the only ones who can protect them from other (racist) whites. In other words, these blacks have chosen (the illusion of) SAFETY over SELF-RESPECT.

Regardless of how many black and white friendships, relationships, and marriages exist, black compliance with white supremacy is NOT voluntary. It has nothing to do with liking, loving, or respecting white people. It has nothing to do with racial superiority – because this superiority does not exist.

This behavior is based on fear and mistrust of white people because whites have the power to devastate non-whites. The black person who surrenders to white supremacy may believe his or her behavior is voluntary – but their confusion and delusions do not change the facts.

When Attacked In Rome, Romance The Romans

Some blacks date or marry whites exclusively even when they (secretly or openly) dislike or distrust whites in general. The same is true of whites in interracial relationships who avoid social contact with unfamiliar blacks because they are not comfortable with blacks in general.

The white partner of an interracial relationship often shuns blacks of the same sex because it is too sexually threatening, and they secretly fear their black partner will (come to their senses and) "go back to black."

It is common for blacks and whites who date interracially to shun romantic partners of their own race YET the majority of interracial couples claim love is "color-blind" and that they didn't "plan" to fall in love with a person of another race. Just because a relationship was not "planned," does not mean our choice of a partner is an accident. Most people would not "accidentally" fall in love with a 400-lb, blind paraplegic, even if that person had all the other qualities they were looking for.

Certainly, a black person who chooses one white lover after another is NOT color-blind, but is acting out ***a skin color fetish*** where white skin represents something (superior) that black skin does not.

Most interracial couples are so uncomfortable talking honestly about racism or facing the racial hang-ups that brought them together in the first place, that just initiating a discussion about racism/white supremacy is enough to send them scurrying into deep denial – or out of the room.

They prefer to pretend the 800-lb gorilla is not in the room, even when it is standing with one huge foot on their (and our) collective necks. If an interracial couple cannot deal honestly with their own racial issues, they will simply spread their sick confusion to their children and to any black person within their area of psychological contamination.

The toxic level of confusion, fear, self-hatred, dishonesty, and denial in most interracial relationships is the abnormal BUT predictable by-product of the most undiagnosed, misdiagnosed, untreated, and destructive mental illness in America:

Racism/White Supremacy

The Dangers Of Black Denial

When we hide our true feelings about racism, we're not protecting white people; we're protecting ourselves from the wrath of white people. We've learned from the painful (and sometimes fatal) experiences of others who have dared to speak out, that many whites cannot handle an honest dialogue about racism, and will deny racism is happening even when it is happening right under their noses.

It is understandable why blacks feel we must mask our anger and outrage in order to function in a white supremacist society. The real danger comes from wearing our masks in private, when we're alone. Our denial of our true reality creates a weak psychological foundation that can easily crack under pressure.

Instead of confronting (and correcting) the source of our pain, we self-medicate with food, alcoholism, and drug addictions, violence, ego trips, risky sexual behaviors, infidelity, promiscuity, poor parenting, obesity, overspending, materialism, violence, irrationality, and over-emotionalism.

The psychiatric community defines depression as rage turned INWARD. What then, is the deadly manifestation of rage turned INWARD AND OUTWARD? Is it racial schizophrenia?

The misdirection, suppression, and self-medication of rage accounts for a majority of high blood pressure, stroke, cancer, mental illness, schizophrenia, drug and alcohol addiction, depression, suicides, and murders that plague the black community.

Many blacks avoid examining their true feelings about racism because they are terrified that once they do, they won't be able to continue functioning (smiling, grinning, tap-dancing, denying, and pretending) as an inferior person within a white supremacist, black-hating society.

We are reluctant to face the truth because once we face our real problem -- racism/white supremacy -- we can no longer avoid the responsibility for fixing it. Without realizing it, our ineffective coping strategy (surrender) actually *extends* the life and the power of the white supremacist system.

Black Amnesia Is Anti-Historical And Self-Genocidal

We must stop being naïve about racism. Racism is not about whites liking or disliking blacks, or about blacks liking or disliking whites. Racism is not about blacks and whites knowing each other better. Racism is not about more blacks living next door, or going to the same schools as whites, or any such nonsense. Increasing the crossover appeal of black entertainers will not end racism. As a famous black comedian (with huge crossover appeal) once observed:

> *"I don't understand what goes on some times, right, 'cause here we are in this theater, we getting along just fine. We go outside and the shit changes." – Comedian Richard Pryor speaking on racism*

Sammy Davis, Jr. was one of white America's favorite entertainers during the 1950s and 1960s yet this famous, wealthy black man could not stay in the same hotels where he received standing ovations. We forgot (or didn't understand) that even the most rabid monkey-hater will pay a fortune to see a monkey sing, talk, and tap dance.

We forgot that in the segregated Deep South, whites and blacks lived next door to each other, and played together as children but that did not eliminate racism. Southern whites certainly "knew" the black women who cleaned their homes, raised their children, cooked their food, and nursed white infants at the black woman's breast.

Black domestics workers were "just like family" to their white employers, but this did not protect them from being victimized by the same racist segregation laws that were condoned by their white pseudo "family members."

Racial sensitivity and diversity training will not end racism. Blacks and whites living, learning, working, or eating together in the same neighborhoods, schools, workplaces, or restaurants will not end racism.

Racism will NOT end until white supremacy ends. White supremacy will NOT end until non-whites in every part of the world CHANGE THEIR RESPONSES to it.

"Whiteness is the empty and therefore terrifying attempt to build an identity on what one isn't, and on whom one can hold back."

David Roediger,
social historian at the
University of Minnesota

Chapter Six

HOW WHITE SUPREMACY DAMAGES WHITE PEOPLE

"I never met a racist who loved themselves." -- A psychologist explaining racism on a TV talk show

Silent Partner: The Crime Of Omission

Matt removed his hard hat and untied the scarf from his blond hair. He swiped the scarf across his face and jammed it into his pocket. It was humid; ninety-three degrees and climbing, but Matt wasn't complaining. It felt damn good to bring home a paycheck after being laid off for four months. Thanks to his sister-in-law, Dee, who was dating a foreman at a new hotel construction site, Matt was making $28 an hour plus overtime, which meant he could catch up on his mortgage and bills. His ulcer hadn't flared up in weeks.

The sound of boots crunching on gravel made him look around. It was Ben, the new guy the company hired last week. Matt greeted the stocky, brown-skinned man with a nod. At first, Matt resented being stuck with the only black guy on the site, but it turned out okay.

Ben was a damn good worker, not like most blacks. They had a lot in common. Both were in their early thirties; had a year or two of college; had married young and had a couple of kids each. Some of the other white guys started ribbing Matt about getting stuck with the colored guy. Matt shrugged it off as if to say, what can a guy do?

But it made Matt feel uneasy. The other guys never said anything when Ben was around, but Matt could tell they didn't like working with blacks. They said, pretty soon the blacks would be taking all their jobs. Ben was only one black guy out of a crew of three hundred plus white guys, but Matt wasn't about to argue the point. *He needed this job.*

Matt was teamed up with Ben since nobody wanted to work with a black. Secretly, Matt was glad. Ben had traveled all over the world as a Marine and had some great stories to tell. They talked about everything -- women, marriage, kids, sex, and the money they would make once they completed their apprenticeship and became journeymen electricians. $38 an hour was the kind of money Matt had only dreamed about. Ben said he was going to move out of the inner city and buy a home in the suburbs with a big yard and good schools for his kids.

Matt figured, once the other guys realized Ben wanted the same things they all wanted -- to provide for their families -- they'd see he wasn't the typical nigger. The funny part was Ben wasn't mad that the other guys snubbed him.

Matt tried to imagine what that would be like; being the only white guy working with blacks who didn't like whites. He knew it would only be a matter of time before he blew his cool and walked out.

They were sitting on a pile of stacked lumber, just the two of them, eating lunch out of paper bags. Matt crushed his empty Coke can with one hand then shot a look at Ben, lips twisted in a silent dare. Ben took the challenge. It took three tries before the cheap tin collapsed. They laughed out loud. Matt couldn't remember the last time he'd felt so relaxed. It felt damn good.

At the end of the workday, after Matt punched the time clock, he ran smack into the foreman of his crew.

"How's it going, young fella?" Houlihan, a beefy Irishman in his mid-50s, clamped Matt on the shoulder in a friendly way, a cigar stub dangling from the corner of his mouth.

"Good," Matt said, nodding.

"Sorry you got stuck with the spade."

"Who?" Matt's stomach muscles tightened.

"The nigger."

"Oh. Yeah."

"The city's giving us bullshit about not hiring enough minorities." Houlihan blew a thick cloud of smoke in Matt's direction.

Matt coughed into a balled fist. *He needed this job.*

"Blacks are lazy, that's why we don't hire 'em."

"Yeah."

"Forget about it, that minority ain't gonna be around much longer." The foreman draped a heavy arm around Matt's shoulders. "We gotta stick together. My grandfather and father worked construction. So will my son. If we let the niggers in, won't be nothing left for us or our kids."

"Ben's alright," Matt said, almost pleading.

"My niece works here. She's a nice girl. Do I gotta spell it out?" Houlihan's calloused hand tightened on Matt's shoulder. "You keep your mouth shut, understand?"

Matt got it, and once he thought about it, it made a hell of lot of sense. Still, he wondered if Houlihan was serious, or blowing cigar smoke in his ear.

The rest of the week passed without incident. The following Friday afternoon, after Matt punched the time clock, he saw Ben storming his way.

"You know what Houlihan just told me?" Ben said, his normally mild brown eyes burning with rage. "He says, all I can work is eight hours!"

"A week?" Matt was genuinely shocked.

"Hell yeah, a week! I'm supposed to feed my kids on eight hours a week?" Ben's watery eyes searched Matt's for the answer. "Union rules says I gotta keep this job or I gotta quit the apprenticeship program. He knows that. To hell with this, this ain't nothing but some racist bullshit!"

Matt dropped his eyes. When he looked up, something hardened in the black man's face. Maybe Ben saw his relief -- that it wasn't him -- or maybe, all he saw was Matt's white skin.

Without warning, a muscled, brown arm shot past Matt's head. Matt flinched as a yellow hard hat bounced off the chain-link fence behind him, and spun across the gravel. Ben stomped toward the parking lot and never looked back.

Laughter exploded from a group of men standing nearby as Ben's Chevy truck squealed out of the lot. Matt averted his eyes as he walked to his truck and climbed inside. He was reaching for his keys when a burning pain bent him in half. His ulcer was back.

THE END

The Universal Conduct Code For White Males (In A White Supremacy Society)

The previous story, *'The Silent Partner,'* illustrates how the crimes of 'commission' AND 'omission' are NECESSARY for racism to function effectively AND efficiency. White males know there are benefits if they remain silent while other whites are practicing racism. They also know there is a price to pay if they don't. Matt's crime was the "crime of omission," which is a form of racism because it enables other whites to practice racism without the victims being able to prove they were victimized.

The system of white supremacy is a male-dominated "brotherhood," where much is GIVEN, but much is also expected from the most privileged people on the planet*: white males*.

Not only are white males programmed to feel superior to non-whites and females; they are programmed to believe they MUST BE superior. This means white males -- who are **LESS THAN 5 PERCENT** of the world's population -- are burdened with the unenviable task of trying to dominate the other **NINETY-FIVE PERCENT**.

The white male's racial isolation isn't due just to the billions of black, red, yellow, and brown people who (rightfully) oppose his unilateral and unjust domination; it also comes from a lifetime of faulty programming under the patriarchal system of white supremacy.

To maintain the white male status quo, there is an unofficial, unspoken, and unwritten code of conduct that white males are expected to follow from the cradle to the grave:

- A white male is superior to all women and all people of color.
- A white male should be professionally, economically, and educationally superior to all women and all people of color.
- White males created everything worth creating on the planet.
- A white male should never be in a subordinate (inferior) position to a woman or any person of color.
- A white male should rebel against the authority of anyone who is not white and male, because they have no right to have any authority over him in a white supremacy system.

- A white male should never willingly take orders from a non-white or female person unless ordered to do so by another white male authority figure (who is really in charge).
- A white male is the biggest victim in America due to reverse racism, and should view affirmative action, civil rights, and women's rights as an attack (threat) against the white male.
- A white male should not share any more information than necessary, except in the performance of his job or business.
- A white male should suppress any sexual or romantic interest in non-white women, in particular brown or dark-skinned black women, unless it is out of eyesight of other whites, in particularly, white females.
- A white male should view any relationships with non-white women as temporary sexual flings.
- A white male should never let his guard down around people of color, especially males, and should avoid close friendships with men of color.
- A white male should restrain his desire to be "cool" lest his white peers label him a "wigger" or worse, a "nigger lover."
- A white male should always assume: a black male is "slick" (if he is confident); "articulate" (if he is well-spoken); and up to no good if women (especially white women) find him attractive.
- A white male should view the black male as a sexual predator who cannot control himself around white women.
- Never treat the "inferior" black female as if she is equal or superior to the white female.
- A white male cannot admit he secretly resents (and envies) the freedom of black men to be with women of any ethnic group without suffering a loss of male peer approval.

The pecking order in a white supremacy system places the white male in a superior position over women and people of color, and programs the white male to assume this is ***the natural order of things.***

The High Cost Of Being White In A White Supremacist Society

What psychological/sexual damage is done to a white male who is told he MUST be superior to 95% of the people on the planet, or that non-white women are NOT desirable because it is taboo to find them sexually attractive?

What about the man who denies another man his God-given right to provide for and protect his family? Does the karmic backlash result in a loss of confidence in his own manhood, or increase the tendency toward homosexuality?

What psychological damage is done to a people who are taught they MUST BE superior to anyone who is not white -- even if there is no evidence of their own superiority? Does it lead to chronic dissatisfaction, insecurity, and rampant materialism -- regardless of what one owns or has achieved?

Does it mean winning at any cost, even if that means attacking (or killing) another parent at a children's softball game? Does it drive a mother to hire a hit man to knock off her teenage daughter's cheerleading competition? Or fuel the compulsion to undergo a series of life-threatening surgeries to fix nonexistent physical flaws?

What psychological damage is done to the white female who feels she must be superior to non-white women, or who believes she must have the "perfect" breasts, nose, chin, and thighs when physical perfection is an impossibility and is based on a man-made (false) standard of beauty?

This (white) obsession with perfection (superiority) may be the main cause of the epidemic of bulimia, anorexia, self-mutilation, promiscuity, divorce, plastic surgery, alcoholism, substance abuse, and suicide that afflicts the white collective. A white supremacist system based on injustice and lies actually INCREASES the odds that the white collective will eventually turn on itself in self-loathing.

> *"The U.S. suicide rate is up for the first time in a decade, and it's rising most among middle-aged white men and women, a new study finds." (SOURCE: U.S. News & World Report – October 21, 2008)*

According to the article, the suicide rate for blacks decreased significantly, while the suicide rates for Asians and Native Americans remained "stable." The rising suicide rates for whites have baffled researchers, who claimed the bad economy was not a major factor. The article also stated that suicide is more common in America than homicide.

There will be no attempt here to unravel the mystery or complexity of suicide. Why some people choose to end their lives so tragically, is beyond the scope of this book and the expertise of the authors. What can be stated with absolute certainty is:

AXIOM #5: IT IS IMPOSSIBLE TO LOVE YOURSELF WHEN YOU ARE MISTREATING OTHERS.

Do not misinterpret the above as a judgment of suicide casualties. However, there is a universal law at work in the universe. If we fail to heed it, we will bring down the wrath of universal karma upon our collective heads.

Why Are Whites Reluctant To Talk Honestly About Racism?

Reason #1: To Maintain White Privilege

When someone benefits from a system, they are understandably reluctant to change that system. For example, Coworker A makes 20% more than Coworker B even though their jobs are identical. Eventually, Coworker B becomes suspicious and asks Coworker A about his salary.

Coworker A avoids the question, by making the claim that Coworker B is getting special treatment and perks that he is being unfairly denied. Coworker A also hides the fact that he is related by marriage to the personnel manager.

Coworker A knows it is to his advantage to avoid direct answers to Coworker B's questions. Otherwise, Coworker B might take some action (like filing a lawsuit) that causes Coworker A to lose his "privileges."

Most people -- including Coworker A -- cling to the (often false) belief that they are honest and ethical people EVEN when they are benefiting from the mistreatment of others. This "belief" requires MASS SELF-DECEPTION on the part of those who benefit, and MASS DECEPTION towards those who are being mistreated. In a system of white supremacy, it is necessary to:

1. convince non-whites they are NOT being mistreated
2. convince non-whites they are disadvantaged ***because*** they are inferior
3. convince whites they have earned advantages ***because*** they are superior
4. convince whites that they are being mistreated by non-whites
5. convince whites that non-whites deserve to be mistreated
6. pressure whites to keep silent even when racism is happening right in front of them

Reason #2: Peer Pressure

Whites are subject to a tremendous amount of peer pressure from other whites (racists) to be racists, or at the least, to not interfere in the business of those who are. Fortunately, there are whites courageous enough to speak against racism and white privilege:

> *"I really believe that she just always thought, 'This is mine. I'm Bill's wife. I'm white, and this is mine. I just gotta get up and step into the plate.' Then out of nowhere came, 'Hey, I'm Barack Obama,' and she said, 'Oh, damn! Where did you come from? I'm white! I'm entitled! There's a black man stealing my show!'" -- Father Michael Pfleger, on the 2008 presidential candidates, Hillary Clinton and Barack Obama at Trinity United Church of Christ. a predominantly black church, (May 25, 2008).*

Father Pfleger, a white Catholic priest, committed the cardinal sin of defining the political aspirations of Senator Hillary Clinton as "white privilege." By doing so he incurred the wrath of the mainstream media, white political pundits, Catholic church leaders, and certain anxiously apologetic black leaders. Nine days later, on June 4, Cardinal George asked Pfleger to take a disciplinary leave of absence from St. Sabina:

> *"I have asked Father Michael Pfleger, Pastor of St. Sabina's Parish, to step back from his obligations there and take leave for a couple of weeks from his pastoral duties, effective today."*

Contrary to what many political pundits claimed, Father Michael Pfleger wasn't punished for mixing church and politics. The Catholic Church has been a strong political supporter of amnesty for illegal immigrants, and has provided safe sanctuaries for illegals fearing deportation.

Father Pfleger's REAL CRIME was daring to break the unofficial, unspoken rule for whites in a white supremacy system: ***never, ever admit PUBLICLY as a white person that white privilege exists.***

Reason #3: False White Innocence

In 1992, Jane Elliott, a white former schoolteacher turned anti-racist activist, appeared on the Oprah Winfrey show and conducted the following experiment without the knowledge of the studio audience:

Before the audience was seated in the studio, they were divided into two groups: the blue-eyed people and the brown-eyed people. The show's producers immediately escorted the brown-eyed people to their seats and offered them donuts and coffee in clear view of the blue-eyed people who were treated rudely and forced to stand for two hours.

By the time the blue-eyed audience members were seated in the studio, they were furious. Mrs. Elliott poured gasoline on the fire by saying their unruly behavior was proof that blue-eyed people were less intelligent and more violent than brown-eyed people.

Even after Mrs. Elliott revealed that the entire audience had been part of an experiment on racism, most of the blue-eyed audience members continued to rant and rave about the way they had been treated. Mrs. Elliott calmly reminded them that being mistreated for two hours was nothing compared to dealing with racism on a daily basis.

> *"White people do not live in the same reality that people of color do," Mrs. Elliott explained. "We think that because we have all these freedoms, everybody else has them, too. That isn't the way it is."*

For the first time in their lives, the blue-eyed audience members got a taste of real-life racism, and discovered that being mistreated for having the wrong eye (or skin) color was an infuriating and demoralizing experience.

Regardless, most fiercely resisted the message because to understand it would mean losing their imaginary "innocence" about the cruelty and realities of racism.

It is logical to assume the white people who fought Mrs. Elliott's lesson the hardest, were most likely, the most guilty of practicing racism themselves.

Reason #4: Guilt (Fear Of Being Exposed)

When non-whites bring up the subject of racism, many whites feel it is a personal indictment (attack) against them. Even when non-whites criticize the government, some whites become angry and defensive because they see these (white) government officials as extensions of themselves.

A week after Katrina devastated New Orleans in 2004, John W, a white employee, asked his black coworker, Joe S, if the government was lax in its rescue efforts because most of the people were black. When Joe said absolutely, Tom became defensive. "Oh, so now you hate all white people?"

This illogical, almost hysterical, response could mean John secretly agreed with his black coworker but still felt the need to justify the (white) government's actions.

In addition, many white males identify with the powerful white males who run Corporate America and the US government in a desperate attempt to distance themselves from the (inferior) female and non-white masses.

This explains why so many poor and working-class white males cling to a Republican Party that has done little to nothing for poor and working-class white males.

The blatant racism of Katrina, the fear of exposing (white racism), and of guilt-by-association fueled John's reaction. Otherwise, there would have been no reason for him to take his black coworker, Joe's, criticism of the government so personally.

Non-whites should not take any comfort in white guilt. Guilt is non-productive for the victims of white supremacy because it rarely results in a change in the behavior of those who benefit from injustice. In fact, too much guilt actually has the opposite effect by creating resentment and a tendency to justify one's behavior rather than correct it.

Reason #5: Indifference

A white woman who identified herself as a "white supremacist" was asked the following question by her black interviewer: *"What do you think white people would do if the US government did to blacks what the German government did to the Jews?"*

"Nothing," she said.

"You don't think whites would say or do anything about it?"

"No, because it wouldn't be happening to us."

While this seems like a chilling response, it is an honest one. This is why it is crucial for non-whites to educate ourselves about the system of racism/white supremacy, and to focus on **CHANGING OUR BEHAVIOR**, rather than wasting energy trying to change those behavior of those who practice racism and benefit from it.

Chapter Seven

WHY RACISM/WHITE SUPREMACY WAS CREATED

Obviously, the reader is free to accept or reject any of the ideas or theories presented in this book. However, one universal truth is undeniable. The system of Racism/White Supremacy -- like everything in the universe -- exists for a reason.

Cress Theory of Color Confrontation

Dr. Frances Cress Welsing, a famous African-American psychiatrist and the author of "The Isis Papers: The Keys to the Colors" (1991), states that White Supremacy is practiced by the global "white" minority on the conscious and unconscious level to ensure their genetic survival by any means necessary.

Dr. Welsing contends that because of their "numerical inadequacy" and "color inferiority," white people may have defensively developed "an uncontrollable sense of hostility and aggression" towards people of color, which has led to "confrontations" between the races throughout history.

Repressing their own feelings of inadequacy, whites "set about evolving a social, political, and economic structure to give blacks and other 'non-whites' the appearance of being inferior."

Whether the reader accepts or rejects Dr. Welsing's theories, it is undeniable that whites are in the "numerical minority" among the people on the planet. Whites are also experiencing a fertility crisis AND a **negative population growth rate** (more deaths than births).

Countries That Made The Negative Population Growth List:

Ukraine	Hungary	Germany
Russia	Romania	Czech Republic
Slovakia	Italy	Greece
Japan	Poland	Austria
Lithuania	Croatia	

Women of Color Are the Most Fertile

The **fertility rate** (the total number of children the average woman is likely to have) ranges from seven or more children per woman in developing countries in Africa to around one child per woman in Eastern Europe.

Certainly, the number of white females who choose to abort, remain childless, or have fewer children, contributes to the low white birth rate. However, the skyrocketing demand for fertility drugs, fertility clinics, sperm banks, sperm donors, artificial insemination, in vitro-fertilization, test tube babies, US and overseas adoption mills tells a different story: *the rate of infertility is increasing among whites.*

Do All So-Called "Races" Practice Skin Color Supremacy?

> *Mr. Neely Fuller, Jr., in his 1969 Textbook for Victims of White Supremacy, described racism as a "universal operating system of white supremacy rule and domination in which the majority of the world's white people participate."*
>
> *Mr. Fuller suggested that economic forms of government such as capitalism and communism were created to perpetuate white domination and that the white "race" is really an "organization" dedicated to maintaining control over the world. In addition, he argued that people of color have never imposed "colored" supremacy on anyone.*

Some might argue that Mr. Fuller is incorrect, and that white supremacy is simply human nature, because it is natural to discriminate against people who look different. They might also add that slavery existed all over the world long before Europeans enslaved Africans 400 years ago.

Certainly, it is true that whites AND non-whites have enslaved other human beings throughout history, but this usually happened after the victors won a war or a conflict. The victors NEVER justified this enslavement with a system of SKIN COLOR SUPREMACY. If one looks at the overwhelming historical evidence, it appears Mr. Fuller's argument may be correct.

Countless battles have been fought between warring tribes throughout human history, but those tribes never justified these wars with a system of SKIN COLOR SUPREMACY. Nowhere on earth does a system of SKIN COLOR SUPREMACY exist EXCEPT among white people (Europeans).

If it was normal (human nature) for ALL ethnic groups to kill and oppress other ethnic groups based on skin color differences alone, there would be a long HISTORY (and evidence) of such skin-color-based conflicts and systems. For example:

- Brown people would have developed a system of brown-skin supremacy
- Red people would have developed a system of red-skin supremacy
- Black people would have developed a system of black-skin supremacy
- Yellow people would have developed a system of yellow-skin supremacy

America -- as we know it -- would be a very different nation, as would most of the world, because Native Americans, Africans, and the first (black) Australians would have ***murdered or enslaved the first European arrivals on sight, instead of helping them survive in the new world.***

Black Is Genetically Dominant/ White Is Genetically Recessive

NOTE: The authors do not pretend to have any scientific expertise. As is true in this entire book, the reader is free to accept or reject any theories or explanations presented here. The following is based on our own research and logically drawn conclusions:

According To The Genetic Phase Of Biology, Black Is Genetically Dominant, And White Is Genetically Recessive.

Ancient fossil discoveries in the late 1970s by Louis Leakey, a British/ Kenyan archaeologist and anthropologist, and his expedition, concluded that the first man and woman originated in Africa.

If Mr. Leakey is correct that all human life began in Africa, it is logical to assume the African man and African woman are genetically capable of making all the colors of humanity, which includes black, red, yellow, brown, and white.

Genetically AND logically speaking, "brown" is just another shade of black; "red" is another shade of black; "yellow" is another shade of black; and "white" is another shade of black.

However, ***politically*** speaking, "white" is NOT a shade of black because white is a "non-color." How do we know this is true? White supremacy classifies ALL non-whites as "people of color," which means ***white cannot be a color.***

Is There A Link Between Melanin And Fertility?

If the FERTILITY RATE per woman in developing countries in Africa ranges from seven or more children, and the fertility rate in Europe is one child per woman, we might draw some logical (but not necessarily scientific) conclusions:

1. Africans have more melanin than Europeans because dark skin has more melanin than light skin.
2. Africans have one of the highest fertility (birth) rates in the world.
3. Africans are genetically dominant (can produce all the skin colors, including black).
4. Therefore, Africans are in the LEAST danger of becoming genetically extinct -- except by artificial, man-made means (genocide).
5. Europeans have less melanin than Africans because light skin has less melanin.
6. Europeans have the lowest fertility (birth) rate in the world.
7. Europeans are genetically recessive (can only produce one color, which according to white supremacy is a non-color: white).
8. Therefore, Europeans are in the MOST danger of becoming genetically extinct (by natural selection).

Therefore, it is logical to assume there might be a connection between skin color, melanin, and fertility.

TRUTH IN CINEMA

"Children of Men" (2006). Plot: A science fiction film set in the year 2027. After two decades of global human infertility, in the midst of societal collapse, a miracle occurs. A young woman is pregnant; the first pregnancy on earth in 18 years. A government agent agrees to transport her to a safe sanctuary where scientists can study the birth of her child and hopefully save humanity from extinction. ***The pregnant female is a young African woman.***

Contrary to white supremacy propaganda, dark skin is NOT a sign of genetic inferiority. In fact, "dark" usually represents the stronger (original) version while "light" usually (but not always) represents a weaker, diluted, or artificial version that is always lacking something found in the original.

> *"If you want bread with no nutritional value, you ask for white bread. All the good that was in it has been bleached out of it, and will constipate you. If you want pure flour, you ask for dark flour, whole-wheat flour. If you want pure sugar, you want dark sugar." -- Malcolm X*

If the African man and woman possess the MOST MELANIN, it could mean Africans, genetically and biologically speaking, are ***the most powerful people on the planet,*** and the ***greatest genetic threat to white survival.***

This would explain why dark-skinned black males are more likely to be unemployed, arrested, incarcerated, assaulted, or murdered by police than light-skinned and non-black men -- AND explains why the darkest-skinned black woman is the most degraded and demonized woman on the planet.

Black Male Sexuality And White Obsession

Fear of white genetic extinction might shed light on the white obsession with black male genitalia and sexuality, and why black males (and their sexual organs) have been frequent targets of white lust and white rage. It also explains where the "big, black bogeyman" myths about gigantic black penises originated and why these myths still persist within the white culture.

This sexual obsession (fear) may explain why whites, historically, have mentally, financially, socially, sexually, and even physically castrated black men. Collectively, black men are the least educated, and are the most likely to be unemployed, incarcerated, die prematurely, or be murdered than any other group in America.

White male police officers have sodomized black men in police custody with broom handles and screwdrivers (a symbolic assault on black male sexuality). The pornographic industry makes millions from movies featuring black males with large penises having sex with (savaging) petite white females.

There are numerous "private" clubs in the US where white men pay black men to have sex with their white wives. (Our research failed to uncover a single sex club where black men pay white men to have sex with their black wives). This widespread fear of (and fascination with) black male sexuality is obvious in the stereotypes of black males on network TV and feature films:

1. the cowardly black male, popular in early films (symbolic castration)
2. the super-hero black male (the virile, masculine, sexually dominate male)
3. the dangerous, violent, animalistic (rapist of white female) black male aka King Kong who must be destroyed
4. The sexless, neutered black male friend or rescuer (symbolic castration)
5. The black male in dresses, high heels, and earrings (symbolic castration)
6. The foolish/ignorant black male buffoon (self-castration)

If black male sexuality is a THREAT to white genetic survival, it will be attacked on all fronts by the white supremacy system. These "attacks" have created generation after generation of fearful and insecure black males who often adopt a fatalistic or selfish attitude about life in general.

To compensate for the relentless attacks on their manhood, some black males attempt to validate their masculinity by sexing and breeding with multiple women, or by abusing and disrespecting women.

Some may pursue non-black women who are perceived as more feminine (easier to dominate), and having more status. Some are sexually conflicted (confused), resulting in bi-sexual or down-low males who lead secret sex lives.

Other males -- out of desperation and fear of the difficult challenges of being black and male in white America -- become self-destructive or violent toward others. The end result is more black victims, more broken families, more fatherless black children, and more black males in jail and in the cemetery.

Added to this devastating mix, is the alarming number of black men spending decades in prison, which ***guarantees a male population whose sexuality is constantly compromised and is, sometimes, forever altered***.

The (racist) mainstream media and entertainment industry cruelly adds to the vulnerable black male's sexual confusion by portraying the most successful black males as super-macho athletes, heroes, and thugs, or as feminine characters wearing dresses, stockings, earrings, and high heels.

Black Males: Enemies Or Allies of White Supremacy?

If blacks are genetically the most dominant, and whites are genetically the most recessive, blacks have the most (genetic) potential to make whites genetically extinct. Therefore, it is logical to assume blacks (and Africans) will be the **MAIN TARGETS** of global genocide.

This black genetic potential has fueled the FALSE belief and fear that the black male who breeds with the white female (and produces non-white offspring) is the biggest threat to white genetic survival.

In reality, it is just the opposite. The majority of these black male/ white female relationships will not last, even if they have children together.

Most of the children of these interracial unions will (1) be raised by single white mothers; (2) will have a closer, more sympathetic bond with the white side of their family, in particular, the white females; (3) will be white-identified; (4) will breed with whites (or other white-identified biracial partners); and (5) will produce offspring who will merge ***undetected*** with the white population.

The future generations of these black male/white female unions will produce whites who will be more fertile (due to melanin from the black male), resulting in an INCREASE in overall white fertility, which will possibly extend the life of **White Supremacy** and **Black Oppression.**

Therefore, the black male who breeds with the white female represents the:

SINGLE BIGGEST NON-WHITE THREAT TO BLACK LIBERATION and **the BIGGEST NON-WHITE ALLY of RACISM/WHITE SUPREMACY.**

This may explain why the mainstream media and entertainment industry promotes and rewards high-profile black males who engage *exclusively* in interracial relationships. They are the most visible role models for impressionable black males -- and the best advertising money can buy when it comes to promoting interracial relationships between black males and white females. *(See Chapter 26 "Operation Jungle Fever" - pg 157).*

The Basic Instinct Of Every Species Is Genetic Survival

What does the smallest microorganism have in common with the most sophisticated human animal? **The instinctual drive to reproduce and perpetuate its own species.** Therefore, non-whites must ask themselves a critical question:

What is the most logical (and desperate) response of any species that fears extinction -- and has the sophisticated brainpower to address their inadequate numbers?

> *"One of the greatest disasters facing the world is the decreasing white population. If we do not take drastic measures to reduce the non-white population, the white race will face extermination or enslavement by these non-white populations." -- A quote from an organization addressing the declining white birth rates (name withheld by request).*
>
> *In the 1970s, South Africa developed race-specific bio-weapons to target blacks and Asians.*
>
> *In September 2000, the Project for a New American Century published a document in which Dick Cheney described race-specific bio-weapons as "politically useful tools".*
>
> *(SOURCE: Alex Jones' "End Game" DVD, www.infowars.com)*

It is up to the readers to decide the truth for themselves.

"A third fear involves a slightly different scenario -- a world in which non-white people might someday gain the kind of power over whites that whites have long monopolized...

And then what? Many whites fear that the result won't be a system that is more just, but a system in which white people become the minority and could be treated as whites have long treated non-whites.

This is perhaps the deepest fear that lives in the heart of whiteness. It is not really a fear of non-white people. It's a fear of the depravity that lives in our own hearts: Are non-white people capable of doing to us the barbaric things we have done to them?"

Robert Jensen, "The Fears of White People"(white professor, University of Texas)

WEÂPON #2

BEÂUTY

(DEMORÂLIZE)

"Once you convince someone to hate the reflection in their mirror, you can convince them of anything."

Anon

CHAPTER EIGHT

THE BEAUTY CON GAME

The old cliché -- "Beauty's in the eye of the beholder" – is no match for the power of white supremacy. Under this system, beauty has become a zero-sum equation for whites and non-whites, which states: (1) If whites are the most attractive, non-whites must be the least attractive. (2) If light skin is a sign of (racial) beauty, dark skin must be a sign of (racial) ugliness.

Black Inferiority Complexes Are Rooted In Our Mirrors

This (false) man-made concept of beauty is used to instill the FIRST seeds of self-hatred and inferiority in non-white children -- in particular, in the darkest-skinned people.

It is critical that we understand how the **second weapon of Mass Mind Destruction – BEAUTY** – functions so we will understand why so many non-whites despise the person in their mirrors.

Debunking White Supremacy Beauty Myths

MYTH #1: We Should Take Credit For An Accident Of Birth

We have no control over the parents we have, the genes we inherit, or the color of the woman that delivered us into this world. Giving ourselves credit for being born white, black, red, or green; light or dark-skinned; six-foot-two or four-foot-one; blue-eyed or brown-eyed; is the same as taking credit for having two hands and two feet.

Our skin color is an accident of birth; a random toss of the genetic dice. To base our superiority on something we had no control over is foolish. We should only take credit for what we have personally accomplished.

MYTH #2: God Made Whites Superior To Blacks

If this is true then the following must also be true:

1. God CANNOT be all-powerful and all-knowing because He made the African man and woman the first people on earth. (He made a mistake).
2. Two inferior human beings (the African man and woman) can produce two superior offspring (the European man and woman).

MYTH #3: Mother Nature Is Clueless And Incompetent

Mother Nature – the physical manifestation of GOD – gave every species – including humans -- the physical traits needed for survival. Europeans have straighter, longer hair that provides protection in a cold climate. Pale skin and light eyes indicates that whites have less melanin than more melanated people (of color), and also indicates a native environment where there was less exposure to intense, direct sunlight.

Mother Nature chose Africa as the birthplace of all humankind and chose the African man and woman to be the first people on earth. She equipped Africans with dark eyes, tightly spiraled hair, and the most melanin, which makes dark skin ideal for Africa's climate and intense heat and sunlight.

Light skin, hair, and eyes are more desirable in a cold climate with less intense sunlight since melanin blocks the absorption of sunlight. Bottom line, the differences in skin color for whites evolved due to natural selection, genetics, and environment, NOT racial or intellectual superiority.

MYTH #4: One Beauty Standard (European) Fits All (Races)

False. The physical differences between different ethnic groups are determined by genetics, the environment, and other biological factors. It is illogical (and insane) to judge all human beings by ONE beauty standard, just like it is insane (and illogical) to expect a Rottweiler to look like a Great Dane just because both are DOGS.

MYTH #5: The European Beauty Standard Is A Universal Standard

False. It is ILLOGICAL (and insane) for the white minority (10% of the people on the planet) to be the standard for what is normal or desirable for the other non-white 90%. In fact, today's (European) beauty standards are the exact opposite of the beauty standards that existed hundreds of years before white supremacy infected the planet:

Pre-Modern Asian Ideas On Race

The text below is reprinted from the article, *"Universal preference of whiteness over blackness?"* by colorq.org. (www.colorq.org/articles/article.aspx?d=1999&x=blackwhite).

Standards of beauty in South and Southeast Asia: Marco Polo reports on the Dravidians of South India: "It is a fact that in this country when a child is born they anoint him once a week with oil of sesame, and this makes him grow much darker than when he was born.

In the Chinese record Nan tsi Chou, a Chinese traveler to Southeast Asia wrote of the people: "...they consider black the most beautiful."

Prior to European colonization, the ancient Visayans of the Philippines considered the very opposite of high noses and oval faces handsome.

Visayans, as well as some other Austronesian peoples in Malaysia and Indonesia, compressed their babies' skulls to achieve broad faces and flat noses.

Old Chinese Views On Caucasians

The text below is reprinted from the article, *"Universal preference of whiteness over blackness?"* -- courtesy of www.colorq.org.

By traditional Chinese opera conventions, a black face is considered nobler. Actors wear masks that denote the character's qualities. A predominantly black face indicates courage, righteousness, and incorruptibility. A predominantly white face indicates craftiness, deceit, and knavery.

Ming Dynasty China records even state that Caucasians, especially blondes, are physically unattractive: "Huihui are shaggy with big noses, and Qipchags have light hair and blue eyes. Their appearance is vile and peculiar, so there are those (Chinese) who do not wish to marry them."

This distaste for blondes is a stark contrast to the worship of European standards of beauty so prevalent among modern Asians today.

The Character And Beauty Of Ethiopians Admired By Ancient Europeans

The text below is reprinted from the article, *"Universal preference of whiteness over blackness?"* -- courtesy of www.colorq.org.

"The Ethiopians," wrote Herodotos, "are said to be the tallest and best-looking people in the world." (In ancient Roman/Greek writings, the term "Ethiopian" is loosely used to refer to all black Africans).

Greek writer Diodoros wrote of the Ethiopians: "Their piety has been published abroad among all men, and it is generally held that the sacrifices practiced among the Ethiopians are those which are the most pleasing to heaven." (Sources and links for pp 58-59 found on website).

If Europeans were living back in ancient times, they might be searching for cosmetic remedies to darken their skin and kink up their hair – like the millions of whites today who flock to beaches and tanning salons to darken their skin; to plastic surgeons to thicken their lips, and enlarge breasts and buttocks; and to hair salons to perm, wave, kink, and curl their hair.

MYTH #6: Africans Worshipped The First Europeans As "Gods"

False. Contrary to the racist delusions of Hollywood moviemakers, Africans did not think the first Europeans were gods (or goddesses). Some Africans believed Europeans were white because they had been skinned alive.

Others, like Olaudah Equiano, was terrified by the appearance of the white men who kidnapped him from his African village and brought him to the New World on a slaveship in 1756.

After ten years of enslavement, Olaudah purchased his freedom and wrote his autobiography, describing the horrors of slavery, the cruelty of slaveowners, and how he fainted with fright the first time he saw the *"white men with horrible looks, red faces, and long hair."*

In pre-colonial Africa, a skin-color inferiority complex was nonexistent. Africans took pride in their skin, hair, and features because it was desirable (normal) to look like their fathers, mothers, aunts, uncles, and grandparents.

Africans never knew they were "inferior" **until the Europeans colonized (conquered) Africa,** and used physical differences to justify enslaving, robbing, raping, and murdering them. Only after four centuries of being FORCE-FED these artificially created (false) European beauty standards, Africans, and their descendants, learned to hate what they saw in the mirror.

MYTH #7: It Is Normal For One Race To Think A Different Race Is More Attractive (Superior)

False. It is ABNORMAL to view another race as more attractive, just like it is ABNORMAL to look into a mirror and see ugliness. A black child will not automatically think pale skin is superior to his skin, any more than a white child thinks his pale skin is inferior. Every child – regardless of race -- has a healthy amount of self-esteem until he or she is ***taught*** to feel inferior.

What Happened To "Black Is Beautiful?"

The slogan, "Black is beautiful," which became popular in the 1970s, was little more than a good idea turned bad fad. By the time non-black merchandisers, the blax-ploitation filmmakers, and the media made a fortune from *Superfly* hats, high-heeled shoes, idiotic films, and afro combs, "black and proud" became synonymous with "black and foolish."

We did not understand why such a wonderful slogan had been doomed from the start. We did not understand that we had to scrape off the rusted paint of self-hatred and inferiority before we applied a new paint job. We did not understand that in order to REDO, we first had to ***UNDO.***

The telltale sign of past or present European colonization of a non-white nation: the people become self-hating.

If European (white supremacy) beauty standards had not been literally rammed down the throats of millions of Asians, it is doubtful a single Asian woman would correct a NONEXISTENT flaw by undergoing eye surgery to make her slanted eyes rounder, and more "Western" (European).

If European beauty standards had not been literally rammed down the throats of Africans and Indians (and their descendants), it is doubtful a single non-white man or woman would even think of using bleaching creams or swallowing poisonous pills, risking skin cancer, leukemia, thyroid disorders, and leprosy to lighten (destroy) the most age-resistant skin on earth.

MYTH #8: Whites Benefit From The White Supremacy Beauty Standard

The BEAUTY CON GAME has boomeranged on the very ones it was supposed to benefit by breeding an unhealthy obsession with the exterior rather than the more important interior. This obsession is the primary reason there is so much unhappiness within the white collective over minor (and nonexistent) flaws in their own appearances.

Ironically, even though whites are supposed to be the most attractive people on the planet (in a system of white supremacy), they are also the most dissatisfied with their own appearance -- and the MOST INSECURE.

This predominantly white obsession with appearance (perfection) can be seen in the endless snake-oil advertisements for the billion-dollar beauty industry. For the promise of whiter (perfect) teeth, perfect noses, chins, thighs, abs, stomachs, lips, hair, skin, bigger breasts, wrinkle-free skin, potions, lotions, and the promise of staying young forever, millions of Americans swallow billions of pills and voluntarily go under the knife.

This obsession with perfection is also apparent in the epidemic of eating disorders that are most common among the white female population, who ironically, are also held up as the standard of feminine beauty for non-white females.

Truth Is Stranger Than Fiction (In A White Supremacy System)

Despite the inferiority programming of non-white females, black and Asian women generally have a more positive body image than Caucasian females, according to a Washington University study.

In addition, black women with **a strong sense of racial identity** actually rated themselves more attractive than pictures of supposedly beautiful white fashion models, and 40% of moderately and severely overweight black women rated their figures to be attractive or very attractive.

Other research indicates that this may be because black women are more flexible in their concepts of beauty than their white counterparts, who express rigid ideals and greater dissatisfaction with their own body-shape. Another survey found black girls were more self-confident in high school than either white or Hispanic girls, and that white girls lost their self-confidence at an earlier age than Hispanic girls.

How can this be true in a white supremacy system where the black female occupies the bottom rung of the beauty totem pole? ***Is the obsession to be "perfect" (superior) undermining the white female's self-esteem rather than building it up?***

Black girls with **a strong sense of racial identity** do not define themselves by (false) white beauty standards. Nor are they totally dependent on looks for self-esteem, but rely on other factors like personality, style, and intelligence. A black girl who is black-identified (instead of white-identified) knows there is nothing inherently wrong with being black; and is less likely to mutilate or surgically alter her body.

Which explains why so many black females view the eating disorders (like bulimia and anorexia) that afflict the white female population with puzzlement and contempt. Black females, in general, do not long for rail thin arms and legs or tiny butts. Their opinion of a sexy body is far more generous and forgiving since perfection is never a requirement.

Black females also have less of a tendency to obsess over minor flaws in their appearance. If a black female is white-identified, she may mimic the self-hating behavior of her white peers, although seldom to the same extreme degree.

White Beauty Standards Are Contemptuous Of ALL Women

Would a culture that truly values its females create a beauty standard that demoralizes and penalizes them? The answer is clear: it does not value them; but in fact, secretly despises, even hates them. This contempt is obvious, given the widespread slaughter of white females **for entertainment and for profit in television, movies, and in real life.**

The white supremacy "beauty standards" actually demonstrate MORE contempt for white females than admiration. A culture that promotes a media-manufactured body ideal -- tall, long-legged, blonde, and bone-thin with zero-body-fat (a boy's body) -- that drives white girls and women to literally starve themselves to death is ANTI-WOMAN -- not woman-loving or woman-respecting.

This is NOT about empathizing with whites, who are victims by their OWN HAND. This is NOT about empathizing with white females who use the same racist standards to elevate themselves above non-white females. ***This is about exposing the BLATANT CONTRADICTIONS of a white beauty standard that even the WHITE CREATORS do not and cannot measure up to.*** The biggest beauty con game victims are non-whites, who have been demoralized by the LIE of white superiority.

Is the epidemic of self-loathing the karmic price the white collective is paying for perpetuating mass self-loathing among non-whites?

America is one of the wealthiest nations in the world YET Americans are plagued by more self-doubt, self-hatred, self-abuse, over-materialism, dysfunctional relationships, broken families, cruelty, jealousy, envy, bullying, vanity, narcissism, eating disorders, self-mutilation, drug and alcohol addiction, mental illness, depression, suicide, sexual deviancy, rape, incest, and homicide – than anywhere else – including the (so-called) Third World.

If the most privileged people on the planet are also the most miserable, they are missing the two most valuable lessons of their lives:

1. There is NO substitution for genuine self-respect and self-esteem. If we are mistreating others, we will have neither.
2. If we escape punishment for our ill deeds and crimes, ultimately, we will find a way to punish ourselves.

CHAPTER 9

STRAIGHT TALK ABOUT NAPPY HAIR

"Don't remove the kinks from your HAIR. Remove them from your BRAIN." -- The Honorable Marcus Mosiah Garvey [1887-1940]

Baby, Let Your Hair Hang Down

Audrey was sitting across a candlelit table from Ernest, a man she met the week before on the commuter train to work. She had dressed carefully for their first date. Not too plain-jane but not too sexy. She didn't want him to think she was willing to trade her body for a glass of wine and a plate of blackened tilapia.

The conversation had been decent but nothing special. Audrey had been hoping for some kind of spark then warned herself to relax and just enjoy the man's company. That was the problem with single women like herself; they expected an instant connection with a man they just met. For all she knew, Ernest was having the same doubts about her.

"This fish is delicious," Audrey said, letting him know she appreciated the meal he was paying for.

"Not as delicious as you," Ernest said, bold brown eyes staring over his raised cocktail glass.

"You know what they say. Appearances can be deceiving," Audrey teased, refusing to take his comment seriously. She was a little flattered by his constant staring, but also a little unnerved. Finally, she asked, "Is something wrong?"

"Wrong?"

"You keep staring."

"Just wondering..." His voice trailed off, a wistful look on his face.

"About what?" Audrey mentally crossed her fingers. *Please don't let this man say something stupid.*

"I was wondering what you'd look like if you let your hair down."

"Let my what down?" She sat back, frowning.

"It's sexy," Ernest continued. "When a woman lets her hair down." He tilted his head back and rolled his shoulders to demonstrate.

"Uh-huh," Audrey said, a self-conscious hand straying to the French roll she'd plastered with hair goo to keep the short, stray hairs lying flat.

"If I was your man, would you let your hair down for me?"

"But, see, you're not my man, so I don't have to answer that," Audrey said firmly.

"I might be one day."

Why was this man going there on their first date? And why was the fool talking about letting her hair down when it barely reached her shoulders?

Unfortunately, Audrey knew exactly what Ernest meant. If she had seen that tired scene once, she had seen it a hundred times:

The prim and proper, plain-Jane white female, hair in a tight bun, glasses, white blouse buttoned up to her chin, who hadn't had sex since the Great Depression. The handsome male hero walks in the door. Bam! Instant attraction! The top buttons of her blouse pop loose. She reaches up and pulls out that one strategically placed hairpin, shakes her head, and her long hair tumbles around her face, transforming her into a raging sex kitten!

When Audrey was younger, she wanted long hair like that, but now, just a few days short of her 40th birthday, she was no longer impressed with Hollywood's idea of sexy. She thought it fake, silly, and too contrived. In fact, spending so much time and money fretting, fixing, and worrying about her hair was wearing on her last nerve.

She was sick of waiting for hours at the beauty salon, sick of hair relaxers, hair straighteners, and hair rollers. She was sick of trying to stretch, pull, and shape her short hair into a decent style every morning. Audrey had decided that this would be the year to throw away the relaxers and curling irons, and start wearing her hair natural. And now this clown wanted to turn her into a piss-poor imitation of a white female?

Ten years ago, Ernest's careless comment would have made her feel inadequate – or it might have driven her to the nearest hair weave salon to accommodate his inappropriate, and frankly, rude expectations. Ernest had no idea how much he had turned her off, or that this would be their last date, because he was still smiling and waiting for her response.

"Ernie," Audrey cooed, giving him a seductive smile. "I'll let my hair down on one condition."

"What?" Ernest leaned forward, an eager look on his face.

"You let your hair grow long and silky, so I can run my fingers through it." Then Audrey's eyes traveled slowly and deliberately up to the balding spot on top of his thinning, close-cropped, nappy fade.

THE END

The "Joy" Of Nappy Humor

Don Imus and his "crew" take aim at the hair and sexual morality of eight black teenaged girls on the Rutgers basketball team (April 4, 2007).

IMUS (host): So, I watched the basketball game last night between -- a little bit of Rutgers and Tennessee, the women's final.
ROSENBERG (former Imus sports announcer): Yeah, Tennessee won last night -- seventh championship for Pat Summitt, I-Man. They beat Rutgers by 13 points.
IMUS: That's some rough girls from Rutgers. Man, they got tattoos --
McGUIRK (producer): Some hard-core hos.

IMUS: That's some nappy-headed hos there. I'm gonna tell you that now, man, that's some -- woo. And the girls from Tennessee, they all look cute...
McGUIRK: A Spike Lee thing.
IMUS: Yeah.
McGUIRK: The Jigaboos vs. the Wannabes -- that movie he had.
IMUS: Yeah, it was a tough --
McCORD (newsman): Do The Right Thing.
McGUIRK: Yeah, yeah, yeah.
IMUS: I don't know if I'd have wanted to beat Rutgers or not, but they did, right?
ROSENBERG: It was a tough watch. The more I look at Rutgers, they look exactly like the Toronto Raptors.
RUFFINO (engineer): Only tougher.
McGUIRK: The [Memphis] Grizzlies would be more appropriate.

Nappy hair has been a frequent target of white ridicule. There is a tremendous amount of pressure for black women to imitate a beauty standard that was designed for white women. This makes hair a sensitive topic for many black females. Even though black males are not pressured to have long hair, straight hair, "good hair," or any hair at all, they are just as obsessive (and conflicted) about "black hair." One only has to turn the clock back 40 years to recall the "conk" hairstyles that were once popular among black males.

A Short Walk Down Memory Lane...

"The "conk" was a popular hairstyle for black men from the 1920s to the 1960s. The naturally "kinky" hair was chemically straightened using lye, and styled into pompadours that resembled white hairstyles. Some men chose to simply slick their straightened hair back to lie flat on their heads (like white males). At home, a "do-rag" (head wrap or scarf) had to be worn to prevent sweat and other situations to prevent the "conked" hair from reverting back to its natural (nappy) state. Relaxers had to be constantly reapplied as new hair grew in.

Malcolm X On The "Conk" Hairstyle

"This was the first really big step toward self-degradation: when I endured all of that pain, literally burning my flesh, to have it look like a white man's hair. I had joined that multitude of Negro men and women in America who are brainwashed into believing that the black people are 'inferior' and the white people 'superior' - that they will even violate and mutilate their God-created bodies to try to look 'pretty' by white standards.

Look around today, in every small town and big city, from two-bit catfish and soda-pop joints into the 'integrated' lobby of the Waldorf-Astoria, and you'll see conks on black men, and black women wearing these green and pink and purple and red and platinum blonde wigs. They're all more ridiculous than a slapstick comedy. It makes you wonder if the Negro has completely lost his sense of identity, lost touch with himself."

If the conk was a form of self-degradation for the black male, are hair straighteners, perms, and hair weaves inflicting the same kind of self-esteem damage on the unsuspecting black female?

A Classic Case Of The Pot Calling The Kettle "Nappy"

Despite the black male's own history of hair obsession, he is quick to belittle black women for all the time and money they spend on their hair, forgetting that HE is the one who rewards black females who come the closest to the white beauty standard. The black male's hypocritical and contradictory "pride" in his own blackness is seldom extended to black women who refuse to straighten their hair (imitate white beauty), and proudly and defiantly wear their natural hair short, braided, locked or dreadlocked.

Black females who wear their naturally nappy hair often run the risk of being labeled as less feminine and less attractive by black males than their long, and permed-hair female peers. When black women try to live up (or down) to the unreasonable standards FORCED upon them by white society and black males (who often openly admire "white features"), they are ridiculed for wearing hair weaves, wigs, and "horse hair."

Some black male comedians -- who wear their OWN hair in locks as a sign of so-called "racial pride" -- often use black women's hair as the butt of their "unbeweavable" and "nappy hair" humor.

> *"Now they aren't 'hos,' but there were some nappy-headed women on that team. Those are some of the ugliest women I've ever seen in my whole life." -- black comic D.L. Hughley on Jay Leno's "Tonight Show" (May 7, 2007), "joking" about the black girls on the Rutgers University Basketball team.*

Three FACTS (some) black males conveniently ignore: (1) the black female's hair is the SAME HAIR THAT GROWS OUT OF THEIR OWN SCALPS, (2) their GENES are ***50 percent responsible for the hair of the black female***, and (3) their ridicule of (and contempt for) the black female's hair is **an ANNOUNCEMENT of their contempt for themselves, their genetics, and the hair on their own heads.**

Men Set the Beauty Standards For Every Culture

In male-dominated cultures (like America) men, NOT women, set the standards for feminine beauty. Once this "beauty standard" is established, the women fall in line by conforming (or trying to conform) to these standards. The most powerful males in a male-dominated society use the most desirable females to enhance their status in the eyes of other males. The women strike a similar bargain, trading their youth (fertility), and beauty (high status) for financial security (marriage).

Do not confuse 'status" with validation. In a male-dominated society, women CANNOT validate men; ***only men can validate other men***. The same is true for women in a male-dominated society. Women ***do not validate*** women; they COMPETE with other women. Only men can validate women.

Make no mistake. The black community is a male-dominated society. It does not matter that black females head up almost 70% of black households. That is an economic and political reality (tragedy), NOT a cultural choice. Like all males in a male-dominated society (like America) most males, in general, reject female leadership. However, most women -- and black women are no exception -- actually welcome male leadership. In other words, most black women will follow black men, but most black men will not follow black women. The proof:

1. the preacher
2. the politician
3. the pimp

Whether it is the church, the meeting hall, or the street corner, black men usually lead; black women usually follow. With a few exceptions, black women are the foot soldiers and seldom the generals in most black organizations.

When it comes to female beauty standards, black males -- like all males in a male-dominated society -- decide what is desirable and what is not. In nearly every culture in the world, women look to the men in their culture to ***validate*** their self-worth and value as women. Why is this so important to understand?

Because males collectively have the power to psychologically devastate females collectively if they do not validate their worth AS females.

For example, the white male supremacist elevates the thin, blonde, blue-eyed, pale-skinned female because she has the highest genetic value in a society that prizes "whiteness" and "lightness." White females are programmed from childhood to accept this narrowly defined beauty standard, and will judge their own beauty (value) as females by this standard.

To attract men (a desirable mate), millions of white females imitate (or try to imitate) the beauty standard set by white males so they can be ***validated*** (and socially, financially, and romantically rewarded) by white males. We know this is true from the astronomical number of white females (of all ages and incomes) who dye their hair blond and starve themselves to be thin.

The black (?) beauty standard for black females -- light skin, long hair, and European features -- is based on the same white supremacy standards. Black females learn the painful lesson at an early age that the most powerful and influential black males – as well as many average and ordinary black males -- "reward" black females who are closer in appearance to the white standard of beauty. The proof: The (very) light-skinned, biracial, Asian, white wives and girlfriends of the most influential and successful (status-seeking) black men.

Black Male Invalidation Of Black Females

Detroit headline: A local DJ and club promoter cancels party that would let "light-skinned" black women into the club for free (2007)

In their attempt to gain status, some black males seek validation from the male with the highest status in a white supremacy society -- ***the powerful white male.***

When the black male deliberately chooses the female with the highest status (the white or white-appearing female) -- he is ***unconsciously reinforcing his own inferiority*** as a non-white person.

Even if she does not articulate it, the black female knows ***instinctively*** that the black male's (foolish) choice of (white) status over honoring his female mirror image is ***unjust***, and is the greatest possible betrayal that a man can commit against the women of his race. This unspoken (but obvious) resentment accounts for a great deal of the black woman's anger toward black men. If the black female cannot depend on the black male to validate her worth as a female, who then can she turn to for protection?

If the black male refuses to validate (and value) the black woman (the black womb), how can he validate and value himself? Perhaps this explains his callous disregard for the black female and why black males slaughter each other without hesitation.

In 2007, when Beyonce appeared on the cover of Sports Illustrated's annual "Swimsuit Issue," angry white readers demanded subscription cancellations. One reason given by a white male subscriber: *"My daughters grew up identifying with the models in the Swimsuit Issue, and wanting to be like them. How is my daughter supposed to see herself in Beyonce?"*

The white male -- collectively -- understands the potentially devastating effect on the white female psyche when a non-white female is elevated above the white female -- even for something as trivial as a magazine cover. White males understand, collectively, that in order to validate themselves, they must validate (and uplift) the white female (the white womb). Together, this reinforces the VALUE of white life. The black male is encouraged to do just the opposite -- uplift white females and degrade black females -- yet the black male does not understand why ***black life -- including his -- is so cheap.***

If black males took a page out of the white male's book, flipped their tragic (and self-genocidal) black scripts, and collectively embraced their female mirror images in all shades of brown and black, wearing a crown of natural hair, the companies that profit from hair weaves, wigs, permed-hair, and skin-bleaching products ***would go out of business***. Black males would then reap the rich psychological and spiritual rewards of LOVING THEMSELVES by elevating and honoring the (black) womb that delivered them into the world.

Bottom line: black males must accept some of the blame for the time, attention, anxiety, and insanity displayed by (some) black women about their hair.

How The Beauty Con Game Penalizes Black Males

> *"When you teach a man to hate his lips, the lips that God gave him, the shape of the nose that God gave him, the texture of the hair that God gave him, the color of the skin that God gave him, you've committed the worst crime that a race of people can commit." – Malcolm X*

The black male's secret shame (of looking and being too black) explains his collective disrespect toward black females, and it explains why so many successful, status-seeking black males deliberately choose non-black females. It has less to do with non-black women being more desirable and more to do with what non-black women represent to the self-esteem-starved black male who measures his success by white (male) standards.

The black man's (unreasonable and self-genocidal) resentment toward the black female may be due in part to him subconciously BLAMING her for delivering him -- literally -- as a black male into a black-male-hating white world.

Where Have All The Shampoo Girls Gone?

Recently, a black male blogger from Chicago wanted to know...

"Where are all the white girls I see in those TV shampoo commercials? I have never seen a white female in person who had the kind of hair I see in those commercials."

The glorious manes seen on TV require hair additions, weaves, falls, wigs, sophisticated lighting techniques, film and photo retouching, and artificial substances and devices to add volume, curl, density, color, and sheen to hair.

These media-manufactured (false) television images are the primary reason so many females (of all races) are so dissatisfied with the hair growing out of their scalps, and why so many women (of all races) chemically treat, process, lenthen, straighten, thicken, curl, wave, kink, and color their hair, or use a battalion of artificial devices to enhance it.

Different Is Beautiful

Black hair is unique when compared to the hair of many other races. It is only through the lens of white supremacy/ black inferiority that this difference becomes a demoralizing focal point for many blacks. Mother Nature – the physical manifestation of God – made us perfect in God's sight. Our hair serves a sacred purpose in its natural state, growing up toward the sun, like a spiritual antenna that connects us to our Creator.

The self-loving black male and female embraces the softness, texture, durability, and versatility of black hair. They know "hair" can't cook, clean, make love, comfort us, earn a living, save a life, nurse us back to health, fix a flat tire or a leaky faucet, or raise a healthy, happy child.

They know that hair – be it long, short, curly, wavy, kinky or straight -- is only a small part of what makes a man or woman desirable. The self-loving black male and black female know from experience that a long head of hair shrinks in importance if what lies beneath the scalp is wholly unappealing.

"A person obsessed with the exterior is already inferior -- in his or her own mind." -- Anon

"The best and most beautiful things in the world cannot be seen, touched...but are felt in the heart."

Helen Keller
1880 - 1968)

CHAPTER 10

STRAIGHT TALK ABOUT BEAUTY

"Civilized" VS Primitive Beauty Standards

Americans (and other technologically advanced societies) spend billions of dollars to artificially enhance what nature did -- or did not -- give them. Body and face paint, artificially produced suntans, hair weaves, wigs, hairpieces, toupees, hair transplants, makeup, lipstick, eye shadow, hair color, tattoos, piercings, and plastic surgery are used by millions of "civilized" people to make themselves more appealing to the opposite (or the same) sex.

What, then, is the real difference between a woman from the Central African Sara tribe with lip plates and a white woman in Hollywood, California with breast implants (breast plates)? How is the New Zealand Maori warrior with facial tattoos and body markings more "primitive-looking" than the white male college student in Paris, France with body piercings and tattoos?

The westernized Beauty Con Game is a multi-billion-dollar industry that has claimed billions of victims -- of all races -- by creating a false standard of beauty for whites and non-whites. In order to keep the billions pouring in, the industry must set the bar for "beauty" (normalcy) impossibly high to keep the white and non-white populations insecure. Then, the industry can sell cosmetic "solutions" for imaginary imperfections.

The World's Biggest Beauty Secret

The biggest beauty secret on the planet cannot be found in a $300 vial of skin cream or in a pair of skilled plastic surgeon's hands. What is this secret?

Could it be the infusion of African genes into the European gene pool that gives pale skin more color (and a deeper tan), makes hair thicker, wavy, or curly, and adds more sensuousness (fullness) to lips, noses, and other facial features?

If one studies the history of Africans (Moors), who traveled the ancient world and conquered Europe long before Christopher Columbus sailed to America, one might imagine that "swarthy" (dark) and "olive" complexions, dark, curly, wavy, and wavy-kinky hair; dark hair, dark eyes, and full lips in ***some*** parts of Europe may be visible evidence of African genetic influences. While this cannot be stated as scientific fact; it is certainly not an unreasonable theory.

If, as scientists have claimed, ALL human life began in Africa -- every man, woman and child is a ***modification of the original African man and woman.*** (Links & sources available on website).

True Beauty Is Not For Sale At The Cosmetic Counter

True beauty is NOT a small, pointy nose, long blond hair, or a bone-thin, pale body. Beauty is the look in a lover's eyes, the curve of a woman's cheek, or a man's broad, strong back. It is a smile that lights up a face, or a laugh that makes us smile. It's the graceful wTaay someone moves or dances. Beauty is eloquence; intelligence; wisdom; kindness; and determination.

God gave all of us something special; a special quality or gift that no one else in the world possesses in the same way we do. God's greatest gifts can be found in a pair of eyes that sparkle, in the hands of a doctor who delivers a new life into the world, or a powerful voice that makes the angels weep. Or it might be the greatest gift of all: a kind, intelligent, loving human being.

Mother Nature Gets The Last Word

Is there a beauty standard that is objective, logical, and can be applied to all human beings, regardless of race? *Absolutely.* Who is qualified to set this standard? The most powerful force on earth: ***Mother Nature.***

She is the ***VISIBLE, PHYSICAL, and TANGIBLE MANIFESTATION OF GOD***. She is the final judge of all that is good and perfect in this world.

Mother Nature does not acknowledge beauty or ugliness based on artificial, manmade standards. Mother Nature does not put more value on an eye because it is blue than she does on a brown eye. Only man and woman, in their endless foolishness, put more value on superficial, useless differences than they do on the value of a human life.

The shape of a nose, the color of an eye, the length of hair, or a jutting chin is a matter of taste, NOT proof of racial superiority. There is NO functional purpose that straight blond hair has that is not also present in dark nappy hair.

Is a blind blue eye superior to a brown eye with 20-20 vision?

What does Mother Nature consider beautiful? A strong body, limbs without deformities; healthy skin, teeth, vitality, good vision, hearing, and speech are beautiful to nature. But the MOST IMPORTANT TRAIT IN EVERY SPECIES is invisible to the human eye: **THE ABILITY TO REPRODUCE.**

Yet, the most fertile woman on the planet – THE BLACK WOMAN – is the most demeaned woman on the planet. Again, the question is:

Could the true emotion that fuels so much contempt for the fertile, full-lipped, full-hipped, curvaceous black female be ENVY?

Mother Nature may have already answered that question.

CHAPTER 11

LEGEND OF THE PURPLE PEOPLE

In a distant place and time on planet Earth, there were two races of people in a tiny country called PURPLE LAND. The PURPLE PEOPLE had bright purple skin, purple eyes, green lips, and thick, green rope hair. The white minority in PURPLE LAND had white skin, blond hair, and blue eyes.

The PURPLE PEOPLE owned and controlled all the banks (and the money), the schools and universities, the businesses, the criminal justice system, and the government. Despite being in a supremely superior position, the PURPLE PEOPLE never missed an opportunity to tell the white people how inferior white people were. The PURPLE PEOPLE even had white statues on their lawns with exaggerated white features, like bulging blue eyes and thin lips that stretched from ear to ear.

PURPLE PEOPLE claimed the white people were too stupid to learn, but just to make sure they stayed stupid, the PURPLE PEOPLE created a separate and unequal school system that was inferior to the PURPLE schools. The white schools were in horrible condition; with leaking roofs, lead paint, broken desks, and the outdated schoolbooks discarded by the better-educated PURPLE CHILDREN.

The teachers who couldn't cut it in the PURPLE schools were sent to the white schools where no one would know the difference. Since the PURPLE PEOPLE had a superior education, naturally they got most of good jobs, while the whites took the menial jobs, or had no jobs at all.

It was a depressing sight to travel through the white neighborhoods. The sidewalks were cracked, the city street sweepers skipped weekly cleanings, and the street lamps stayed broken. On every third corner, there were liquor stores that stayed open 24 hours a day – some within blocks of white grammar schools. Young white males openly sold crack, heroin, and reefer on the street corners but the police seemed oblivious to their criminal activity.

In the morning, the commuter trains from the PURPLE suburbs would pass through the white neighborhoods. The PURPLE PEOPLE on the train would shake their heads and say, it didn't make sense for people to live like animals. Of course, PURPLE PEOPLE never said it when white people were around.

The white women were horrible and overweight from eating cheap junk food since fresh fruits and vegetables were too expensive. The men were worse, always standing on street corners and drinking out of paper bags, and blaming the PURPLE MAN for all their problems. Even the movies and television were depressing because white people were always playing fools or criminals.

White people never saw white people kissing, hugging, or making love on TV. Secretly, some whites believed that love and romance were reserved for PURPLE PEOPLE. Some whites resented the PURPLE-PEOPLE-ONLY images, and started a white civil rights organization to fight PURPLE racism. Some complained to their church leaders, and were told to stay on their knees, pray, and to stop worrying about this life because they would be rewarded in the next one.

This confused the white people because no one told PURPLE PEOPLE, who read the same Bible, to stay on their knees. After a while, the white people were too confused and demoralized to fight the powers-that-be. They figured, if they couldn't beat the PURPLE PEOPLE, maybe they better join them.

They hung framed pictures of their savior, a PURPLE MAN with green hair, on their living room walls. They didn't understand why so many young white people were turning their backs on religion and on the PURPLE MAN.

If only, white parents lamented aloud, they hadn't been born with such ugly white skin, blond hair, and blue eyes, their lives, and their children's lives would have been much easier.

White women began using green dye on their blonde hair so they would look more PURPLE and less white. They bought makeup that would turn their pale pink skin a deep purple and green lipstick to wear on their lips. They wore purple contacts to hide their blue eyes then swore they weren't wearing any. Upon seeing the white people strutting proudly in their new get-ups, the PURPLE PEOPLE would chuckle, shake their heads, and say under their breath, *"Isn't it sad to be white? No matter how hard they try, they'll never be as good as PURPLE PEOPLE."*

The white women suffered the most because white men thought PURPLE WOMEN were the absolute sex bomb. The PURPLE WOMEN loved to sneak into the white community to get some of that big, white, you-know-what that the white men were more than happy to give them.

The white man's self-esteem was so battered and bruised, he didn't feel much like a man, so he decided the easiest (and safest) way to be equal to the PURPLE MAN was to find ***any*** PURPLE WOMAN who would have him, so he could be less white and be more acceptable (more purple).

Unfortunately, the people who suffered most were the white women who were left to pick up the pieces and raise their children alone, while the demoralized and frightened white man sought validation in a pair of PURPLE arms. The poor white woman hid her hurt and bewilderment behind a wall of hostility because she was too proud to admit her own men thought she was inferior.

White women didn't know what to do or where to turn. They had tried looking as PURPLE as they could, but the white men wanted the REAL THING. More and more white women turned to religion. They prayed every night to the framed picture of the PURPLE SAVIOR above their empty beds and asked Him to wake the white man up and tell him to come back home where he belonged.

THE END

"A climate of alienation has a profound effect on the Black personality, particularly on the educated Black, who has the opportunity to see how the rest of the world regards him and his people.

It often happens that the Black intellectual thus loses confidence in his own potential and that of his race.

Often the effect is so crushing that some Blacks, having evidence to the contrary, still find it hard to accept the fact we really were the first to civilize the world."

Cheikh Anta Diop
(1923-1986)

WEÂPON #3

WORDS

(CONFUSE)

"The power of the white world is threatened whenever a black man refuses to accept the white world's definitions."

James Baldwin
(1924 - 1987)

Chapter 12

WAR OF THE WORDS

"The most powerful weapon in the known universe is the written and spoken WORD." -- Umoja

Words create thoughts, paint pictures, provoke actions, infuriate, sicken, harm, heal, inspire, soothe, confuse, condemn, deceive, divide, and deliver death with one stroke of a pen. When President Bush said Iraq had "weapons of mass destruction," his WORDS led to the costliest war in US history.

Sticks And Stones May Break Bones But Words Might Kill Our Babies

In September 2005, former US Education Secretary turned talk show host, William Bennett (who served under the Reagan and George Bush, Sr. administrations) said, *"If you wanted to reduce crime, you could -- if that were your sole purpose -- you could abort every black baby in this country and your crime rate would go down."*

Then, he added in a futile (and false) attempt to backtrack from what he really meant, "That would be an impossibly ridiculous and morally reprehensible thing to do, but your crime rate would go down."

There was the predictable outrage from public officials, politicians, talking heads, pre-paid civil rights activists, and the black collective. Instead of reacting emotionally (our usual response), we should appreciate those rare moments of honesty when a member of the elite voices a sincere opinion. We knew this was not the first time (nor will it be the last time) these kinds of sentiments were expressed in public or behind closed doors.

After 400 years in America, we (blacks) should be past the time for "political correctness." We need information we can use. We must develop a thicker skin and less tender feelings. Every time the elite reveal their true feelings and intentions toward the black collective, the black masses BENEFIT.

Bennett need not apologize. He said what he meant, and he meant what he said. Once WORDS are spoken over the public airwaves, they cannot be retracted. Our minds do not work like blackboards that can be erased every time a public figure "misspeaks" (says what he or she really means). Just for argument's sake, let's analyze what this kind of statement really means:

1. Blacks commit more crimes per our population than whites.
2. Blacks are (genetically) more inclined to commit crimes than whites.
3. Fewer black babies mean less crime.
4. Dead (aborted) black babies are good for society.

If blacks are genetically more inclined to commit crimes than whites, middle-class and upper-class blacks would commit the same percentage and the same types of crimes as poor blacks AND poor whites commit. This is false, according to US Justice Department statistics:

1. The typical male inmate – *regardless of race* -- has a substance abuse problem, dropped out before 10th grade, has a fifth grade reading level, and no marketable skills or continuous job record.
2. The majority of male inmates – *regardless of race* — were physically and/or sexually abused as children.
3. The majority of male inmates – *regardless of race* — came from impoverished backgrounds.

Poverty, childhood abuse, and family dysfunction are the greatest predictors of criminal behavior NOT skin color. Yet, with a few (deliberately) spoken WORDS, all black babies were dumped into the same concentration camp pot, regardless of their economic or family circumstances. Bennett's words actually framed a more lethal solution: ***aborting (mass-murdering) black babies is a logical and permanent solution for a crime-free society.***

A More Logical (And Moral) Proposal To Reducing Crime In America Would Be:

> *"If you wanted to reduce crime, if that were your sole purpose, you could increase the number of jobs in poor communities that pay a living wage, have a real war on drugs – not a war on poor black people, stop outsiders from selling guns and supplying drugs to poor black youth, abolish ten-year mandatory sentences for non-violent drug users, abolish three-strikes-you're-out laws for petty and non-violent offenders, provide more drug and alcohol rehabilitation centers, stop police brutality, and provide a decent education for all children, regardless of income or race – and your crime rate would go down."*

Then, the white supremacists would counter (in private) with:

> *"That would be an impossibly ridiculous and morally reprehensible thing to do, because we don't want the black crime rate, poverty rate, prison populations, drug trafficking, or corporate corruption rates to go down."*

Flipping The Logic, We Could Make A Parallel Argument:

"If you wanted to reduce the victims from racism, injustice, unjust and illegal wars, imperialism, corporate greed, and global poverty, you could – if that were your sole purpose – you could abort every white baby in this country and the number of people who are devastated financially, medically, environmentally, and militarily would go down."

After the predictable outrage from internet forums and bloggers, public officials, politicians, political pundits, religious leaders, newspaper and TV journalists, socio-political commentators, shock jocks, and indignant (and terrified) professional blacks, all calling for our black heads on a silver platter, we would issue a public apology, say we *"misspoke;"* that our words were taken *"out of context;"* and that aborting white babies *"...would be an impossibly ridiculous, morally reprehensible thing to do."*

In reality, NO black public official, politician, celebrity, TV journalist, social commentator, or any black professional in any capacity would ever DARE suggest over the public airwaves OR privately that *"...white babies could be aborted."*

NOR ARE WE SUGGESTING THAT ANYONE SHOULD ABORT ANY BABIES OF ANY RACE FOR ANY REASON.

However, if the impossible happened, and some high profile black -- in a moment of insanity -- actually said, *"We could abort white babies in order to have a more peaceful planet,"* they wouldn't have to worry about apologizing. Their high-profile careers would be over permanently...

...like **Tim Hardaway**, a black former NBA player, who was banished from All-Star Weekend and stripped of product endorsements after he said:

"Well, you know I hate gay people. So I let it be known. I don't like gay people and I don't like to be around gay people. I am homophobic. I don't like it."

Not once did Hardaway ever talk about killing, hurting, or maiming gays, or about aborting innocent babies of any race. He never singled out a single gay person by name. He never demeaned or ridiculed a gay person's physical or racial characteristics. Yet, his punishment was swift, severe -- and permanent. Now compare Hardaway's comments to Don Imus SINGLING OUT eight black girls and their racial features for public ridicule.

After weeks of public protest initiated by the National Black Journalists Association, Don Imus was fired. In angry response, hundreds of news, TV, cable, radio commentators, and Internet bloggers, expressed more sympathy for Don Imus, ***the perpetrator***, than they did for the ***real victims:*** eight black teenage girls.

Some people blamed Al Sharpton and Jesse Jackson. Some blamed the NAACP. Some blamed the girls' tattoos, or all blacks in general. The only person who escaped the (irrational) wrath of the Don Imus fan club was the same person ***who had initiated the incident***: *Don Imus.*

> *"Do we really live in a country where we can't call black lady b-ballers "nappy-headed ho's" and keep our jobs?" – www.jossip.com*

> *"Everyone I talk with about the Imus comments knows what he is saying. When one sees the garish, vulgar display of huge women athletes sporting tattoos, the normal human response is one of disgust." – white poster on an Internet forum.*

"I'm no Don Imus fan but the double standard from organizations like the NAACP has got to end. This phony outrage is so typical of our ratings hungry society. GET OVER IT, enough already!" – white poster on an Internet forum

Somehow, in a strange, racist twist of logic, Don Imus became the "victim" of eight black girls whose only crime was being born black, female, and playing basketball on that particular day. It didn't matter that the girls didn't initiate the incident, or that it wasn't their idea to fire Don Imus. Somehow, the black girls became responsible for the racist comments of a sixty-plus white male who should have known better.

The feelings of these academically and athletically talented college students didn't matter to the indignant Don Imus fans, even though Imus had a history of making racist slurs against black women, and had once referred to Gwen Ifill, the black moderator of the highly acclaimed show "Washington Week" as "the cleaning lady."

"Isn't the Times wonderful? It lets the cleaning lady cover the White House."
-- Don Imus speaking about Gwen Ifill (1993)

Later that year Don Imus – the new freedom-of-speech poster child -- was rehired, a richer, more popular personality.

"Citadel Broadcasting Corporation and 77 WABC Radio announced today the return of radio's lone cowboy Don Imus as the station's new morning host beginning Monday, Dec. 3. Imus signed a 5-year deal with Citadel that pays him between $5 and $8 million annually."

"We are ecstatic to bring Don Imus back to morning radio," said 77 WABC President and General Manager Steve Borneman.

Could Don Imus's popularity be due to the vicarious thrill some of his listeners get from hearing Don Imus say the kind of racial slurs PUBLICLY that they only dare use PRIVATELY?

We will never know how much damage was done to the self-esteem of the eight black girls who were publicly humiliated at what must have been the biggest moment of their lives. We will never know how much damage was done to the collective self-esteem of millions of black girls and women who had just received one more public confirmation of their "black female inferiority."

What we do know is the Don Imus incident once again confirms:

AXIOM #6: "THE BLACK VICTIM = A VICTIMLESS CRIME" THEORY. A BLACK PERSON IN A CONFLICT WITH A WHITE PERSON (OR WHITE SYSTEM) CANNOT BE THE VICTIM IN A WHITE SUPREMACY SOCIETY. THE BLACK INDIVIDUAL IS ALWAYS AT FAULT, REGARDLESS OF WHO INITIATED THE CONFLICT, OR WHAT FACTS OR EVIDENCE ARE PRESENT.

Let's Flip The Don Imus Script

John (a fictitious black male ESPN sports announcer) and his black co-host, Tim, are watching a girl's college basketball game where School B's team is made up of white players:

John: Look at those rough-looking white girls with all them tattoos–
Tim (laughs): Them some hard-core hos, man.
John: Whoo! They are some ugly, stringy-haired, pasty-faced, flat-assed hos there--
Tim: The black girls are cute.

Had this exchange occurred on national television, would the Don Imus fan club consider the words of John and Tim "harmless?" Would the Don Imus fan club defend the freedom of speech of two black males who used racial slurs to publicly demean eight white girls on national television? Or would they demand John and Tim's black heads on a platter?

Who's To Blame? Don Imus Or Black Gangsta Rappers?

When Don Imus blamed black gangsta rappers (half his age) for his "nappy-headed hos" comment, he was half right. As long as black males continue to demean black females for profit, we have NO MORAL GROUND to stand on when a white man does it.

"The gangsta rap is raking in billions of dollars saying much more graphic lyrics than Mr. Imus did...that's alright because they are predominantly African American. Here's the bottom line: If you are black, it's fine to call other blacks "nigger." Rap artists and black comedians have been doing that all the time. Jesse and Al aren't crusading for any of the rappers to lose their livelihood. What a country!" -- A white poster on an Internet forum.

The black collective's dangerous double standard of demeaning black people, especially black women, for fun and profit gives license to the Don Imuses of the world, who are simply mimicking the lack of respect black males have for black women and for ourselves.

Every time we spend our money on music, videos, comedy shows, and movies that degrade black people, we become the eager (and foolish) co-conspirators in the ***war of the words*** being used against ourselves.

We are the co-creators of the degraded images of black men and women that are seen all over the world. Until we learn to play on the right side, we will continue to lose the game.

"All around me I saw black men, from the sweeper to the president. As I sat in the hotel lobby and looked around, a voice in my head said to me, 'Richard, do you see black people all around you?'

To which I replied, 'Yeah, man, black all around, I have never seen so many black people in my life.'

Then the voice said, 'Richard, do you see any niggers around you?' I looked around again and said, 'No man, I don't see any niggers, only black people.'"

Comedian Richard Pryor speaking about a trip to the continent of Africa in 1983.

CHAPTER 13

NIGGER REDEFINED

"If America didn't have niggers, they'd have to invent them."
-- James Baldwin (1924-1987)

"Nigger" is the most debated and misunderstood word in the English vocabulary. As long (and as often) as this word has been used, most people do not understand it at all. For those who are uncomfortable with the word, it's time to take the NIGGER out of the closet and strip away its power to devastate us.

The Definition Of "Nigger" In A White Supremacy System:

1. "Nigger" is NOT a racial identity.
2. ALL non-white people are niggers – by default – in a system of white supremacy.
3. "Nigger" is NOT a personality defect.
4. "Nigger" is a political term that defines a social, economic, and political REALITY.
5. A nigger cannot decide who is a nigger and who is not.
6. All black people are niggers but all niggers are not black people.
7. All non-white people are niggers (in a system of white supremacy).
8. There is no place on earth called "Nigger Land," therefore niggers are NOT born (niggers), they are CREATED.
9. White people cannot be niggers in a system of white supremacy.
10. There is NO racial slur for whites that is the social, economic, or political equivalent of "nigger" in a white supremacist system.
11. There is no such thing as "acting like a nigger."
12. Being a nigger has nothing to do with being ignorant, backward, country, poor, or uneducated. Those qualities are found in every ethnic group.
13. No amount of education, professional achievements, or fancy table manners will transform a nigger into a white person in a system of white supremacy.
14. Nigger is not a lifestyle or behavior, it's a condition. Accusing someone of acting like a "nigger" is like saying, "Stop acting poor!" If you're poor, you act poor. In other words, your behavior reflects your conditions NOT your race.
15. If we eliminated poverty and white supremacy, there would be no poor folks or niggers.
16. "Nigger" should never be a term of endearment. This is like greeting a friend who just lost his job by saying, "How you doing, you 'out of work person'?"
17. In the absence of white supremacy, niggers would not exist.

18. In the absence of white supremacy, there would be no need for niggers.
19. A moral and just society is "nigger-proof." (because there would be no need to invent niggers).

Once we understand what a "nigger" is, we will understand that a made-up word **DOES NOT DEFINE WHO WE ARE; it defines WHAT IS BEING DONE TO US.**

Once we understand what the word "nigger" means, we will stop being afraid of a word we did not create. Once we understand that "nigger" does not define (or limit) our humanity, we will stop being ashamed of a word that says more about the creator than it does about us. Then, we will have the time and energy to turn our collective focus to eliminating the conditions that have created "niggers" all over the world.

"Nigger" According To Mr. Neely Fuller, Jr.

"A nigger is a non-white person who is subject to white supremacy. That's the truth. So, people have asked me, 'Do I fit that description?' I say yes, but now, everything in the codebook is supposed to be of constructive value. Otherwise, it's not supposed to be in there.

So, a person may ask how is that constructive, for a white person to call you a nigger and you admit that you are one? You give the definition. Now what have you done when you say the definition of me being a nigger is that I am subject to white supremacy.

Now, what you are doing is indicting the white people who are white supremacists. You have taken the word and made it an indictment, not of yourself, but just of a description of yourself because of what is being done to you.

And then I elaborate on the word 'nigger' by taking it further so people get a dimension of the implications for the word. I call it when a black person is taken under white supremacy and taken through the process of 'niggerization.'

*To end this process you have to end white supremacy through codification and that is the process of de-niggerization. If you're looking for a word that's equivalent to **the word 'nigger'** as applied to a non-white person, it just **means a prisoner of injustice."***

The Origins Of The Most Common Racial Slurs For Whites

1. "Honky" -- a term (created by whites) from the words, "bohunk" and "hunky" to describe Polish and Hungarian immigrants who worked in the stockyards of Chicago during the early 1900s. Blacks began applying the racial slur to all Caucasians, in retaliation for the racist epithets used against blacks.

2. "Cracker" – dates back to the white field bosses who used bullwhips to discipline African slaves. The sound of the whip was described as 'cracking the whip'. The white field bosses who cracked whips were known as 'crackers.'
3. "Redneck" -- originated in 17th century Virginia, because indentured servants were sunburnt while tending plantation crops; having a red neck was caused by working outdoors in the sunlight over the course of their lifetime. Also referred to poor white dirt farmers in Alabama who worked in soil mixed with red clay that was hard to clean off skin.

Bottom-Line Differences Between "Honky" And "Nigger"

1. No white child has an inferiority complex because of the word "honky."
2. When a white adult dredges up his or her most painful childhood memories, being called a "honky" probably isn't one of them.
3. No white person has ever been shot by police, castrated, burned alive, hung from a tree, run out of town, infected with syphilis by their own government, falsely imprisoned, denied housing, a decent education, a home loan, employment, the right to own land, to buy an insurance policy, to rent an apartment, to use a public toilet, to sit in the front of a bus or movie theater, sit in a restaurant, get treatment at a hospital, or denied anything else they wanted because of the word "honky."
4. "Honky" has no legacy (history) of provoking non-white people to brutalize white people. There is NO historical evidence of black people collectively mistreating white people because of the word "honky."
5. "Honky" does not imply a deficit of character, intelligence, or humanity.
6. "Honky" has absolutely NO effect on the quality of white people's lives. It is bland; meaningless; colorless; odorless; white. "Honky" is an empty vessel that holds no collective white pain – which is exactly why the word is tolerated when used by black entertainers.

In contrast, here's a partial list of what "nigger" signifies in a white supremacist society:

Ignorant, dirty, dishonest, foolish, violent, stupid, dangerous, defective, illiterate, incompetent, inferior, unequal, undeserving, idiotic, ghetto, welfare, stealing, dope-dealing, unemployed, lazy, trifling, white-woman-raping, home-invading, car-jacking, crack-smoking, gang-banging, bling-bling-wearing, baby-momma-and-baby-daddy-making, fast-food-fried-chicken-eating, loud-talking, watermelon-chomping, ebonics-writing, gangster-rapping, spear-chucking, jive-talking, promiscuous, hustling, swindling, coons, apes, pimps, chimps, hos, fools, buffoons, gorillas, and porch monkeys.

"Niggers" have been burned alive and hung from trees while white picnickers and their children looked on in amusement. "Niggers" have been run out of town, burned out of black towns and forbidden to live in all-white towns. "Niggers" have been deliberately infected with syphilis and secretly sterilized by their own government.

"Niggers" have been falsely imprisoned, beaten, and murdered by authorities. "Niggers" have been denied decent housing, a decent education, home loans, jobs, a burial plot in a cemetery, medical care, and service at restaurants and hospitals. "Niggers" have been denied the right to own land, buy a life insurance policy, use public toilets, or sit in the front of a bus or movie theater. Even in the 21st century, unarmed "niggers" are still being shot by police, and sodomized with broom handles (NYC), and screwdrivers (Chicago) in police precincts.

"Niggers" have been denied anything and everything that is humanly possible for one human being to deny another human being all because of one word: "nigger."

Some WORDS (like "nigger") CREATE REALITY, while other words (like honky) are just...WORDS

A thorough search in available English language dictionaries in print or on-line failed to turn up a single derogatory word created by blacks to degrade whites or a word that negatively affects the quality of life (or death) for white people. We can safely assume (until proven otherwise):

1. There is no word for white people in the English language that is equivalent to "nigger" because white people cannot be "niggers" in a white supremacy system.
2. A word that has the power to reduce whites to "niggers" cannot exist in a white supremacy system because non-whites do not have the collective power to name, rename, define, or redefine white people collectively in a white supremacy system.
3. In a white supremacy system, only whites have the power to name, rename, define, or redefine any non-white person on the planet. We know this is true because THEY HAVE ALREADY DONE IT.

The Myth Of The Double Standard

> *"If it had been a black man on stage, he'd call them a nigger in a heartbeat and the crowd would have loved it. Chris Rock calls us white folk a cracker, honky and all sorts of things and gets away with it every time he's on stage and no one gets pissed. We went through all the racial things in the 60's and now a black man gets pissed off if a white guy calls him a nigger? Give me a break." – A white male's comment after Michael Richards ("Kramer") screamed racial insults at blacks at a L.A. comedy club in 2006.*

Whites often accuse blacks of having a double standard when it comes to who is allowed to use racial slurs and who is not. This white resentment resurfaced after Michael Richards and Don Imus were forced to apologize publicly for their racial remarks. The accusation of a double standard seems valid until one makes a comparison between comedians Michael Richards and Chris Rock:

"Never go to clubs with metal detectors. Sure, it feels safe inside. But what about all those niggas waiting outside with guns? They know you ain't got one." (Chris Rock entertaining a racially mixed audience)

"Fifty years ago we'd hang you upside down with a fucking fork up your ass. You can talk, you can talk, you're brave now, motherfucker. Throw his ass out. He's a nigger! He's a nigger! He's a nigger! A nigger, look, there's a nigger!" (Michael Richards angrily taunting blacks in the audience)

It is impossible not to question the true motives (or intelligence)- of anyone who doesn't understand the difference between a racial assault and racial humor, however tasteless that humor may be. Despite the readily available video evidence, the media deliberately distorted the sequence of events by (falsely) reporting that the black males initiated the conflict by heckling Richards. However, if one views the actual video, it is clear what really happened:

Two black males who were part of a racially mixed group that entered the club the middle of Richards' act. This disturbance enraged Michael Richards, who focused his rage on the black males, instead of the entire group. In return, the black males heckled Richards, who fired back with racial taunts.

The media labeled the black males as "hecklers" in order to shift the blame for Richards' racist rant to the "victims," which, once again confirms:

AXIOM #6: THE "BLACK VICTIM = A VICTIMLESS CRIME" THEORY. A BLACK PERSON IN A CONFLICT WITH A WHITE PERSON (OR WHITE SYSTEM) CANNOT BE THE VICTIM IN A WHITE SUPREMACY SYSTEM. THE BLACK INDIVIDUAL IS ALWAYS AT FAULT — REGARDLESS OF WHO INITIATED THE CONFLICT, OR WHAT FACTS OR EVIDENCE ARE PRESENT.

Who Benefits From The Racial "Double Standard" In Entertainment?

"Who you calling crazy, honky?" -- George Jefferson, addressing his white neighbor, Tom Willis on The Jeffersons (TV sitcom, 1976)

Why are black entertainers allowed to use racial slurs against whites when white entertainers cannot use them against blacks? Because this creates the (false) perception that blacks are "mistreating" whites as much or more than whites are mistreating blacks, and that whites are the victims of "black racists".

This Premise Is Illogical For Five Reasons:

1. Whites control the entertainment industry, broadcast and cable television,
2. Whites are the radio, TV, and movie censors who decide which words are obscene and which words are not.

3. 99% of the television and Hollywood screenwriters are white.
4. There is no such thing as black racism in a system of white supremacy, therefore...
5. ...whites cannot be victimized by something ***that does not exist.***

From Victimizers to Victims

The black entertainer who is allowed to use racial slurs against whites only adds fuel to the (false) white "argument" that blacks are racist. This idea is most reassuring to certain segments of the white collective because it allows them to be victims, rather than victimizers, and it invalidates the racism claims that blacks legitimately have against whites.

Whites may feel vindicated (and relieved) to be "victimized" (entertained) by "black racists" instead of always being accused of being the racists. In their minds, the black comic who uses racial slurs against whites has "evened the score" despite the lack of a logical and intelligent connection between an hour-long comedy routine and real-life racism.

Whites can afford to laugh at the black comic throwing (harmless) racial jabs because they know at the end of the day (or the end of the routine) that there is nothing that black entertainer can do that will adversely affect the quality of life for a single white person.

In addition, racial humor can be entertaining, occasionally profound, but always harmless when it is directed at white people. When a black entertainer playfully insults or ridicules whites, it allows whites to pat themselves on the back for having such a good sense of humor. Certainly, this is proof – some whites may think -- that not only can whites dish out racism; they can take it!

"Yes, I am a honky. Yes, I love this shirt!!! This shirt gets looks everywhere you go." -- A review by a white poster who purchased a "Shut up Honky" George Jefferson T-shirt on Amazon.com.

Not Everyone Sees The Humor In White Racial Slurs:

"Blacks get a pass when they bash whites, no whites in the Rainbow PUSH Coalition, no White History Month, no White Expo, why?? Whites are the most racially discriminated group in this country and it is pathetic." -- Posted on internet after Michael Richards' racist rant.

Bottom line: It is whites – not blacks – who decide what comedy is and what comedy is not. Whites own and control the majority of television and cable networks, radio stations, newspapers, magazines, awards shows, comedy clubs, studios, distribution companies, and the entire mass media publicity machine.

Had Eddie Murphy never been in the cast of Saturday Night Live or landed a role in a major motion picture, he would not be a household name or one of the most successful black entertainers in America today.

If "Nigger" Is Such A Demeaning Word, Why Do Blacks Use It?

> *"Why was 'nigga' so damn funny when Dave Chappelle did his 'niggas' routine? I saw a whole lot of black people on that show thinkin that was hilarious. How can what Michael Richards did be any worse than a black man pulling in 20 million dollars making nigger jokes?"– Posted on an internet forum.*

A good question; one that many blacks do not want to think about, let alone answer. We demand respect from others even while we continue to disrespect ourselves. A better question: Why are we (blacks) so hooked on self-degradation? Maybe another, more insidious explanation needs to be examined:

> *"Slaves often pandered to racist assumptions by using the word "nigger" to their advantage in the self-deprecatory artifice of "tomming." Implicit was an unspoken reminder that a presumably inferior person or subhuman could not reasonably be held responsible for work performed incorrectly, a fire in the kitchen, or any similar offense.*
>
> *It was a means of deflecting responsibility in the hope of escaping the wrath of an overseer or master, and a self-referential term used to avoid suspicion and put whites at ease." (SOURCE: Stephen Railton, author of 'Tomming in Our Time' (2005).*

In other words, a slave (or a slave-minded black person) who referred to himself or another black person as a "nigger" was telling whites that he accepted his inferior (subordinate) role and posed no threat to white authority.

Could black people calling other black people "nigger" or "nigga" in public in the 21st century be a subconscious attempt to appease whites and deceive whites into thinking we are harmless? Or, are we so clever (and foolish) that we have literally outsmarted ourselves?

The Art Of Self-Niggerization

Referring to other blacks (or ourselves) as "niggers," and using the word "nigger" to define who or what black people are, and what black people do, is little more than our VERBAL and VERY VOCAL ACCEPTANCE of our inferior status (and racial inferiority) in a white supremacist society.

It is the same as saying, *"White people, you are absolutely right to see me for what I am: a nigger."*

When blacks call each other "niggers" in public, at school, at home, in movies, music, and videos, we are ANNOUNCING TO THE ENTIRE WORLD that black people have waved the white flag of self-respect and pose no real threat to anyone but ourselves.

"Refugees? You mean they took away our citizenship, too?"

-- A black Katrina survivor, after hearing the press refer to Lower Ninth Ward residents as "refugees." (2005)

CHAPTER 14

WORDS MORE DEADLY THAN A CATEGORY-5 HURRICANE

HURRICANE KATRINA; Refugees overflowing Baton Rouge
FOXNews.com - Half Katrina Refugees Have Records
USATODAY.com - Americans open doors to Katrina Refugees
Barbara Bush on Hurricane Katrina Refugees
Katrina Refugees Overstay Their Welcome

When the word **"refugee"** instead of **"evacuee"** appeared in the headlines above to describe Katrina survivors, there was an immediate outcry:

> *"It is racist to call American citizens refugees," said the Reverend Jesse Jackson after visiting the Houston Astrodome. Congressional Black Caucus members expressed similar sentiments.*

While our outrage was understandable, we made a critical error. We convinced ourselves that the **most professional news organizations in the world,** like the New York Times and the Associated Press (AP), did not know the difference between the words "evacuee" and "refugee". Despite our protests, some news organizations remained unapologetic about their continued use of the word "refugees" to describe Katrina survivors:

> *"The AP is using the term 'refugee' where appropriate to capture the sweep and scope of the effects of this historic natural disaster on a vast number of our citizens," said (Associated Press) Executive Editor Kathleen Carroll.*

> *"We have not banned the word 'refugee,'" said (NY Times) spokeswoman Catherine Mathis. "We have used it along with 'evacuee,' 'survivor,' 'displaced," and various other terms that fit what our reporters are seeing on the ground.*

What's The Real Difference Between "Evacuee" And "Refugee?"

An "evacuee" is a civilian (non-military ***citizen***) who has been evacuated from a dangerous place OR removed from ***a place of residence*** for reasons of personal security.

A "refugee" -- according to the UN Convention -- is a person (a non-citizen) who, owing to a well-founded fear of persecution for reasons of race, religion, nationality, or political opinion, is ***outside her or his country of nationality*** and is unable or unwilling to return. ***In other words, a "refugee" is NOT a "citizen."***

Winding The Historical Clock Back 163 Years...

1846: Dred Scott, a slave, sues for his freedom. His case goes all the way to the US Supreme Court. The **Dred Scott v. Sandford** decision ruled that people of African descent imported into the United States as slaves, and their descendants – whether slaves or not – could ***never*** be citizens of the United States.

1865: The ***13th Amendment*** is adopted to the United States Constitution officially abolishing slavery *except as punishment for a crime.*

1866: The proposed ***14th Amendment***, which overturns the ***Dred Scott Decision***, and (supposedly) guarantees full rights and citizenship to blacks, is ***rejected*** by 15 states: Texas, Georgia, Florida, Alabama, North Carolina, Arkansas, South Carolina, Kentucky, Virginia, Louisiana, Delaware, Maryland, Mississippi, Ohio, and New Jersey.

When an amendment is proposed by the Congress, it must be ratified (passed) by 3/4 of the states as per the Constitution. At the time the ***14th Amendment*** was proposed, there were 37 states in the Union. Since 22 states passed the ***14th Amendment,*** and **22** is LESS than the required 3/4 of the existing states (as required by the Constitution), ***the 14th Amendment failed.***

1868: Even though the Secretary of State expresses **doubt** about the validity of the ***14th Amendment***, the US Congress passes the ***14th Amendment***.

1875: The US Congress passes the ***Civil Rights Act of 1875*** to protect blacks from private acts of discrimination. The ***Civil Rights Act of 1875*** is invalidated by the US Supreme Court in 1883.

Was the 14th Amendment Unconstitutional?

Yes, according to former US Congressmen John Rarick, attorneys Gene Healy, and Raoul Berger, who have formerly challenged the ***14th Amendment,*** on the grounds that it was never constitutionally ratified because ***less than 3/4 of the existing states of the union at that time*** passed the amendment.

If Rarick, Berger, and Healy are correct, and the ***14th Amendment*** is invalid, the Dred Scott Decision is still the LAW of the land. In other words, ***formers slaves AND the descendants of former slaves are not, and cannot be US citizens -- ever***. (Links/sources can be found on website).

Are Blacks In America 'Citizens' Or 'Refugees?'

The ***Emancipation Proclamation of 1863*** formally abolished slavery, but it did NOT free all slaves from bondage, or automatically grant citizenship to former slaves. To clarify this point, let's define the words, **"immigrant" and "citizen."**

> **Immigrant:** *a legal, permanent, non-citizen who is subject to conditions set by immigration laws. In other words, a legal immigrant is a "free" individual, but all "free" individuals are NOT citizens.*

Citizen: *a member of a state, or a naturalized person who goes through a formal process of naturalization, owes allegiance to a government, and is entitled to protection from that government.*

In other words, for ***non-citizens*** (a refugees or a legal immigrant) to become a US ***citizen***, they MUST complete a formal citizenship or naturalization process. ***What formal citizenship process did former slaves (and freed blacks) complete to become US "citizens?"***

Was Katrina A Clue To The True Status of Black America?

"They are not refugees. They are citizens of the United States."
-- Civil Rights Activist, Al Sharpton.

Is Sharpton correct? A possible answer to the true status of blacks in America may be found in the inhumane response by the US government to Katrina survivors. Why? Because ***citizens are entitled to protection from the government. Non-citizens are not.***

Do not be confused or deceived by the white Katrina victims who were abandoned by the government. During times of war, there are always innocent casualties. Poor people -- even poor whites – are always expendable.

If our analysis sounds too outlandish, the reader is free to find a better explanation to explain why (black) Katrina survivors were called "refugees" by the mainstream media -- and why the US government's response to Katrina survivors was so severely lacking.

Three Critical Questions To Consider:

1. If the Fourteenth Amendment was constitutionally ratified (passed), and it guaranteed ***full rights and citizenship*** to former slaves and free blacks, why did blacks need the ***Civil Rights Act of 1875***?
2. If the rights of blacks (both former slaves and free blacks) were already guaranteed by the US Constitution and the ***14th Amendment***, why did blacks need the ***Civil Rights Act of 1964***?

The Third Question Is One That Has Baffled Black America For Four Decades:

3. If the Fourteenth Amendment guaranteed the descendants of slaves and free blacks FULL US citizenship with all the unalienable rights of citizenship -- **including the right to vote** -- why do black people STILL need a ***Voting Rights Act*** in the 21st century?"

Once we master the WORDS, we will understand exactly what is happening and why it is happening to us.

"If thought corrupts language, language can also corrupt thought."

George Orwell
(1903 - 1950)

CHAPTER 15

CODE WORDS IN A WHITE SUPREMACY SYSTEM

Code Words For Whites

1. **Mainstream, Mainstream America, and Main Street** – standard (white) values, (white) institutions, and (white) individuals that are defined as the most normal.
2. **All-American** – wholesome and normal (white) institutions, values, and people.
3. **Lower class** – lower-income whites. Poor whites are never referred to as the "white underclass" because white skin privilege guarantees that poor whites will always have more status than poor non-whites.
4. **Middle Class** – the assumed status of most whites, regardless of income.
5. **Middle America** – (white) individuals whose values and lifestyle are considered the most normal.
6. **Mom and Apple Pie** – the most wholesome (white) Americans.
7. **Regular** – normal as opposed to abnormal or undesirable. Often used to describe (white) facial features in popular fiction. For example: *"...the deep tan of his skin hinted some Indian or Negro blood but the regularity of his features gave lie to this."* (from the novel "Lila" by Curtis Lucas, © 1955).
8. **Patriotic** – a term that usually refers to (white) US citizens, especially those who support US foreign policies (and aggression) against third-world nations, even if those actions are unjust.
9. **Taxpayers** – (white) US citizens whose taxes support the government.
10. **The Civilized World** – First World people, Europeans, whites.
11. **First World** – new term (created by whites) to refer to the U.S., Western Europe, Japan, & Australia (where non-whites are in the minority and occupy an inferior position). "First" signifies most important, i.e., superior.
12. **Second World** – new term (created by whites) that refers to the Soviet Union, Eastern Europe, China, and Turkey.

13. **Citizen** -- An inhabitant of the US who entitled to the rights, privileges, and protection of their government, distinguished from legal and illegal immigrants and refugees. A naturalized person (immigrant or refugee) who goes through a formal process of naturalization, owes allegiance to a government, and is entitled to protection from that government.

14. **Person** -- a human being, individual, partnership, or corporation that is recognized by law as having rights and duties.

15. **Suburban** – a code word for whites, regardless of income or location, used by the mainstream (white) media and advertising industry.

16. **Gentrification** – when city officials allow affluent people (usually whites) to displace poorer (usually black) inner-city residents from desirable inner-city neighborhoods by raising taxes and declaring imminent domain.

17. **Reverse Discrimination** – a term used by whites who claim affirmative action gives special preference to (unqualified) non-whites over (qualified) whites.

18. **Eurocentric** – a world view and perspective that assumes white people, white culture, and white values are superior to non-white people, culture, and values. Eurocentrism is practiced throughout the world, even in countries where non-whites are the majority.

19. **Evacuee** – a citizen who has been evacuated from a dangerous place OR removed from a place of residence for reasons of personal security.

20. **Pro-Life** – individual and/or organized opposition to the abortion of (white) babies for religious and/or political reasons (such as the declining white birth rate.)

Code Words For Blacks (And All Non-Whites)

1. **Nigger** – a racial slur created by whites to describe blacks and other non-whites, i.e., Arabs are often referred to as "sand niggers."

2. **Negro** – a (made-up) word used from the early 1900s to the late 1970s to describe American-born blacks -- obviously from "Negro-land."

3. **Colored** – any non-white person; a person of color.

4. **Underclass** – blacks who occupy the lowest possible rung of the socio-economic ladder.

5. **Urban** – a code word used by the media and advertising industry for blacks, regardless of income or location.

6. **Inner city** – a predominantly black area of a city, regardless of income and education.

7. **Diversity** – a code word that implies the token inclusion of "minorities" in corporate, educational, and government environments, often for appearance's sake.

8. **Articulate** – an "unusual" black person who is able to express themselves intelligently as opposed to the black "norm" (who is not). An example is the comment former Senator Joe Biden (D-DE), made about former Illinois Senator, Barack Obama, in 2007: *"I mean, you got the first mainstream African-American who is articulate and bright and clean and a nice-looking guy."*

9. **Ebonics** – describes the type of "black English" spoken by (some) black children and adults. Note that no "word" has been created to describe the speech patterns and mispronounciations of English by poor or uneducated whites (to the authors' knowledge).

10. **Overpopulation** – refers to the increasing (and undesirable) populations of non-white people.

11. **Third World** – a term that describes people of medium to dark complexions in Africa, Middle East, Central, Latin, and South America, South Asia, North Korea, Saudi Arabia, and Oceania. The word "Third" versus "First" implies the inferior status of the darkest-skinned people on the planet.

12. **Fourth World** – a (new) term that describes the indigenous people (non-white natives) living within colonized countries, such as American Indians (Moors) and Aborigines from Australia. Again, this term minimizes people of color.

13. **Afrocentric** – a lifestyle and/or perspective that is decidedly pro-black but not necessarily anti-white. Afrocentrism -- in self-defense -- challenges the myth (lie) that African people are inferior and redefines African people and their contributions from a more accurate historical perspective.

    Afrocentric blacks identify with the black collective and support those things that benefit the black collective. Afrocentrism does not promote hatred of whites, and has no historical legacy of victimizing white people. It is important to note that this philosophy might not exist if racism/white supremacy (Eurocentric) did not exist.

14. **Tribe** – more than two non-whites occupying a specific geographical area at the same time. Note that whites are never referred to as "tribes."

15. **Natives** – describes the non-white original habitants who have been colonized (conquered) by European imperialists. (Not surprisingly, the word "native' is never used to describe indigenous whites.)

16. **Aborigines** – a term created by the invading English around the 17th century, meaning "first or earliest known." It describes the original, dark-skinned inhabitants of the Australian continent and nearby islands.

17. **Indigenous** – a term created by whites for (non-white) people who inhabited a geographic region before Europeans "discovered" and colonized them.

18. **Non-white** – anyone who is not classified as "white."

19. **People of color** – anyone who is not classified as "white."

20. **Exotic** – a non-white, usually a female, who is part white and is, therefore, more physically appealing. For example a "Eurasian" (Asian and Caucasian) female is usually described as exotic and attractive. The official definition of exotic: "Somebody or something unusual and striking; an exotic species; *a person or thing that is foreign or unusual."* Whites are never described as "exotic" since they are considered the most normal.

21. **Minority, minority group, minorities** – non-whites living within a larger white population. (It is worth noting that whites are a "minority" of the world's population).

22. **Barrio** – a Hispanic (non-white) neighborhood.

23. **Oriental** – a politically incorrect term for Asians and Asian Americans, Pacific Islanders, Eskimos, etc.

24. **Baby's Momma** – a word popularized by the mainstream media that stereotypes and dehumanizes single black mothers, by referring to them as nameless breeders (animals).

25. **Baby's Daddy** – a word popularized by the mainstream media that stereotypes and dehumanizes single black fathers, by referring to them as nameless studs (animals).

26. **Ho** – a word popularized by black male rappers and the mainstream media to stereotype (degrade) young black women as naturally promiscuous and immoral.

27. **Dawg (dog)** – a word used by unconscious black males to stereotype themselves as animalistic, oversexed, and immoral. Popularity of the word among black males is due to collective low self-esteem and a false view of manhood.

28. **Ghetto** – a low-income black or brown neighborhood. Never used to describe poor white neighborhoods.

29. **Ghetto fabulous (ghetto rich)** -- low or moderate income (black) people whose lifestyle is above and beyond their financial means.

30. **Refugee** – defined by the UN Convention as *"a person (non-citizen) who is outside her or his country of nationality and who is unable or unwilling to return."*

31. **Wilding** – a (new) word used to describe the alleged rape & assault of a white female jogger in NYC's Central Park by several black youths in the late 1980s. Other (animalistic) terms used by the mainstream (white) press to describe the black male defendants: a pack, predators, animals, preying, and wolves.

    Several years later, after the black males were convicted and serving their sentences, DNA evidence and an unexpected confession from the real Central Park rapist cleared them of all charges. Not surprisingly, the mainstream media was largely silent and unapologetic for crucifying – and convicting before trial – these young black males.

Code Words For "Pro-Black" Whites And "Anti-Black" Whites

32. **Liberal** – a word that is used to reassure (deceive) blacks into thinking that a particular white person, policy, or organization is not racist and is "supportive" of blacks as a group. Also used as a coded word by other whites to imply that a particular white is a "nigger-lover" (aka traitor).

33. **Conservative** – a word that is used to alarm (frighten) blacks by implying that a particular white person, policy, or organization is hostile to blacks as a group (is racist). Also used as a coded word to (falsely) imply that a particular white person is a "nigger-hater."

34. **Bleeding-Heart-Liberal** – a code word used by whites to describe a white person who makes excuses for the bad or criminal behavior of "niggers."

35. **Law-and-Order** – a code word that is used to reassure (con) the white collective that a particular political candidate will be hard on "niggers," especially niggers who break the law.

WEÂPON #4

EDUCÂTIONÂL GENOCIDE

(PROGRÂM)

If you can control a man's thinking, you don't have to worry about his actions. If you can determine what a man thinks you do not have worry about what he will do.

If you can make a man believe that he is inferior, you don't have to compel him to seek an inferior status, he will do so without being told and if you can make a man believe that he is justly an outcast, you don't have to order him to the back door, he will go to the back door on his own and if there is no back door, the very nature of the man will demand that you build one.

Carter G. Woodson (1875-1950)

CHAPTER 16

THE THREE STAGES OF EDUCATIONAL GENOCIDE

A Short History Lesson:

> *In 1954, the United States Supreme Court ruled in the case of* ***Brown v. Board of Education of Topeka*** *that "separate educational facilities are inherently unequal."*
>
> *As a result, separate and unequal schools were ruled a violation of the* ***Equal Protection Clause*** *of the* ***Fourteenth Amendment*** *of the United States Constitution. This court ruling paved the way for school integration and the civil rights movement.*

55 years later, (most) US schools are still segregated and unequal, and our children are still the tragic victims of educational genocide.

Reading, Writing, And White Supremacy 101

Educating black children is seen as an unnecessary (and dangerous) expense, NOT a benefit in a white supremacy system. Any group (or race) in power will NEVER eliminate the economic, educational, and political advantages that have kept them in power. If the reader takes anything away from this book, it will be a greater understanding of how the American anti-education system works.

Three Stages Of Educational Genocide

I. Introduction
II. Reinforcement
III. Refinement

I. INTRODUCTION STAGE

The Foundation For Educational Genocide Begins The Second A Black Child Sits In Front Of A TV Set

All children — regardless of ethnicity or economic class -- are born with a healthy amount of self-esteem. This does not change until something or someone says that child is NOT OK. This creates a foundation for the low self-esteem that will follow the child into adulthood. The early years are critical because some experts believe a child's personality is formed by age three.

For the black child, the outside world becomes an emotional landmine. All the things young children adore – children's TV shows, cartoons, movies, comics, popular toys, books, dolls, magicians, stuntmen, clowns, action heroes, Nancy Drew, the wildly popular Harry Potter, Disney characters, and a host of magical, mythical, and fantastic human beings – show black children ***a wonderful world that is 99.99% WHITE.***

Even the most harmless household items, like "flesh-colored" crayons and Band-Aids become weapons of mass self-esteem destruction for black children. If they are old enough to understand that human beings are "flesh-colored," they might ask, *"If human beings are pink, and my skin is brown, what does that make me?"*

The recent trend over the last decade of mainly casting bi-racial boys and girls in TV commercials reinforces white superiority by making brown and dark-skinned children invisible (and inferior). It is well-known within the television industry that casting directors who want to cast a black boy or black girl in a TV commercial, prefer the biracial children of white females over the brown and dark-skinned black children who look "too black."

Black Doll/White Doll

The infamous "Black Doll/White Doll" experiment proves that by the age of four, black boys and girls have already internalized the belief (lie) that "white is good" and "black is bad." In the experiment, black children are asked to pick the doll that best fits the questions asked:

> *When the tester asked a four-year-old black girl to pick the "nice doll," she chose the white one. When asked to pick the "bad doll," she chose the black one. When asked to pick the doll that looked most like her, her big, dark eyes turned sad as she picked* ***the black doll.*** *(Over 90 percent of the black boys and girls picked the white doll as the nicer, smarter, and prettier doll).*

A Black By A Less Black-Sounding Name Sounds Sweeter

> *In September, 2006, ABC's primetime news show, "20/20", ran a segment called "The Impact of Your Name." Jack Daniel, a professor at the University of Pittsburgh, tested a group of four- and five-year-olds to see how they matched the black or white-sounding names based on the questions asked.*
>
> *When asked who the smartest girl was, or what child the children would like to play with, they chose "white-sounding" names like Sarah or Megan. When asked what child was more likely to do something bad, "Adam" or "Jamal," they picked the "black-sounding" Jamal.*
>
> *According to the professor, both black and white children reacted more positively to the white-sounding names. If skin color had nothing to do with their choices, and the children simply favored the more familiar-sounding names, how does one explain the black children making the same choices as the white children?*

By age four, black and white children have already internalized the white supremacy value system: *white is superior/black is inferior*. If a black child at that tender age already knows he is inferior to a white child, what happens to that black girl or black boy's self-esteem?

If a little black girl believes the doll with the pale skin, straight blond hair, and blue eyes is the prettiest BUT she is brown-skinned and dark-eyed, with a head full of soft, nappy hair, what does that do to her self-image, self-esteem, and later, her opinion of herself as a black woman? What about the little black boy who picks the white doll as the "nicest" doll even though his mother, sisters, aunts, and grandmothers are black? How does he view (or respect) them if he already believes black females are inferior to white ones?

Where Do Black Children Get All These Crazy Ideas?

1. The Mainstream Media Via TV, Videos, Music, & Movies

Black children watch MORE TV than any other single demographic group in America. This means black children are reading FEWER BOOKS, LEARNING LESS, ***and getting a fatal overdose of white supremacy/ black inferiority programming*** at the most critical brain-development stage of their young lives.

Children don't have to understand the content or the context of the media's subliminal messages to absorb them. Young brains are like sponges that lack the ability to filter out the lies from the truth, or the sense from the nonsense.

2. White Images In The Media

The images of whites in the media are overwhelmingly positive. Whites are scientists, doctors, animal experts, magicians, super-heroes, and the wildly popular Harry Potter. Whites are kind, decent, educated, smart, creative, ambitious, successful, generous, passionate, sexy, and all around lovable human beings.

3. Black Images In The Media

The media images of blacks are overwhelmingly negative. Blacks are poor, angry, resentful, violent, uneducated (and proud of it), defiant, boastful (when there's nothing to boast about), ignorant, ghetto, slick, unkind, selfish, scheming, whorish, primitive, vulgar, needy, pathetic, unsuccessful, lazy, apathetic, criminal, unloving, and all around unlovable human beings.

4. Unbalanced Commercial Images About Beauty

Nearly all the images of beauty – pale skin, straight or long hair, and blue, green, or gray eyes – show the necessary prerequisites to be worthy as a romantic partner. Black children seldom see black males and females holding hands, kissing, or making love on the TV or movie screen. Black girls never see commercials for hair products that represent their own natural (un-straightened, un-processed, un-permed, un-weaved or un-wigged) hair.

5. The Educational System From Pre-School To Graduate School

Black schoolchildren are taught that everything and anything of any value was done by white people. Black history – if it is taught at all – is the least accurate part of any school curriculum, and focuses on the same handful of "facts," starting with slavery, as if blacks did not exist on the planet until Europeans "discovered" and enslaved them.

Once a year, during Black History Month (the shortest month of the year), there are the same whitewashed and uninspiring stories about the "peanut guy", Booker T. Washington, with a little Harriet Tubman, and Martin Luther King, Jr., thrown in for good measure. It is not until later in adult life -- after the self-esteem damage has been done -- that some blacks learn that the human race and ***the foundation for arts, science, architecture, and literature began in Africa.***

None of today's history school books mention the thousands of black adventurers, inventors, scientists, builders, and craftsmen before, during, and after slavery, OR that blacks WERE ALREADY IN AMERICA, long before Christopher Columbus set sail for the "new world," OR that "Native Americans" were the original black inhabitants of North America.

Nor will black children ever read about the more than 50, prosperous, all-black towns from the late 1800s to early 1900s like Tulsa, Oklahoma's *"Black Wall Street,"* that were destroyed by whites, who were unable to tolerate the success of their "inferiors."

6. Black Male Images In The Media

Black men are more likely to be seen wearing handcuffs (than a tailored suit); in prison; in the back of a squad car; riddled with bullets on a city street; or lying on a slab in the morgue. Most movies and TV shows aimed at black youth depict black men as thugs, pimps, drug dealers, hustlers, struggling, poor, criminals, deadbeat baby daddies, clowns, court jesters, athletes, entertainers, buffoons, fools, and animalistic brutes. ***In short, black males are losers.***

The few positive images of black males are limited to entertainment: actors, athletes, comedians, entertainers, and politicians. If a black male is shown in a serious or positive light, he is ALWAYS isolated from other blacks; for example, the token black in a lily-white primetime drama, who is NEVER shown loving black women or nurturing and protecting black children.

7. Black Female Images In The Media

Black women – especially if they're dark-skinned – are usually portrayed as single, overweight, mean, jealous, low-down, loud, untrustworthy, deceitful, disagreeable, greedy, treacherous, ignorant, ghetto, promiscuous, unattractive, materialistic, unsexy, and downright unlovable human beings.

If they are light-skinned and attractive, they are unstable, troubled, self-destructive, and always lusting after white males, aka the "Tragic Mulatto" roles created for the minstrel show audiences during the 1800s and 1900s.

When these sick images are fed to black children on a daily basis, what do black girls internalize about themselves, black men, and their future possibilities as women, wives, lovers, and mothers?

What do black boys internalize about themselves, black women, and their future possibilities as men, husbands, lovers, and fathers? No wonder so many young black females have such low expectations for their male counterparts and why so many black boys have NO expectations for themselves.

No child is born thinking he or she is defective. An inferiority complex is something that must be taught.

II. THE REINFORCEMENT STAGE

Once the early foundation for racial low self-esteem is firmly set into place, the ANTI-EDUCATION forces gear up for the next stage of war: *using the classroom to sow the seeds of white superiority/black inferiority in children.*

Blue Eyes, Brown Eyes, And (False) White Innocence

In her famous "blue-eyed/brown-eyed" exercise in 1968, Mrs. Jane Elliott, a white schoolteacher, divided her third-grade class into two groups: the brown-eyed children and the blue-eyed children.

The brown-eyed students were given extra recess time, second helpings at lunch, and praised for being more intelligent than the blue-eyed students. The blue-eyed students were forced to wear crepe paper armbands; were not allowed to drink from the same fountain as the brown-eyed children; and were told they were not as good as the brown-eyed students.

> *"The brown-eyed people are the better people in this room," Mrs. Elliott told her class. "They are cleaner and they are smarter."*

By the end of the first day, the brown-eyed children could do schoolwork they had been unable to do before. The blue-eyed students became withdrawn and made mistakes on the same classwork they had been able to do. On the second day of the exercise, Elliott had the brown-eyed and blue-eyed students switch places. After the exercise ended, the children had to write essays about what they had learned about discrimination and what it felt like.

> *"I think these children walked in a colored child's moccasins for a day," said Mrs. Elliott.*

Mrs. Elliot's two-day experiment confirmed what many black educators and parents had always suspected: that black underachievement is a DIRECT REFLECTION of a white supremacy system that teaches black inferiority from cradle to grave.

After only EIGHT hours in the classroom, the blue-eyed children who were told they were inferior, began to BEHAVE as though they were inferior to the brown-eyed students.

When word spread of Mrs. Elliott's experiment, she was invited to appear on the Johnny Carson show. Following her appearance, hundreds of viewers called in and wrote letters to the show, most of which read like the following:

> *"How dare you try this cruel experiment out on white children! Black children grow up accustomed to such behavior, but white children, there's no way they could possibly understand it. It's cruel to white children and will cause them great psychological damage."*

What the letter writer didn't say (and didn't have to) was he or she understood that racism causes "great psychological damage," but it was all right (normal) for ***black children to grow up damaged.*** These "confessions" by outraged viewers are proof that whites are well aware of the "great psychological damage" racism causes to its victims – because they objected to white children being treated IN THE SAME RACIST MANNER.

Yet we, as a nation, blame black children -- the youngest and most defenseless victims of racism -- for their intellectual and emotional underachievement.

The local community's response to Mrs. Elliott's appearance on the Johnny Carson show was equally telling. Teachers at her school shunned her; her children were harassed and assaulted; and her father's store was boycotted, forcing him into bankruptcy. The white outrage completely contradicts the ***false white innocence about the deadly effects of racism.***

$500,000 Ways To Guarantee An (Un)Equal Education

When school systems base their funding on the real estate tax base, this GUARANTEES that schools in poor neighborhoods will have fewer (inferior) educational resources than those in more affluent areas.

Even a half-million-dollar home in a black area is always be less valuable than the same home in a predominantly white area, simply because black people live there. Not only do blacks lose valuable home equity (wealth), black children lose in the educational game of real estate tax-based schools. The obvious conclusion: **America's UNEQUAL educational system is by DESIGN, not by DEFAULT.**

What's Money Got To Do With It?

Social "scientists" like **Richard J. Herrnstein**, author of *The Bell Curve*, claimed intelligence (IQ) was due more to genetics than environment. He is not alone:

> *In the February 2003 issue of New Scientist magazine, DNA Researcher* James D. Watson *said, "If you are really stupid, I would call that a disease. The lower ten percent who really have difficulty, even in elementary school, what's the cause of it? A lot of people would like to say, 'Well, poverty, things like that.' It probably isn't."*

It would be interesting to ask Mr. Herrnstein and Mr. Watson how much money mattered when it came to their own children's education and environment. Obviously, money matters a great deal when it comes a quality education for white or affluent children -- otherwise, every prestigious, invitation-only preschool, boarding school, private school, and Ivy League University would have to CLOSE THEIR DOORS.

How Poverty Affects The Academic Performance Of Poor Students

It doesn't take a Harvard degree (or the Nobel Prize) to understand:

- If a child goes to school hungry, his schoolwork will suffer.
- If a child's home has no heat in the winter, his homework will suffer.
- If a child lives in a noisy, chaotic environment without a safe, quiet place to study, his thinking will become chaotic, and his schoolwork will suffer.
- If a child has to travel through dangerous gang territory, going to school might not be the most appealing option.
- If a child is ridiculed, threatened, ostracized, or beaten for "acting white" (being smart), good grades might be a luxury that child cannot afford.
- If a child is exposed to violence at a young age, his or her untreated post-traumatic stress syndrome might affect the way they perform in school.
- If a parent lacks the financial resources for SAT tutoring classes, the child may not do as well on their SATs as those who had special help.
- If a teacher has outdated books, inadequate equipment, and supplies, her students will not get the same quality of education as the students who attend state-of-the-art schools with the latest equipment and books.
- If schoolteachers have to buy school supplies out of their own pockets, this particular school IS NOT FUNDED to deliver a quality education.
- If a teacher has a class of 40 students crammed into one classroom, he can't give struggling students the individual attention they may need.
- If a white school spends twice the money per student than a black school on the other side of town, the white child will receive a superior education.
- If a black school has metal detectors and security guards, black children may think black schools are for bad, stupid kids.
- If a black boy has no black male teachers, he may decide that higher education is something black men don't (or can't) do.
- If a child's experiences are limited to a poor inner-city neighborhood, he might have a hard time imagining himself being successful at anything.
- If black children believe being smart is "acting white," they may think being black means the opposite.
- If a black child is always reminded by the media that black children don't do well in school, he or she might start to believe it -- about themselves.
- If a black school has outdated books, peeling paint, broken toilets, leaking roofs, and teachers with low or no expectations, black children will come to a logical conclusion: ***they don't count.***

Three Common Myths About Black Students

1. They are less intelligent than white students.
2. They don't care about education (too lazy).
3. Blacks schools don't need more money to provide a quality education.

What happens to the self-esteem and motivation of children who realize the most influential adults in their lives -- their teachers, school administrators, the media, and sometimes, even their parents -- think they're incapable of learning? Could the answer be found in the high dropout rate for black, Hispanic, and poor white students?

School Curriculums Are Outdated, Irrelevant, and Criminal

It's a crime that a student can spend 12 years in the American school system without acquiring a single life or job skill like **changing a tire, balancing a checkbook, or filling out a job application.**

Most inner-city students suffer under a school cirriculum that either ignores or whitewashes the significant contributions of African people. The high-school dropout rate among black students may be an instinctive reaction by young blacks to TUNE OUT (reject) a (false) racist curriculum that rejects their true humanity, history, and self-worth.

Fewer Qualified Teachers In High-Poverty Schools

A 2008 report by the Education Trust found schools in poor minority areas are twice as likely to have math teachers who do not have adequate knowledge of math, did not major in math in college, and are not certified to teach math. It is logical to assume unqualified teachers are teaching other subjects besides math. In fact, it is common for incompetent or emotionally disturbed teachers to be assigned to minority schools where educating the students is a low priority.

Cheating, Tracking, And 'Rithmetic

While black students get a merciless pounding in the press for low academic scores, the teachers, school administrators, and board members at some of America's best (white) high schools and Ivy League universities are falsifying grades and test scores: (links/sources can be found on website)

- Cheating Scandals Rock Three Top-Tier High Schools
- National Survey Finds Two-Thirds of Students Admit Cheating
- Cheating is Epidemic, say School Experts
- Duke's B-school cheating scandal
- Most High School Students Admit to Cheating
- North Carolina High School suspends students for stealing exams

Even Within The Same Integrated School System, Black Students Received An Unequal (And Inferior) Education.

In 1998, the news program *"60 Minutes"* (CBS), exposed the racist practice of "tracking" in an integrated school system in Georgia. Black students were systematically excluded from college-prep courses, regardless of their test scores, while white students were "tracked" into the Advanced Placement and Honors Classes, regardless of their scores.

The Advanced Placement and Honor Class students take the courses that prepare them for college-level classwork and are required for college admission. The students on the vocational-bound track do not receive the classes necessary for most college placement. It should be no surprise that these students don't do as well on their SATs as honor students, or that many never make it to college.

In Addition, Black Boys Are More Likely To Be:

- Tracked into special education classes
- Labeled as "mentally disabled" (when they are not)
- Tracked into vocational courses
- Excluded from gifted programs and college preparatory classes
- Suspended or expelled more often than white students for same offenses

We cannot ignore the facts: There is a national agenda to drive black boys out of school. While white boys (of privilege) are trained to be masters of the universe, black boys are trained to be future candidates for the prison-industrial complex.

III. THE REFINEMENT STAGE: POPULAR CULTURE & THE MEDIA

By the time black girls and boys reach the young adult stage, many will:

- believe blacks are inferior to whites
- be demoralized by their poor academic performance
- feel they are less intelligent than whites
- have few goals other than being an entertainer or athlete
- believe they will never amount to anything

Once the foundation for intellectual inferiority has been laid and set, the media REFINES the white superiority/black inferiority complex by:

- showing black males as buffoonish and criminally inclined
- showing black females as ignorant, whorish, and undesirable
- feeding black youth a steady diet of profanity, sexuality, vulgarity, and degrading black images
- teaching black youth that BLING-BLING defines their self-worth

- showing 99.9% of successful black men as athletes, criminals, & entertainers
- never showing black lawyers, doctors, scholars, educators, architects, and inventors in the mainstream media and schoolbooks
- creating reality-TV crime & prison shows "starring" black, brown, and poor white men so the viewers will think this is the natural order of things
- promoting stereotypes of black men as more BRAWN than BRAINS and white men as more BRAINS than BRAWN
- showing educated men as WEAK and violent men as STRONG
- showing "baby-mommas" and "baby-daddies" on trash-talk TV shows as normal behavior for black males and females
- creating children's cartoons and movies that show blacks as inferior to whites, or that show dark-skinned animal characters that are dumb, criminal, or both
- rewarding blacks with fame and fortune for degrading other blacks
- ***placing the entire blame for all of America's social, moral, and financial ills on poor black youth***

The Trojan Horse Called "Education"

It is difficult to view the systematic mis-education of black children without anger or emotion, but that is EXACTLY what we must do. It is naïve to expect black children to receive the same quality of education that white children receive in a white supremacy system.

The educational system is designed to maintain the white status quo. ***It is unrealistic to think otherwise.*** We cannot afford to ignore what is happening to black children all over the nation. We cannot afford to wait for someone (else) to "do something." We cannot afford to let any more time pass before black children get the quality education they DESERVE.

Black Parents Must Step Up To The Educational Plate

Black parents must educate ourselves about the ANTI- EDUCATION AGENDA against black children that INTENTIONALLY destroys their intellectual potential, self-esteem, and self-confidence. It is time to STOP asking, *"What is wrong with black kids?"* and start asking, *"What is wrong with us?"*

We must replace the television, DVD players, videos, and video games with books that do not reinforce white supremacy; toys that use the imagination; and a school cirriculum that tells the TRUTH about our history, along with a lot of hugs, kisses, and praise that will build our children's self-esteem and intellectual skills -- starting at age two or three.

If all the above sounds like too much work, instead of bringing more abused and neglected black children into a world overflowing with abused and neglected black children, we should save ourselves the time and trouble required to raise a mentally sane, high-self-esteemed black child, and adopt a goldfish.

CHAPTER 17

AFFIRMATIVE ACTION & THE MYTH OF BLACK INFERIORITY

Debunking The Seven Most Common Affirmative Action Myths

MYTH #1: Affirmative Action Is An Entitlement Program Created By Blacks For Blacks

Black people did not create affirmative action, the terminology, or the where, when, or how it became a policy. Blacks do not control Corporate America's or the US government's hiring or affirmative action policies. Blacks do not have the power to implement any policies, just or unjust, at any white-owned corporation, college, or university.

MYTH #2: Blacks Benefited The Most From Affirmative Action.

According to the US Labor Department, the biggest beneficiaries of affirmative action were white women. Between 1972 and 1993:

- women architects increased from 3% to nearly 19% of all architects
- women doctors more than doubled from 10% to 22% of all doctors
- women lawyers grew from 4% to 23% of all lawyers
- female engineers went from less than 1% to nearly 9% of all engineers
- female chemists grew from 10% to 30% of all chemists
- female college faculty went from 28% to 42% of all college faculty

White women are the biggest beneficiaries of affirmative action yet it is still seen as a "black program" by most Americans -- including white females(!)

White females refuse to credit affirmative action for their sorely needed boost up the corporate and professional ladder. White females also shy away from taking any heat for one of America's most unpopular policies, even as they line up to claim their "minority" status under affirmative action. Most ignore the FACT that the civil rights movement preceded the (white) women's movement AND paved the way for (white) women's rights.

However, the facts -- and the timeline -- cannot be disputed. Before the civil rights movement and affirmative action, there were ***few (to none)*** white female CEOs, executives, surgeons, lawyers, judges, university deans, governors, mayors, dentists, managers, technicians, electricians, carpenters, supervisors, politicians, or US Secretary of States.

Before the civil rights movement and affirmative action, most female workers – white and non-white -- were segregated in the "pink ghetto" of clerical, domestic, teaching, and service-related jobs.

Affirmative action programs opened doors for people of all ethnic groups, including Native Americans, Arab Americans, Latinos, Asian Americans, and whites. For example, in the late 1970s, the Federal Aviation Administration (FAA) created an upward mobility program (affirmative action) that allowed government employees to train as air traffic controllers and electronic technicians. The majority of people in the FAA's "affirmative action" program were white men and women.

The lion's share of the highest-paying jobs and university seats still go to whites. The handful of blacks who break past the color barriers in the highest-paying professions are a minority in more than one sense of the word – and often face relentless racism behind closed corporate doors. While whites are busy grumbling about "affirmative action" and the small number of blacks making more than $75,000 a year, the nation's workforce is being devastated by outsourcing and downsizing.

MYTH #3: Blacks Need Affirmative Action To Compete With Whites

Affirmative action is a lot like child support. It was supposedly created because some employers -- like some parents -- wouldn't do the right thing on their own. Affirmative action was a legal remedy that opened doors to minorities and women that had been previously closed to all but white males.

Even though affirmative action is seen as "giving" blacks something they haven't earned, there's a limit to what affirmative action can do. It cannot attend classes, or pass college or bar exams. It does not get dressed in the morning, drive the car to work, or do any work at all. Affirmative action is little more than a ticket of admission to the wildly successful party that's been going on for centuries.

Affirmative Action = A Lose-Lose For Blacks

While affirmative action opened some doors for blacks, it created a wall of white resentment. If blacks strive for higher education and take a coveted university seat, some whites cry, *"Reverse discrimination!"* Once they graduate from college and land a good-paying job, they're accused of using affirmative action to cheat whites. Behind closed doors, their hard-earned credentials are routinely dismissed as "dumbed-down affirmative action degrees."

If blacks don't go to college, and attempt to join the skilled construction trades, they're confronted by abrupt rule changes and impossible hurdles. If they attempt to join the police or fire department they're accused of *"reverse racism."* If they don't pursue higher education, a trade, a profession, or find adequate employment that pays a living wage, they're labeled parasites who feed off the labor of hard-working (white NEVER black) taxpayers.

Clearly, it's a case of damned if we do, and damned if we don't do any damn thing at all.

MYTH #4: America Was A Meritocracy Before Quotas, Affirmative Action, And Blacks Polluted the Workplace.

Quotas are nothing new for white males, who have always received preferential treatment in the workplace. Before the civil rights movement, there were ironclad 95-100% "quotas" for white males when it came to the most prestigious and best-paying jobs. It was not only who you knew that counted, it was WHAT (race or sex) you were that mattered more than education, skills, or qualifications.

It is illogical to believe that ***every*** white person who gets into college got there on merit, and not because her politically powerful father places a personal call to the dean, or a rich grandather donated a wing to the university library, or simply because fewer non-whites qualified financially or educationally (due to substandard living conditions) -- leaving more seats for white students.

It is equally ludicrous to believe that ***every*** white person with a good paying job got that job on merit. What about the boss's son (or daughter) who shoots up the executive ladder ahead of senior employees; or the neighbor who gets her neighbor's son an internship at her corporation; or the foreman who hires his sons to work at the construction site and refuses to hire blacks?

Let's not forget the druggie son of a powerful family who manages to graduate with a 3.0 grade point average, and lands a corner office with a prestigious investment or law firm. To pretend that favoritism and quotas STARTED with affirmative action and minorities is dishonest and illogical.

MYTH #5: Affirmative Action Is Reverse Discrimination (Racism)

What is the most common UFO sighting in America? *The* ***U****nqualified* ***F****or* ***O****ccupation* minority, aka "the black person who stole a job or promotion from a more qualified white person." Many whites know of some white person who was passed over (cheated out of a) job in favor of an ***U****nqualified* ***F****or* ***O****ccupation* minority.

However, if asked for the NAME of the **unqualified minority person**, the usual response is SILENCE. If questioned about the **unqualified minority person's** QUALIFICATIONS, like his or her college degrees, grades, or previous work experiences, the silence is followed by a BLANK STARE.

What do these non-responses really mean? ***That whites are always more qualified than non-whites, regardless of experience or education.***

In fact, just the mere presence of non-white job applicants and employees automatically casts suspicion on the "quality" of the workforce:

> *"NY Police Commissioner Bernard B. Kerik said that by loosening the eligibility requirements for these employees, the department gains a pool of 1,300 potential applicants, many of whom are members of minority groups."*

The implied assumption? Minorities are the ONLY people who can benefit from "loosening the eligibility requirements" -- ***because whites are always eligible and qualified.***

Less Than ALL Equals Nothing For Some Whites

Whenever blacks or non-whites are hired or promoted, cries of "reverse racism" usually follow, unless the job is a low-paying or low-status occupation. For example, there are no cries of "reverse racism" when black males take 99% of the airport shoeshine jobs.

Overall, non-whites represent ***less than 15%*** of police and firefighters in the US -- even in cities where blacks and Hispanics are the majority -- yet this 15% OR LESS is still seen as massive "discrimination" against white males.

The widespread cheating scandals on police and fire department exams across the nation leads to an obvious question: *Who scores the tests?* ***The same fire or police department officials that refused to hire non-whites in the first place.***

If blacks (or other non-whites) are consistently scoring lower than whites, perhaps there are reasons other than intelligence or ability that explains their "scores." In New York State alone, there have been landmark judgments after discovering computerized police sergeant exams results had been falsified.

Other Employment Cheating Scandals

BOSTON: Allegations of Cheating on Boston Firefighters Exam

BALTIMORE: Baltimore firefighter exam results stand after cheating scandal

ALBUQUERQUE: Albuquerque Firefighters Fired Following Exam Scandal.

CHICAGO: Illinois Cheating Scandal Leads To New EMT Test

ORLANDO: City Fire Fighters' Scandal Isn't Over

BOSTON: Ex-Policeman Tells of Boston Test Thefts. A former senior police captain testified in Federal District Court how he and other officers (including police chiefs) systematically stole advance copies of civil service promotion examinations and sold them over a six-year period (Boston).

MYTH #6: Blacks Have A Monopoly On Being "Unqualified"

If this was true, there would be no Enron, WorldCom, Arthur Andersen, Lehman Brothers, or a subprime mortgage crisis. There are thousands of incompetent and corrupt employees, managers, officials, politicians, and CEOs of every race and ethnicity. Incompetence respects no racial or sexual boundaries.

MYTH #7: Blacks Are Intellectually Inferior To Whites

If this was true, there would be ***no need*** to create inferior school systems or artificial employment barriers. **A truly superior race will ALWAYS rise to the top -- without holding another race to the bottom.**

"The need to cheat actually reveals the cheater's secret fear that he is inferior to his competitor." -- Anon

CHAPTER 18

ARE BLACKS LESS INTELLIGENT THAN WHITES?

Let's cut to the chase. Are blacks (really) less intelligent genetically than whites?

Yes!

Blacks are less intelligent, according to Adolph Hitler, Charles Darwin, Dr. William Shockley (a Nobel Prize Winner in Physics), Richard J. Herrnstein, co-author of the controversial "The Bell Curve," Arthur Jensen, James D. Watson (a Nobel Prize winner in medicine), and many others too numerous to list here.

This "racial superiority" argument has been used for centuries to justify slavery, murder, rape, exploitation, imperialism, and the oppression of non-whites all over the world. It was used to devastate millions via the African and the Jewish Holocausts. Today, this same "science" is used to promote black inferiority/white superiority by ignoring the unequal educational playing field between whites and non-whites.

With a heavy, collective sigh, reasonable (black and non-black) people wonder why (some) whites are so obsessed with the need to be superior. The best answer might be found in the definition of a "superiority complex." According to Alfred Adler (1870 – 1937), one of the most respected psychoanalysts of his time, a ***"superiority complex"*** is:

"A subconscious neurotic mechanism of compensation developed by the individual as a result of feelings of inferiority."

The theory of "white intellectual superiority" was put to the test during a televised debate between Dr. William Shockley and Dr. Frances Cress Welsing on "Tony Brown's Journal" in 1973. Dr. Frances Cress Welsing, a brilliant, black, medically trained doctor of psychiatry, confidently gutted Dr. Shockley's "theories" on black intellectual inferiority.

Unfortunately for Dr. Shockley, this was done in front of a national audience. He succeeded in debunking his OWN theories of superior white intelligence by losing the debate to a truly superior black intellect – Dr. Welsing's.

Perhaps this very public loss of face explains why Dr. William Shockley disappeared from the national scientific scene after being humiliated on national TV by an "inferior" black female. *(For info on ordering a DVD of debate, go to Resource Section, pg 324).*

Just for argument's sake, let's assume Dr. Shockley is correct when he says blacks are intellectually inferior to whites. That would mean...

EVERY black scientist, geneticist, mathematician, architect, dentist, author, engineer, scholar, doctor, chemist, builder, astronomer, astronaut, inventor, Pulitzer Prize winner, computer engineer, businessman, student, computer programmer, pilot, business owner, electrician, plumber, network engineer, demolition expert, Secretary of State, Supreme Court justice, lawyer, judge, pharmacist, MBA, PhD, and Rhodes Scholar is the intellectual inferior of EVERY white high school dropout because...

...genetic intellectual superiority is a constant.

EVERY elephant is more intelligent than EVERY earthworm, because it is genetically impossible for a less intelligent species (earthworms) to be occasionally more intelligent than a more intelligent species (elephants).

If Charles Darwin, William Shockley, and Adolph Hitler are correct, intellectual superiority is not affected by family income, environment, nutrition, educational background, or a prestigious pre-school. Intellectual superiority does not skip generations, city blocks, or occur randomly.

If genetics is the MAIN factor in determining a person's IQ then the academic performance of a white child from the poorest part of Appalachia should be equal to that of a privileged white child who lives on NYC's Park Avenue and attends private school.

If Richard J. Herrnstein, Charles Murray, and James D. Watson are correct that blacks are intellectually inferior to whites, every poor white high school dropout from rural Appalachia would be the intellectual superior of every black Harvard graduate because...

...genetic intellectual superiority is a constant.

However, if the two things being compared (like black people and white people) are similar enough, measuring the differences between them can be done ONLY IF ALL THINGS ARE EQUAL.

In other words, to accurately compare the intellectual capacity of black children with white children, the white child and the black child must have EQUAL access, EQUAL exposure, EQUAL environments, EQUAL nutrition, and EQUAL cultural affirmations over a set period of time until the effects of any prior disadvantages have been **completely neutralized**.

For example, if two men are betting that each can run the faster race, and one man breaks his leg before the race, the race must be postponed. In order to have a FAIR race to determine which man is the faster runner, the healthy man must wait until the other man fully recovers.

Only then can we fairly and accurately determine WHO is the faster, superior runner of the two. Only by comparing one apple with another apple, can we determine which is the superior piece of fruit.

Fake Science Masquerading As Real Science: Debunking IQ And Standardized Intelligence Tests

Even Alfred Binet (1905), a French psychologist and **the creator of the Binet-Simon intelligence scale** (which IQ tests are based on), did not believe IQ test scales accurately measured intelligence:

> *"The scale, properly speaking, does not permit the measure of intelligence, because intellectual qualities are not superposable, and therefore cannot be measured as linear surfaces are measured."*

In other words, intelligence cannot be measured the same way we would measure a cup of flour.

Binet argued that with proper remedial education programs, most students, regardless of background, could catch up and perform quite well in school. He did not believe that intelligence was a measurable fixed entity. He concluded:

> *"We must protest and react against this brutal pessimism (that an individual's intelligence is a fixed quantity); we must try to demonstrate* ***that it is founded on nothing.****"*

Who Tests The IQ Of The IQ Test Makers?

After revising some IQ tests in the 1940's, women began outscoring men, even though women were considered genetically less intelligent than men. In response, the test makers did the "intelligent" thing. They changed the IQ tests until the men were scoring equally.

Some Facts About IQ:

- **Every word in our vocabulary is LEARNED not INHERITED**. The more words spoken around children, the larger the vocabulary. A child who grows up around educated adults will have a larger vocabulary than a child who does not, and will score higher on IQ tests. A large vocabulary is NOT proof of any genetic superiority; but may be proof of a superior (learning) environment.
- Proper maternal childhood nutrition is critical for fetal development. Malnutrition and other environmental factors, such as prenatal exposure to toxins and lead, duration of breast-feeding, the health of the mother and father, and vitamin deficiencies can affect IQ.
- Obviously, poverty, the lack of prenatal care, fresh food, and clean air will affect fetal development. Premature, underweight babies are common among poor, teenage mothers. Fortunately, in many cases, the damage can be reversed if environmental conditions improve.

- A study of French children adopted between the ages of four and six shows the connection between nature and nurture. The children came from poor backgrounds with IQs that initially averaged 77, putting them near retardation. Nine years after adoption, they retook the IQ tests and all the children did better. The amount they improved was directly related to the adopting family's **financial status**.

Some Final Words On Manufactured Intelligence Tests

It is illogical to believe intelligence can be accurately measured by ONE PAPER TEST. It is just as illogical to believe an intelligence test can be completely objective because there isn't a single human being on earth who is capable of complete objectivity or fairness.

Any scientist (with a normal IQ) and a healthy respect for science knows it is ***impossible*** to measure the effects of nature VS nurture with a single man-made test since intelligence is much more complex than the ability to mark the "best" answer on a sheet of paper.

Those Who Rely On Intelligence Tests May Not Be As Intelligent As They Think

James D. Watson, who believes in white intellectual superiority, also believes stupidity can be and should be cured. We agree wholeheartedly, Mr. Watson. To end stupidity, we propose starting with those people who believe intellectual superiority can be measured by a paper test -- even when one group has had superior economic, social, and educational opportunities for 400 YEARS that have been DENIED to another group.

Ending stupidity should start with eliminating the (neurotic) NEED to be superior to ANYONE, let alone, everyone of another race. If we could all agree to end the unnecessary (and frankly, embarrassing) "intellectual" debate about "white racial superiority" in a white supremacy society that stacks the deck AGAINST non-whites, perhaps we would have the time and the will to eliminate racism/white supremacy for good.

CHAPTER 19

LET'S TELL THE WHOLE TRUTH ABOUT PARENTING

"The lower economic people are not holding up their end in this deal. These people are not parenting. They are buying things for kids -- $500 sneakers -- for what? And won't spent $200 for 'Hooked on Phonics.'"
-- Bill Cosby at Howard University in May 2004

Whether we agree or disagree with Mr. Cosby, we must be careful not to blame the victims of racism/white supremacy and let the wrong people off the hook. It is illogical to analyze the parenting problems of poor Black America without analyzing the effects of racism, poverty, unemployment, the drug/prison culture, and the educational apartheid that created the problems in the first place.

This is not about making excuses for poor parenting, but ignoring the social conditions of poor blacks is like the doctor who treats an infection in the baby toe but refuses to examine the entire foot to see where the infection might have originated.

The black poor are symptoms of a much bigger disease in America, NOT the disease itself.

We cannot underestimate the roles of the most powerful people in the nation who control the quality of life for everyone in America, especially the black collective. We should always be suspicious when the mainstream media is eager to broadcast comments that condemn poor blacks -- the biggest victims of racism.

It is unjust to paint all lower-income black families with the same tar-soaked brush. There are single parents who are working two or three jobs just to put food on their tables. To say they are not doing enough when we don't know the details of their circumstances is UNJUST.

To say the black poor are not doing enough in an economy where even middle-class white families are struggling is UNJUST. To allow Corporate America to make enormous profits by paying less than a living wage to millions of workers is UNJUST. To turn our collective backs on women and children living in poverty then criticize them for not measuring up to our "standards" is UNJUST.

The issue of poor parenting in America is like a giant cherry pie. There are plenty of people passing plates of blame around but no one wants to stick around and clean up the mess.

' people bear the greatest responsibility for the .east (powerful).

ɔ Not Have A Monopoly On Poor Parenting

.renting cuts across all economic, religious, political, and racial . most profound difference between affluent parents and poor parents ,oor face more challenges when money and resources are scarce.

ın reality, more money does not compensate for the poor parenting of the .ffluent. Professional status and executive titles cannot substitute for love, discipline, good role modeling, and the moral guidance that many children of affluence are obviously lacking from their parents.

We know this is true because there is a list too long to print here of wealthy, powerful people who would have done the world a great service had they NOT produced any offspring at all.

The Most Notorious Deadbeat Fathers In US History

Poor black males are routinely condemned for being "deadbeat fathers," and while some of this criticism is valid, the most prolific "deadbeat fathers" in American history are the white slaveowners who over a 400 YEAR period raped and impregnated MILLIONS of African slave women. All one has to do is look at the wide range of skin complexions of American blacks to know this is a FACT.

Recent scandals, like the one involving former **US Senator Strom Thurmond**, a staunch segregationist, and the public appearance of Essie Mae Washington-Williams, his ***"illegitimate"*** black daughter shortly after Thurmond's death, only scratch the surface of America's shameful racial past.

Ms. Washington-William's mother, Carrie Butler, a black maid who was only 15 at the time she gave birth, led many to believe she was the victim of rape. This was a tragically common fate for thousands of black girls and women in the Deep South who had no legal protection against rape or the unwanted sexual advances of white males.

Ms. Washington-Williams did not meet her father, Senator Thurmond, until she was 16 years old (his choice). Even though he offered financial support, Thurmond ***never publicly acknowledged*** his black daughter while he was alive. Strom Thurmond's story is typical of many rich (and poor) white males who have refused to acknowledge or support their "illegitimate" black offspring -- all while throwing hypocritical stones at black males.

The Extreme "Poor Parenting" Of The Rich

We openly criticize the poorest parents, but remain completely mute (cowardly) when it comes to the richest. It is easy to understand the difficulties of parenting when resources are limited, but what excuse do the wealthiest individuals have for raising children who grow up to rob pension plans, bankrupt formerly robust corporations, and put thousands of people out of work?

What about the offspring who loot the savings and loans industry or defraud the public? Certainly some criticism is warranted for raising children who start unnecessary wars, create a subprime mortgage crisis, and allow thousands of Americans to die without adequate medical treatment because they can't afford health insurance.

What kind of extreme "poor parenting" produces offspring who grow up to devastate the entire world socially, economically, politically, and militarily? Or who murder their parents in order to speed up their inheritances?

Yet we feel justified in criticizing the parenting skills of the poorest people in one of the richest nations on earth and fail to see the hypocrisy in that. We place all the blame for a failed educational system at the feet of those parents who have the least power, ignoring that the exact opposite is true:

It is the poor parenting of the rich and powerful that CREATED the poor parenting by the poor in the first place.

Think about the major problems facing this nation -- then decide which group causes the most widespread damage: the poorly parented children of 100 of the most rich and powerful, OR the poorly parented children of 100 single black mothers?

Who Really Controls America's Educational System?

The white elites at the local, state, and federal level control every educational school system in America. They determine which schools will resemble state-of-the-art college campuses and which schools will have decrepit buildings with leaking roofs and peeling paint.

The elites decide which students (white and black) will be enrolled in which schools; how all the schools will be funded (ensuring an unequal education for blacks and whites); and which students (black or white) will be "tracked" into vocational courses or college-prep courses. The formula for every American school and education institution is:

- Black schools = unequal (inferior) funding, facilities, equipment, and staffing.
- White schools = unequal (superior) funding, facilities, equipment, and staffing.

No matter how many black figureheads are placed in a prominent (public) position of authority within the school system, black people -- regardless of title -- do not control anything in America; least of all the education of black or white children.

Not a single black politician, preacher, activist, entertainer, or millionaire has the power to change a school system that consistently and persistently under-educates and mis-educates the overwhelming majority of black students.

For all the dedicated teachers, school administrators, private, and corporate citizens who are working to provide a quality education for ALL students -- regardless of race or income -- they deserve all the credit and respect we can give them because they are clearly fighting an uphill battle.

Black Parents Must Bear Some Of The Blame

Parents are the ***first line of defense*** -- sometimes the ONLY defense – against the systematic, educational, and intellectual genocide of black children. Unfortunately, too many parents have forfeited the game due to a lack of interest.

Where are all the missing-in-action parents who should be cheering their children on to academic victory during the critical family time between six to ten pm?

Here's One Answer:

Go to any bar, club, tavern, motel, hotel, or riverboat casino in any big city or small town and you'll find thousands of black mothers and fathers -- single and married -- spending too much family money and family prime time in the company of intoxicated strangers.

Six to ten p.m. are the hours most children are home (or should be) eating dinner with the family, doing homework and chores; or, if they lack parental guidance, watching (too much) television, or running the streets. Racism is NO excuse for making our pleasure take priority over the welfare of our children.

If we don't care about our own children, no one else will.

CHAPTER 20

FLIPPING THE EDUCATIONAL SCRIPT

SCENE: A giant meteor explodes in space, and showers cosmic dust over every square mile of the United States. By morning, black people have traded places with white people in all areas of human activity, and both think it has always been that way...

SETTING: A small town in the heartland of America.

From kindergarten to high school, white children are taught history from a made-up, SUPER-AFROCENTRIC viewpoint – meaning black people created, discovered, and invented *everything* of any importance.

The white students are secretly ashamed because their history books "prove" whites contributed nothing to art, history, medicine, science, or civilization. All they have is February – the shortest month of the year – to learn the same tidbits of "white history." Most stopped caring years ago.

The teachers are harder on the white students even though the black students goof off and can't answer the teacher's questions, either. By grammar school, 25% of white boys are in special educational classes because the teachers say they don't read and write as well as the other (black) students.

The little white girls prefer black dolls because they are "prettier" and love reading about the adventures of (black) Nancy Drew, wishing they were black, too. Little white boys play with (black) army men and read comic books about black superheroes (since there are no white ones).

On Saturday afternoons, the little white boys and girls in town line up to see the latest (black) Harry Potter movie, and cheer when good (black) triumphs over evil (white). In the evening, after supper, they watch their favorite TV shows. Most of the faces are black, sprinkled with a few white faces and a handful of white women who are mostly fat and unattractive.

By the age of six, the little girls and boys believe that the prettiest women are black because that's what they see on TV, in movies, and magazines. Once in a while, there are one or two pretty white women, but they look more black than white. The children never question this because they believe this is "**normal.**

In the integrated high school, most of the white students are tracked into the vocational courses while most of the black students take college-bound courses. There was a cheating scandal about the placement tests that got their previous principal fired last year but it was swept under the rug by the powerful school board made up of mostly black parents. As a gesture of good will, the girls' athletic coach chooses a white girl to be a cheerleader even though most of the football and basketball players are white.

When the black parents discover one of the history teachers -- the only white teacher -- created a "White History" course to motivate the white students, the black parents threaten to boycott the school.

At the local school board meeting, one of the black parents explains her opposition to teaching "white history" by saying, *"I don't think any one group should be studied. Plus, it makes whites feel really bad about their race when they actually did not have anything to do with it."*

A black father adds, *"Isn't white history already taught in history class? As far as I know, my kids learned about Tom Sawyer and Frank Sinatra, so what's the problem?"*

To appease the black parents, the school board suspends the white teacher for a week. The white parents retreat in angry silence, hesitant to push the issue because some of the black parents in the room are their employers and bosses.

Upon learning of the white teacher's suspension, the white students become even more demoralized than before. A month after the school board meeting, a white boy and a black boy get into a fight. Neither one was hurt but the principal calls the police anyway.

The white boy was arrested and permanently expelled but the black boy only got a week in detention. The white kids are angered, scared, and shocked that that a simple schoolyard fight could result in a felony conviction and a permanent criminal record for their 17-year-old white classmate.

After their schoolmate was expelled, the "slow" white boys, who had been in the special education classes since grammar school and were *permanently* labeled as "educationally challenged," start dropping out of high school.

The white boys said they were "tired of being put down" in front of the other kids. Besides, what was the point of staying in school when everyone said white boys had no future?

THE END

Can you imagine white parents tolerating this kind of abuse against their children from their school system?

THEN WHY THE HELL ARE WE?

Chapter 21

THE LITTLE ESKIMO WHO WANTED TO BE POLYNESIAN

The following is ENTERTAINMENT SATIRE and a work of fiction. The race, people, places, and incidents are the product of the authors' imaginations. Any reference to the Eskimo and Polynesian people is done in the interest of fiction, and is not intended to demean or ridicule either group.

The terms "black" and "white" carry so much racial baggage that we felt they would intrude on this fictional tale. Thus, we apologize in advance if we offend any readers by the terms "Eskimo" and "Polynesian." We hope you will bear with us as we try to illustrate the psychological damage done by racism.

Imagine You're A Little Eskimo Boy...

While you are still a toddler, your family moves from Alaska to Polynesia where Eskimos are only ten percent of the population. For the next 12 years you grow up with the Polynesian people, eat whatever they eat, shop wherever they shop, watch Polynesian TV, listen to Polynesian music, attend Polynesian schools, and your parents work for a Polynesian employer. Polynesian people own all the banks and businesses. Polynesian people also run all the schools, courtrooms, and penal institutions, and determine the quality of life for all Polynesian citizens; including the Eskimos, who own and control very little.

Let's add one more bone to the simmering Polynesian soup: It is common knowledge that the Polynesian people despise Eskimos. The Polynesian TV networks, as well as the major Poly-Wood movie studios, usually portray Eskimo women as ugly and fat, and Eskimo men as irresponsible, cowardly, and lazy. In the Polynesian school system, the only history that is taught is Polynesian history.

According to your schoolbooks, Polynesian people accomplished, created, and invented everything. Eskimo history is seldom mentioned, and the people are always portrayed as primitive and backwards. You and all the other Eskimo kids believe Polynesian people are smarter than Eskimos because your history books say so. You are embarrassed any time the history of Eskimos comes up.

Once, you heard a Polynesian college professor on a television talk show say he had scientific proof that Eskimos had a genetic personality defect. Shortly after that, a Polynesian author wrote a best-selling book claiming he had scientific proof that Eskimos were intellectually inferior to Polynesian people.

This news terrified you because you didn't want to spend your life going in and out of jail, ignorant and uneducated. In your poor neighborhood, a lot of Eskimo boys and men are in prison. Your Eskimo friends aren't the least bit phased, because they think it's normal for Eskimos to be in jail. Everyone in the Polynesian criminal justice system – the prosecutors, the judges, the parole agents, the prison wardens, even the guards, who were mostly Polynesian people, said Eskimos were natural-born criminals.

A former Polynesian government official once said if they wanted to reduce the crime rate, they should abort Eskimo babies. Then, he added, "That would be an impossibly ridiculous and morally reprehensible thing to do, but our crime rate would go down."

You stay indoors, read books, write poems, and watch a lot of television, instead of spending time with your Eskimo friends. You are convinced that they will wind up in jail one day because they are Eskimos, despite them being no better and no worse than you are.

You're 14 now; a freshman in high school. You confide in your Eskimo buddies that the Polynesian girls are finer than the Eskimo girls. They laugh when you confess that you have a crush on the most popular Polynesian freshman girl in your class.

You don't tell them that she reminds you of the girls you see on the television screen you spend hours looking at night after night, and the girls on the covers of glamour magazines next to the supermarket checkout aisle. You don't tell them that you have written dozens of love poems that you'll never give her.

Nor do you tell them about running into her last Saturday at the shopping mall. She was walking with some of her Polynesian friends and when you said hello, she looked right through you. Secretly, you don't blame her. Most Eskimos are poor, uneducated, ignorant, and violent. How does she know you aren't one of them? Even you question the wisdom of associating with other Eskimos.

On your way home from the mall, your humiliation sours into disgust. Everywhere you look, the Eskimo neighborhoods are rundown. Eskimo men stand on street corners drinking from bottles concealed in brown paper bags. The Eskimo women are fat and angry; always talking loud and yelling at their kids. It is so noisy, so grimy, and so hopeless where you live that you can hardly stand it. You can hardly stand *them*.

Your block is nothing like the Polynesian neighborhoods with pool table-green lawns, trimmed trees, big houses, clean sidewalks, and modern schools. There are no liquor stores or drug-dealers standing on those pristine corners. It never occurs to you that the same people who won't permit liquor stores and drug dealers in their Polynesian neighborhoods are the same people who allow them in yours.

You pass by two Eskimo men being frisked by police officers. At first, you are relieved, because one is an Eskimo who will be fair to the Eskimo men. But, that is not the case. The Eskimo policeman seems to be the angriest of the three. He shoves one Eskimo man down on his knees and makes him lie facedown on the dirty pavement with his hands behind his back.

You hear the man protesting; saying, *"What I do wrong, officer?"*

"Shut up, filthy, stinking Eskimo!" The Eskimo policeman shouts with rage. There is a loud crack followed by a cry of pain. You run as fast as you can and never look back. The idea of being humiliated like this terrifies you.

That day you decide to go college to become a journalist and get out of the ghetto. Maybe one day you'll write stories about the "good Eskimos" who don't cause any trouble so Polynesians will know all Eskimos aren't bad. You work hard to bring your grades up, and volunteer for the student newspaper. You're thrilled when they ask you to join since that means you'll be the only Eskimo on the staff. It doesn't occur to you that there is something wrong with that, since Eskimos make up 32% of the student body.

You think you're a pretty good writer but all you do is run errands and make copies. In the meantime, you fill out every student grant and loan application you can get your hands on, and pray that your grades will be good enough to get a scholarship to a good Polynesian university.

On the day of the modest graduation party your parents throw for you, everyone makes a fuss over your full scholarship to an Ivy-league Polynesian university. Five years later, you graduate with a Masters in Journalism as a diploma-carrying member of the Polynesian status quo. You dress like a Polynesian, walk like a Polynesian, talk like a Polynesian, think like a Polynesian, and love all things Polynesian.

All your girlfriends have been Polynesian women. When people ask why you don't date Eskimo girls, you explain as nicely as you can that you have "more in common" with Polynesian women. You say, you can't find an Eskimo woman on your "level," even though Eskimo women outnumber Eskimo men three to one at your university.

Some family members and the childhood friends you dropped a long time ago call you a stone pineapple: *Eskimo on the outside; Polynesian on the inside.* They say you are a Polynesian man trapped inside an Eskimo skin. They ask you why you hate yourself. You dismiss their criticisms as ignorance and jealousy.

You are not confused. You are not seeing other Eskimos through a "Polynesian lens," like one uncle sadly informs you. You are secretly contemptuous of his opinion about anything because he never went to college. You tell him that you made something of your life -- unlike most Eskimo males (including your uncle, although you are too polite to say it aloud).

After six months of a frustrating job search, you are hired at a prestigious Fortune 500 Polynesian firm. You are determined to make it to the top, in spite of your recent (and painful) discovery that your starting salary was twenty percent lower than the Polynesian men who were hired at the same time you were. The following year you proudly announce that you are getting married. No one is surprised that your future bride is a Polynesian woman.

You have finally achieved the Polynesian dream.

THE END

WEÂPON #5

INTEGRÂTION

(WEÂKEN)

"The Negro is like a man on a luxury commuter train doing ninety miles an hour. He looks out of the window, along with all the white passengers in their Pullman chairs, and he thinks he's doing ninety, too.

Then he gets to the men's room and looks in the mirror—and he sees he's not really getting anywhere at all. His reflection shows a black man standing there in the white uniform of a dining-car steward. He may get on the 5:10, all right, but he sure won't be getting off at Westport."

Malcolm X
(1925-1965)

CHAPTER 22

THE CURSE OF BLACK SKIN AND WHITE EYES: THE WHITE-IDENTIFIED BLACK

"It is impossible to achieve equality when one group has the power to deny rights to another group. Until we understand that distinction, we will not understand the difference between tolerance and acceptance." -- *Umoja*

What Is A "White-Identified" Black?

A black person who views the world through a "white lens," and judges most or all events, people, places, actions, and things from a **white perspectiv**e.

What Is The "White Perspective?"

The beliefs, opinions, behaviors, and value systems of whites as a group. The **white perspective** is based on what is normal, desirable, and beneficial for white people collectively. An example is the Rodney King beating case. In spite of VIDEOTAPED evidence of police brutality, an all-white jury decided collectively that what benefited the white police officers benefited white people collectively. That perceived "benefit" resulted in an acquittal.

Had it been the other way around – an unarmed white male beaten by black police officers -- it is certain that an all-white jury would have convicted the black officers. The white collective would have (correctly) viewed an unarmed white person's beating by black policemen as potentially dangerous to ALL white people collectively – because that meant it could happen to ANY white person. The white collective would have acted in their collective best interest by punishing the black officers.

In a racially divisive society (like America), it is NORMAL for the white collective to set standards that benefit their group, and affirms their self-worth as white people collectively. This does not mean all white people think the same, or share the same perspective in all things.

What Is The "Black Collective" Perspective?

The black collective operates on a similar principle; that black people collectively view most or all events, people, places, actions, and things from a perspective that assumes whatever benefits or harms a black person benefits or harms all blacks collectively. This does not mean all blacks think the same, or share the same perspective in all things.

From the black collective perspective, the beating of an unarmed black man by white police officers would have been (correctly) perceived as harmful to ALL black people – because the same thing could happen to ANY black person. Therefore, a black jury would be more likely to convict the white officers.

The OJ Simpson trial is another example of how the white collective and the black collective perceive their self-interests differently. The white collective assumed OJ Simpson was guilty (even before any evidence was heard), while the black collective saw Simpson's acquittal as justice for all blacks, not just Simpson.

This does not mean all blacks believed that OJ was innocent, or that all whites believed OJ was guilty. An individual may not agree with the group perspective on any or every issue, but it is undeniable this kind of group mentality exists within a racially divided society.

It is NORMAL for the black collective to set its own standards, according to what benefits black people and affirms their self-worth as black people. However, due to black-inferiority programming, which was accelerated by the integration and assimilation into a black-hating white culture, the black collective often acts against its own self-interest without understanding why they are doing it.

It also explains most of the black collective's self-destructive behaviors. This inferiority programming is the main reason many blacks refuse to identify with the black collective because it *is* the black collective.

AXIOM #7: ANY GROUP (OR RACE) WHOSE COLLECTIVE ACTIONS PENALIZES THEIR OWN GROUP (AND REWARDS ANOTHER GROUP) IS SELF-GENOCIDAL AND SELF-DESTRUCTIVE.

For this reason, the white-identified black is a liability, NOT an asset, to the black community. Before we go further, let's define what a white-identified black is NOT.

What A White-Identified Black Person Is Not

This is not a condemnation of blacks who are often unfairly labeled as not "black enough." All (or most) blacks are white-identified to a smaller or a greater degree, because we were raised in a white-supremacist culture (America). It is the degree of white-identification that determines the degree of the problem.

Being white-identified does not mean you prefer Beethoven to Beyonce, or Madonna to Master P. It is not about our tastes in food, music, art, or literature. It is not about the way we dress; wear our hair, walk, talk, sing, or dance.

It is not about our level, income, or education, or the type of work we do. It is not about being smart, or educated, or speaking standard English, or several languages that makes us white-identified.

ALL people – regardless of race – have a wide range of talents, skills, and tastes, and are capable of enjoying a wide range of things for the simple sake of enjoyment. Black people are not monolithic (the same), nor are all white-identified blacks the same.

What Is A 'White-Identified' Black?

A white-identified black person is a black person who views the world through a white perspective ***even when*** it conflicts with his or her own self AND group interests. A white-identified black pursues interests, activities, and relationships ***primarily because white people are associated with them*** – and often avoids or looks down on certain people, places, and things ***primarily because black people are associated with them.***

White-identified blacks can be found anywhere, at every income level, from the most exclusive gated community or Ivy League campus, to an inner-city housing project.

How a black person sees black people, talks about black people, treats black people, feels about being a black person, and treats white people determines ***the degree*** of white-identification.

White Supremacy Is The Foundation For The "White Perspective"

The collective white perspective is based on the following principles:

1. white is superior to non-white
2. white life is more valuable than non-white life
3. white people created everything worth creating
4. white is the most normal (the standard) for ALL human beings

If white is the most **normal**; black **must be the most abnormal**. For those who doubt that this white standard exists, there is one INDISPUTABLE piece of evidence that can be found in every medicine cabinet in America: **the 'flesh-colored' Band-Aid.**

In other words, the "normal" color for human flesh is the color closest to the skin color of white people. What does this say to the non-white person? ***That their skin color is NOT normal.***

AXIOM #8: BLACK NORMALCY CANNOT EXIST IN A SYSTEM OF WHITE SUPREMACY.

White-Identified Blackness = Psychological Suicide

By viewing the world through "white eyes," white-identified blacks are in the unenviable position of embracing their own inferiority and abnormality, and have no choice but to be anti-black – and ANTI-SELF.

If the white-identified black is observed interacting with whites or blacks, he or she will eventually reveal their OWN racial bias and inferiority complex by the things they say or do.

Their confusion comes from trying to straddle the precarious line between the black world and white world, by serving two opposing masters at the same time: **white supremacy and black normalcy.**

It is ***unnatural and perverted*** for a race of people to adopt a perspective and a set of standards that does NOT benefit their group AND denies their own NORMALCY and self-worth as members of that group. Unfortunately, this kind of distorted thinking is exactly what has led to the personality disorders and self-hatred issues that plague the black population.

Curing The 'Disease' Of Black Abnormalcy

If whiteness is the norm, blackness must be the disease. The ONLY cure is the assimilation of (inferior) blacks into a (superior and normal) white value system in order to reduce their "black abnormalcy." This fear of being "abnormal" is the main reason some blacks become assimilated (white-identified), so they will be **"normal"** by white standards. Unfortunately, white-identified blacks will never be as normal as white people because they will **never be white**.

By accepting the (false) premise that white is the most 'normal,' the white-identified black is confirming his or her own genetic and intellectual inferiority.

The white-identified black person will never admit to being white-identified, but will do anything to avoid being perceived as too "black." When pro-golfer Tiger Woods created a new term -- "**Cablinasian**" (coined from the words **Ca**ucasian, **Bl**ack, American-**In**dian, and **Asian**) – to describe his racial heritage, some people wondered why a man with a black father and an Asian mother would put "Caucasian" first in the racial pecking order.

Ironically, despite Woods' attempt to racially reclassify himself, he is still known as a "black golfer." In a white supremacist society, non-whites cannot racially reclassify themselves. Those who choose to forget this fact will be reminded.

A blatant reminder occurred in 2008, when a solution was proposed by Kelly Tilghman, a white female sports anchor, for younger golfers who wanted to challenge Tiger's title as the world's No. 1 golfer. She suggested that they, *"Lynch him in a back alley."*

Tiger's response: *"Kelly and I did speak. There was no ill intent. She regrets saying it. In my eyes, it's all said and done."*

The real question is not whether Tilghman had ill intent; it's whether the word "lynching" would have been used to refer to a white golfer. It is similar to Fuzzy Zoeller's comment at the 1997 Masters tournament when he called Tiger *"that little boy"* and told him not to serve *"fried chicken or collard greens."*

The irony is these blatant "racial reminders" make the white-identified black more uncomfortable than the whites who had an unfortunate slip of the tongue. White-identified blacks are quick to forgive these kinds of comments because they are desperate to reassure whites that they are not "angry" black people – even when they are being mistreated.

This kind of behavior is more common for black males than black females, perhaps because showing anger is taboo for black males who want to succeed with the white public. The downside of allowing racist comments to appear innocent is the black masses -- who do not have millions of dollars to insulate themselves from everyday racism – are expected to suffer the same racist treatment without protesting:

> *"Look at that black XYZ celebrity. He doesn't make a big deal out of a harmless comment about lynching (niggers), so why should you (an ordinary nigger) get upset?"*

A columnist for a major sports magazine also casts some doubt on the wisdom of Tiger's response:

> *"Woods doesn't have to become a civil-rights spokesman, but he could have at least acknowledged that he understands the meaning of the word, and how powerful and hurtful it remains." -- Farrell Evans, Writer-Reporter, Sports Illustrated*

This desperate desire to distance themselves from themselves (and their despised blackness) is what drives many white-identified blacks to deliberately seek out a white or Asian spouse to rid their offspring of the racial 'abnormalities' that exist within themselves. This is why it is critical to recognize the symptoms of black denial and self-hatred, so their "disease" will not infect us.

The Poisonous Effect Of White-Identified Black Celebrities

White-identified black celebrities are extremely dangerous to other blacks because they VALIDATE black inferiority/white superiority by the kinds of lifestyle and romantic choices they make. These "successful" white-identified black celebrities are more likely to be rewarded by the white supremacy system with lucrative book deals, talk shows, movies, and TV shows ***because they are the best advertising white supremacy can buy.***

Their fame, awards, and desperation to be embraced by the white elite and the white collective sends a DEADLY MESSAGE to the black masses -- especially to black youth: ***if you want to be rich and successful, be less black.***

The white-identified black person is the ADULT victim of the black doll/white doll experiment. White-identified blacks understand how tragic it is for the little black girl or boy to pick the white doll as the nicer doll, but cannot see how damaged they must be to do the SAME THING.

If black is "inferior", how does the white-identified black exempt him or herself from the same judgment?

Some white-identified blacks adopt external gimmicks to maintain the illusion (and delusion) of "black pride" -- like wearing African clothing, coconut beads, dreadlocks, and talking incessantly about the "black struggle," all while imitating, (secretly) identifying with, sexing, and loving ***white.***

Because white-identified blacks usually get more crumbs from the "white" table than their black-identified peers, they are convinced that their external achievements (and white validations) are proof of their internal self-esteem, when in reality, it is just the opposite.

Wealth, fame, status, titles, material things, or wearing dreadlocks and African clothing, have nothing to do with **SELF-ESTEEM**. However, **SELF-ESTEEM** does require RESPECT for the truth:

AXIOM #9: A NON-WHITE PERSON CANNOT BE EQUAL TO *OR* THE SAME AS A WHITE PERSON IN A WHITE SUPREMACY SYSTEM.

To maintain the level of self-deception and denial needed to maintain their (false) white identity, the white-identified black person must create even more delusions (lies) as to their TRUE status as a black person (a nigger) in a white supremacy system.

This is why white-identified blacks are more vulnerable to the emotional devastation caused by racism -- because they don't think they will ever be victims of it.

CHAPTER 23

THE COLOR OF SUCCESS

Miranda is a senior software programmer for a Fortune 500 company and earns a six-figure salary. She drives a luxury car, lives in a downtown condo just blocks from her job, eats out twice a day, and is always stylishly attired. Five foot-six, and attractive; Miranda maintains her trim 140-pound frame by exercising three times a week at the pricey health club in her apartment building.

Miranda avoids interacting with the black copy clerks, messengers, and secretaries at her firm since she has nothing in common with them. She has a handful of black friends and associates -- all Ivy League grads like herself -- who work for other Fortune 500 firms.

She attends most company functions, and occasionally joins her white coworkers for happy hour at the bars near their office. She dated a white consultant for a few weeks the previous year but they went their separate ways after he said he wasn't "looking for anything serious." She hasn't met anyone since, and is dateless most weekend nights.

Miranda has dated only a few black men over the last ten years; but after one or two dates, they never called again. She assumed she intimidated black men, after one black jerk told her at the end of their first and only date, that if he wanted to date a white woman, he'd find a real one. Miranda assumed he meant she wasn't the typical black woman, and took that as a compliment. And, if Mr. Right turned out to be white, she was okay with that.

The truth is, Miranda feels more comfortable around whites, which is why she lives in a predominantly white area. She grew up in a predominantly white neighborhood and attended schools where she had been one of a handful of blacks. She hadn't stayed in touch with her black classmates, and sometimes wondered what had become of them.

Although Miranda's midwestern city is one of the most segregated cities in the nation, she swears she has never personally experienced racism, except for the occasional white ignoramus who disliked blacks. Shoot, there were plenty of blacks she didn't like herself!

She refuses to be manipulated by all that "brother" and "sister" crap blacks use as a crutch. All blacks had to do to overcome white misgivings and negative stereotypes, was to be more prepared and work harder than their white peers. No, it wasn't fair, but life wasn't fair. It was just that simple.

Either a person was up to the challenge, and if they weren't, they had no one to blame but the person in the mirror. If they succeeded, the rewards were well worth it. The proof was the retirement party three weeks ago for the black vice-president of public affairs. The company bigwigs went all out for McCabe.

A rented hotel ballroom, a catered five-course meal, a six-piece jazz band, balloons, and champagne. Miranda had never seen anyone, let alone a black man, get such a royal send-off. It definitely beat a 30-year pin from the post office.

When Miranda announced to a small group at the retirement party that she was a proud, card-carrying Republican and had never once voted Democratic, she was secretly pleased by their surprised reactions. It was a prudent career move, she added, since the firm's biggest client was a staunch Republican.

The truth was, she despises being typecast as a black Democrat. She hated the patronizing way the Democrats threw out an occasional ham hock to get the black vote. Just what had Democrats done for black people like her lately?

What was even more aggravating was the way the Republican Party ignored the thousands of blacks who thought the way she did. People who were educated, successful, intelligent, and understood the value of an unregulated free market, free trade, and minimal government regulation. Her lifestyle and stock portfolio was living proof of how well it worked.

When the firm eliminated an entire division last year – mostly blue-collar jobs -- Miranda saw nothing wrong with it. Every company had the right to find cheaper labor, even if that meant outsourcing jobs. Management had an obligation to maximize profits for the company and for stockholders—like herself. Any workers who were displaced had to find new jobs. *It was just that simple.*

On the day Miranda receives an outstanding job review, the firm announces plans to cut another 10,000 jobs to boost profitability. Since the firm employs over 61,000 workers worldwide, Miranda isn't too worried, but assumed the people junior to her had better watch their backs.

Miranda is the only black person in her department, but that small detail hardly causes a wrinkle in her powder-smooth forehead. After chatting with a Human Resources manager, a black woman she was only marginally friendly with, Miranda discovers that she is the only one in her department with a Master's degree. It feels good to know her job is secure; not that she ever doubted it for one second. Miranda feels appreciated at the firm, gets along well with her coworkers and boss, and always gets excellent performance reviews. She is confident they see her as an equal and a valuable team member.

The following Friday pink slips are handed out in her department, and there is one with Miranda's name on it! Her entire department is being downsized, and the rumor is their jobs are being outsourced to India. No explanations or apologies were issued with the separation package that included three months severance pay. Miranda packs her belongings in boxes under the watchful eyes of a security guard. She is furious, humiliated, and profoundly confused because she never saw the hammer coming.

A few weeks after she was laid off, Miranda runs into one of her former coworkers, Beth, an accountant who still works for the firm. She tells Miranda that the programmers in Miranda's department had been transferred to other branches. Miranda is stunned. Why wasn't she offered a job when she had the most experience? And why didn't the sister in Human Resources warn her? The look of pity on Beth's face stops Miranda cold before the questions slip out.

Then Beth says something that catches Miranda completely by surprise. She says Miranda should file an EEOC suit against the firm. Two of the senior black accountants in Beth's area were laid off while she and three of the least experienced accountants were shuffled into different jobs. Miranda didn't ask if the three were white. She didn't have to. Beth was.

Eight months after losing her job, Miranda is still unemployed. The few job offers she receives pay a third of what she used to make. Miranda refuses to consider them but is too proud to pound the pavement for a new job, even after her unemployment benefits run out.

Eventually, the headhunters stop calling. A year later Miranda is still unemployed, 35 pounds overweight, and is taking medication for depression. Her savings are exhausted so she is forced to give up her condo and move back home to live with her bewildered parents.

An Epidemic Of Mirandas

Miranda is a classic case of the white-identified black professional. She did everything right. She went to college, graduate school, remained childless and single, and associated with the "right" (white) people. Miranda's false sense of security allowed her to be blindsided and her career to be permanently derailed.

There are thousands of male and female Mirandas in America, some of who were raised in predominantly white environments; attended predominantly white schools; and their closest friends and romantic partners -- if they were lucky enough to have any -- were white. It is understandable that these blacks identify with whites, however, this is a problem for three reasons: (1) They are NOT white, (2) They will NEVER be white, and (3) They believe they are equal to whites (which is never true in a white supremacy system).

White-identified blacks are often fooled by the ease in which they sometimes move about in predominantly white settings. In reality, they are such a small minority, they pose no threat (or competition) to whites. Unfortunately, white-identified blacks can't tell the difference between tolerance and acceptance. They are so determined to fit in, whites find their admiration and imitation flattering, and thus allow them to be in their company.

This does not mean there aren't sincere friendships between blacks and whites, but that usually depends on the black person **remaining white-identified**. Since most white-identified blacks believe whites are the ONLY people who can validate them, they will do whatever it takes to get white approval and distinguish themselves from the (unwashed) black masses, even if that means reinforcing racial stereotypes against other blacks (and themselves).

The End Of Affirmative Action

Miranda thought the extravagant retirement party for the black vice-president was proof that blacks were equals at her company. She didn't know McCabe had been forced into premature retirement, or that the firm used the bad economy as an opportunity to eliminate the affirmative action positions -- including hers -- that had been created in order to secure government contracts.

Miranda didn't know about the countless humiliations McCabe had suffered at the hands of his white colleagues. She didn't know that the day after his first promotion a decade ago, McCabe came to work the following morning and found his desk had been moved into a small closet by the white supervisors who resented sharing their office space with a black man. She didn't know that McCabe's permanent smile, which earned him the (dubious) nickname of "Smiley," had almost cost him his health and his marriage.

The male and female Mirandas do not understand (or accept) that ***skin color always overrides*** education, degrees, professional credentials, cars, clothes, white lovers, and white spouses, when it comes to the CORE pecking order in a white supremacist society. That's why, when they encounter racism, they have a tendency to ignore it unless they are forced to deal with it. They interpret this denial as confidence and strength, but it is just the opposite. *Denial is the height of weakness.*

To Be Young, White-Identified, And Black – Ain't Where It's At

Being white-identified is extremely dangerous for naïve young blacks. Because they lack life experience, they believe having white friends means they will not be as vulnerable to racism as less "assimilated" blacks. However, once they leave the nest of familiar surroundings and people, they are unprepared for the racism they will encounter socially or in the workplace with unfamiliar whites.

After high school or college, young white-identified blacks often discover their white friends are dropping by the wayside. Of course, this is not always due to race, but race increases the likelihood that their white friendships will bite the dust. As whites make the transition into adulthood and compete for jobs, lovers, and peer approval, the lines separating black and white become more distinct.

The peer pressure for whites to not be too friendly with blacks will come from a variety of sources; including their white neighbors, relatives, coworkers, employers, or even from their intimate partners. This may force some whites to realize their black friendships are more disposable than white peer approval. Unfortunately, the only one left in the dark (pun unintended) is the white-identified black who never saw it coming.

White Supremacy And Black Abnormalcy

Racial schizophrenia accounts for a significant percentage of the emotionally traumatized, mentally disturbed, and self-hating black population. In its extreme form, it can lead to the kind of suppressed rage that suddenly explodes one day on a Long Island commuter train; like the murderous rampage in 1993 by Colin Ferguson, who shot and killed six whites and wounded 19 others.

This type of black-on-white crime is extremely rare. What is more likely is the black "victim" of rage and racism turns on other blacks; on his or her family; or on him or herself (commits mentacide) by discarding a black identity to create a new, more acceptable (and false white) one.

Mentacide = Psychological Suicide

To be white-identified and black is MENTACIDE – the destruction of what should be a black-centered, self-respecting, and self-loving mindset. The late Dr. Bobby Wright, who popularized the term, defines ***"mentacide"*** as *"the deliberate and systematic destruction of a group's mind with the ultimate objective being the complete extermination of the group."*

Scholar and author Mwalimu K. Bomani Baruti offers this explanation: *"When you willingly think and act out of someone else's interpretation of reality to their benefit and against your survival. It is a state of subtle insanity, which has come to characterize (more and more) Africans globally."*

The Hazards Of Being A 'Good Black'

Despite the good black's loyalty to the white status quo, he or she is more likely to be overlooked for promotions, fired, or laid off. It is the good black whose competence is routinely dismissed, and whose education is referred to as a "dumbed-down affirmative-action degree" behind closed doors, even if that degree came from Harvard Law School.

It is the good black who is more likely to file a discrimination lawsuit against his or her employer, and is more likely to have a career-related nervous breakdown. The good black is in so much denial, they believe their race "problem" can be solved by getting more education, or becoming more assimilated (more white).

A Plumber For All Occasions (A True Story)

Several years ago, my manager (a white male) came to me out of the clear blue, and asked me to unclog a stopped-up toilet. There I was, in a nice suit and tie, and I was senior to most of the people in the office. We have a janitorial service that cleans the office and handles minor plumbing problems, so I still do not understand to this day, why I was singled out for the job.

I am a black male, have over ten years experience in my field, and a Masters degree. I feel I am well-spoken, competent at my job, and carry myself like a professional – or so I thought until that day. No one said it but everybody knew why I was picked to fix the toilet. I was the only black person in the office. Of course, nobody offered to help me. Not that I blame them. Well, maybe I do, a little bit...

I still work for the same company but I have a different manager. He's white and older than me. I can tell he's not comfortable dealing with black men. I am positive he's blocking my advancement but I haven't confronted him because I can't prove it. It's just a feeling I have.

Just thinking about that toilet incident still makes my blood boil. I would never say this aloud but I understand why that black man -- Ferguson -- started killing white people on that Long Island commuter train. A lot of black men feel like that, wanting to get even for all the dirt white people have done.

I decided to go back to school, and beef up my resume with a foreign language or two. I never want to be in the position where somebody even thinks of telling me to fix a toilet again." – Albert, 44

The Good Black Is The Most Delusional Of All Blacks.

Despite the mountains of overwhelming evidence to the contrary, good blacks (like Albert) believe MORE education, more degrees, designer clothing, fancier homes, addresses, fancy manners, cars, white spouses, and biracial offspring will accomplish what Michael J. with all his millions failed to do: ***Erase the imaginary stigma of being black.*** Good blacks refuse to accept that no one – least of all, the white supremacists – respects a man or woman who is willing to do anything, say anything, be anything, or betray anyone just to belong to a club that doesn't want them as a member.

A Healthier, Black-Loving Perspective

The psychological opposite of the "white-identified" black is the **black-identified black**. The black-identified individual sees the world as it really exists and does not blame black people for being victims of racism. Since they are NOT in denial about racism, they are seldom caught completely off guard because they keep their expectations at a reasonable and realistic level.

They understand that getting along with whites in the workplace does not mean whites see blacks as their equals. This is why most black-identified blacks seldom pursue friendships or relationships with white coworkers outside of work — to the relief of their white coworkers.

Good Blacks, Black Suspects, and Bad Blacks

The black-identified black person's unwillingness to grovel (kiss ass) or assume an inferior position can cause him or her to be viewed as a "suspect" (potential problem) or a "militant" (a bad black). A black person who cannot immediately be identified as a **"good black,"** is often viewed with suspicion, and will be eliminated from the workplace as soon as the opportunity presents itself.

Black-identified blacks are well aware of their prickly dilemma. They know a black-loving perspective will likely hamper their progress in Corporate America, and may even result in them being terminated without just cause. However, their clear-eyed, self-respecting, black-self-loving perspective makes them more ADAPTABLE to change and enables them to recover more quickly from a setback.

A Universal Perspective For All Humanity

The ideal (and most humane) perspective is a universal perspective that acknowledges ALL human beings, regardless of color, as normal and worthwhile. This would mean the end of race, and racism/white supremacy, the creation of the universal man and universal woman, and replacing the system of racism/ white supremacy with a system of universal justice.

CHAPTER 24

OUR SELFISH WAYS

A holy man was having a conversation with the Lord one day and said, "Lord, I would like to know what Heaven and Hell are like."

The Lord led the holy man to two doors. He opened one of the doors and the holy man looked in. In the middle of the room was a large round table. In the middle of the table was a large pot of stew, which smelled delicious and made the holy man's mouth water.

The people sitting around the table were thin and sickly. They appeared to be famished. They were holding spoons with very long handles, that were strapped to their arms and each found it possible to reach into the pot of stew and take a spoonful. But because the handle was longer than their arms, they could not get the spoons back into their mouths. The holy man shuddered at the sight of their misery and suffering.

"You have seen Hell," the Lord said.

They went to the next room and opened the door. It was exactly the same as the first one. There was the large round table with the large pot of stew, which made the holy man's mouth water. The people were equipped with the same long-handled spoons, but here the people were well nourished and plump, laughing and talking.

"I don't understand," the holy man said.

"It is simple," Lord said. "It requires but one skill. You see they have learned to feed each other, while the greedy think only of themselves."

In a materialistic society where resources are plentiful but unequally and unfairly distributed, greed and selfishness are the predictable by-products. A culture that defines "success" as accumulating more things than we need instead of sharing our excess with those in need, will breed a population that believes it is normal -- even desirable -- to be greedy and selfish.

What is written here is NOT a condemnation of black America, but we cannot afford to ignore the epidemic of materialism and selfishness that is systematically destroying black marriages, black families, and black communities.

We were not always this way. The civil rights movement was a living testimony to our willingness to make personal sacrifices for the common good of all black people.

During the depression, white vagrants often relied on the generosity of poor, rural blacks for a hot meal or a handout, even when they could not count on their own kind. Despite our limited resources, black people once had a reputation for being the most generous and forgiving people in the nation.

What Happened To Us? Several Things:

1. Integration

We adopted the majority culture's value system and began to worship money and material things instead of God. Some of us got a taste of the "good life" and began to embrace (poisonous) individualism, forgetting that our safety, progress, and prosperity in a hostile white nation ALWAYS came from us STANDING together.

Thanks to the 24-hour, 7-days-a-week media machine, we were bombarded by fraudulent images of happiness, sexiness, status, and success -- always defined in materialistic terms. The rampant materialism of celebrities, athletes, and an increasing number of handpicked "showcase" blacks with their interracial spouses taught us what "real success" looked like -- and it didn't look like us.

We began to define ourselves and our self-worth by what we owned instead of who we were.

The more we assimilated into (surrendered to) the white majority culture, the more materialistic, self-centered, and black-self-disrespecting we became. Those of us who managed to achieve a bigger slice of the American pie began to look down on those who hadn't. Some blacks, many of whom were first-generation, college-degreed, white-collar, business-suit-wearing employees, began to separate themselves from those who weren't: *"I wear a suit and tie) to work, which means I'm better than someone who gets their hands dirty."*

As more of us achieved professional and financial success, we became arrogant and vain, and bought into the myth (lie) that poor blacks were poor because they wanted to be poor. We ***"integrated"*** (surrendered) our round black identities to fit into a square black-hating white culture, and some of us desperately sought racial redemption in a pair of white arms.

Then Katrina slammed the Gulf Coast, and should have ripped off the rose-colored glasses of "black progress." Some of us got it; some stayed in denial, explaining away the blatant racism as the fault of those poor, ignorant black folks who didn't have the sense to leave New Orleans sooner.

We forgot that our enemies always put aside their "individualism" and move against us as a well-organized and well-financed group.

2. Black Migration From Rural Communities To Cities

The great migration of blacks from the South to the North resulted in the breakdown of the extended family and the second, third, and fourth generation communities that made our families strong.

We traded open space, fresh air, homegrown and homemade food for concrete jungles and Northern-style racism and poverty. We were forced to live in the most impoverished, segregated neighborhoods; often stacked on top of each other in urban, high-rise ghettos from which there seemed to be no escape.

What happens when you force rats into a crowded cage? They turn on each other.

3. The Systematic Attack On The Black Family

In 1925, only three percent of black families were headed by women. The marriage rate for blacks during the depression was higher than the marriage rate for whites, even though blacks were more likely to be poor than whites.

The strength of the black family WAS our extended families of aunts, uncles, grandfathers, grandmothers, sisters, cousins, nieces, nephews, and neighbors who were just like family. It was common for two or three generations to live in the same home or on the same street.

After slavery ended, freed slaves traveled hundreds, even thousands, of miles to find family members who had been sold to other plantations. Even though slavery and racism irreparably damaged the "African family," the family meant everything to former slaves and free blacks.

In the pre-integration South, there were no "latchkey kids." There was always a neighbor or a relative willing to fill in where the parents left off so no child came home to a cold, empty house.

Black children reaped the benefits of experience and wisdom that spanned two or three generations, from grandpa and grandma to the elderly Mr. and Mrs. Jones, who lived down the block. Black children learned to respect their elders ***because no one gave them a choice***. Now, MTV, BET, VH-1, gangster rappers, and the streets are raising much of the next black generation.

4. The Black Man Was Forced From The Home

When blacks fled the racist, segregated South and migrated north for a better life, they faced rampant discrimination in employment and housing. Unable to find work that paid a living wage, many blacks were forced to seek government assistance.

As more blacks became dependent on welfare, the rules were changed, forcing the black man to leave the home if the family received benefits. The black man was stripped of the ***main thing*** every man needed to feel like a (real) man: *the ability to protect and provide for his family as the head of his household.*

Unable to find work, some black fathers and husbands were faced with two gut-wrenching choices: (1) stay, and let their children go hungry, OR (2) leave, so their wives and children would have food and shelter.

Of course, there was a third, more humane, and moral option: allow black men the SAME opportunity to work, earn a living wage, and support their families, as white men were allowed to do.

Comparing Rotten Apples To Elephants

"Look at those boat (Vietnamese) people in New Orleans. They're already rebuilding their homes and businesses instead of complaining like those lazy blacks." -- comment on newspaper article about struggling Katrina survivors.

There's no end to the negative comparisons between blacks and non-white immigrants. There are differences, but these differences have NOTHING to do with racial superiority. It is illogical (and unjust) to compare blacks (who were enslaved and brutalized for 400 YEARS), with immigrant groups who came to America ***voluntarily*** with their cultures (and self-esteem) intact.

Cultural "Assets"	***Descendants of Slaves***	***Immigrants***
Identity	Destroyed	Intact
Language	Destroyed	Intact
Religion	Destroyed	Intact
Customs	Destroyed	Intact
Family Structure	Destroyed	Intact
History/Family Tree/Origin	Destroyed	Intact

Lessons We Can Learn From Non-White Immigrants

Instead of wasting time and energy resenting their success, ***we should be studying and imitating them.*** Blacks, collectively, should:

1. stop seeking social acceptance (validation) from whites because ***we will never get it*** (will never be white).
1. focus on growing businesses NOT on getting "a good job" in corporations we will never own.
2. understand that ETHNIC UNITY (black men and black women building strong families and prosperous communities) is the key to survival for non-whites in a white supremacy society.

If we could turn the civil rights clock back 45 years, which one would we choose? Social integration OR economic empowerment?

The answer can be found in the successful, tight-knit communities of many non-white immigrants. That being said, the ***unsung (civil rights) heroes*** of these success stories are the (black) people who marched, protested, boycotted, sat-in, and sacrificed; who were beaten, kicked, bitten (by police dogs), firehosed (by police), bombed, imprisoned, and murdered; so that 10, 20, or 50 years later, immigrants from all over the world could come to America, buy 7-Elevens and Citgo stations; send their children to an Ivy League university; check into a nice hotel; sit in the front row; eat at any restaurant; and enjoy any number of "civil rights." Had it not been for the "lazy" and "inferior" blacks, non-white immigrants would still be riding in the back of the bus, *right behind us.*

Chapter 25

THE ZEBRA AND THE LIONS: A TALE OF POISONOUS INDIVIDUALISM

"OJ Simpson Guilty of Armed Robbery, Kidnapping." (10/4/2008)

One day, Horace, the Zebra, got the craziest notion in his large, elongated head. He decided he didn't want to be part of a herd any longer. He was tired of grazing where all the other zebras grazed. He was tired of the smells, and the endless grunting and snorting. Zebras were absolutely disgusting!

Horace spent most of his days staring for hours at his reflection in the river. He was the most handsome zebra in the herd; too handsome to be an ordinary zebra. Whenever one of the more comely females flicked her skinny tail in his direction, Horace turned his big snout up in the air. He wasn't about to bring any more smelly zebras into the world.

Horace wandered away from the herd toward a shady grove of trees. To his delight, there was the sweetest green patch that had not been burned brown by the blistering African sun. Horace looked back at the rest of the herd chewing blissfully on the dry tufts underneath their hooves and snorted loudly in contempt. Look at those dumb zebras, eating dry grass like manna from zebra heaven.

Horace moved deeper into the grove and faced the herd so he wouldn't be seen but could see them if they came too close. If they discovered his tasty find, there would be less for him. Unbeknownst to Horace, fifty yards from the shady grove was a pack of lions; one male and three females. As Horace came closer, they strategically kept their distance. They wanted the zebra to think he was safe, so far away from the herd.

"What a dumb zebra," they growled deep in their throats with amusement. The pack licked their huge teeth in anticipation. The zebra was nice; thick around the middle with a big, fat ass.

"He doesn't do much running," a lioness chortled with contempt. She had no use for a lazy male of any species, and was looking forward to ripping that striped hide with her sharp teeth until the blood flowed.

"He's such a stupid zebra," the second lioness agreed, "to wander off by himself. Doesn't he know there are hungry lions in the fields just waiting to take him down?"

"Ho, look at him," roared the male lion, shaking his magnificent, golden-brown mane. "Chowing down like there's no tomorrow—and there won't be after we rip his striped ass apart."

The lions laughed quietly, so they wouldn't alert the blissfully grazing zebra. They were in a good mood. There was nothing predators loved more than a big-headed, stupid animal, so arrogant it forgot its own safety lay in unity of the herd.

In a herd, the zebras' stripes created an optical illusion that confused the lions. To make matters worse, the more devious zebras would zigzag back and forth in front of their herd to make it more difficult to single one zebra out. Together, the zebras were smarter than they looked – but apart – they became a lion's happy meal.

Oblivious to the danger beyond the trees, Horace ate until his big belly bulged. A shifting wind rippled the bristly hairs along his ridged back. His head jerked up and around. In an instant, he recognized the scent. *Lions!* He sniffed again, taking in large gulps through his flared nose. They must have seen him hiding in the trees!

Horace trotted out of the shady grove and paused on trembling legs. Nervously, he looked back and spotted the top of a magnificent brown and gold mane moving low through the grasses – coming in his direction!

Horace broke into a full gallop, his big belly swaying from side to side, toward the herd grazing in the distance. His eyes widened with terror when he looked back and saw the lions, four deep, in hot pursuit.

Horace brayed at the top of his lungs, calling the herd's attention to his plight. When the other zebras lifted their heads, and saw the lions., they took off, leaving Horace in a huge cloud of dust.

Horace couldn't believe these cowardly zebras weren't willing to risk their lives when he needed their help! How could they abandon such a proud, stately, handsome zebra like himself? Wasn't he just like them – only a little better?

Before Horace could make another sound, one of the lionesses leaped in the air and landed on his back, followed by another, bringing him crashing down on his front forelegs. The male lion rushed in, snapped his powerful jaws around the thrashing zebra's neck, and clamped down until the zebra suffocated.

By the time the last tremors rippled through Horace's body, the lions were already feasting. One lioness tore off a bloody chunk of zebra flesh and chewed happily. Poisonous individualism sure made one hell of a tasty meal!

The End

"Even the weak become strong when they are united."
– Johann Friedrich Von Schiller (1759-1805)

Integration was the worst thing that could have happened to black people.

You can't "integrate" into a culture that despises you.

You can't "integrate" when you have to ask (beg) for everything you need.

That's not integration, that's subjugation.

And if you don't know the difference between being equal and wanting to be equal, you never will be.

Umoja

WEAPON #6

INTERRACIAL RELATIONSHIPS

(DIVIDE & CONQUER)

"Therefore kill all that are of the male sex, even of the children." -- Numbers 31:17-18 (King James)

****

How do you destroy a race of people?
You destroy the family.

How do you destroy the family?
You divide (and conquer) the male and female.

How do you divide (and conquer) the male and female?
You destroy the bond between them.

How do you destroy the bond between the male and female?
By destroying the self-respect of the male.

How do you destroy the self-respect of the male?
By turning him against himself.

How do you turn the male against himself?
By turning him against his woman. No fruit can be superior to the tree it came from. No plant can be superior to the soil that nurtured it. And no man can despise the womb (or woman) that gave him life without despising himself.

Umoja

CHAPTER 26

OPERATION JUNGLE FEVER

ANOTHER HOLLYWOOD SUCCESS STORY

The Players:

WW TV EXEC – White female television executive who "green lights" (approves) new TV shows.

BW WANNA-BE -- Black female writer trying to sell her script for a black hour-long drama about three black actors trying to make it in Hollywood.

The Script:

WW: (flashes the pearly whites). "So nice to meet you! Thanks for flying down on such short notice!"

BW: (big smile). "Thank you for inviting me!"

WW: "Your script is exactly what we're looking for!

BW: "That's great!"

WW: (still smiling). "Of course, we'll need to make a few changes."

BW: (smile slides sideways like warm Jell-O). "What kind of changes?"

WW: (flips open a script covered in red ink). "We *love* your idea of an interracial cast. Black audiences love that. Only, we think the Kelly character should be married to one of the men."

BW: (resists temptation to roll eyes. Kelly was the only white female). "But, the show is about three single men and three single women."

WW: "We think Kelly should be married. Our sponsors are very conservative, when it comes to couples shacking up. Naturally, we'll have to take that into consideration.

BW: "So, Melanie should be married, too?"

WW: Oh no, Melanie can be still be live-in girlfriend of man number two. The third man should be a dog -- I mean, dawg -- or whatever; so black males can relate to him."

BW: (wonders why the "sponsors" wouldn't object to Melanie, the black female, "shacking up", but doesn't ask). "What about the third female, Victoria?"

WW: (trying to sound hip). "I'm just not feeling that name."

BW: "What do you mean?"

WW: "We should make her name more urban, like Krackshonda, only we spell it with a 'k' instead of a 'c'!"

BW: ('urban' was code for ghetto). "I don't think a name no one can spell would work for a three-year medical student..."

WW: (enthusiastic). "I completely *agree!* Krackshonda should be a high school dropout who just got her GED but can't keep a job or a man. Just for comic effect!"

BW: (hiding her frustration). "But it's not a comedy, it's supposed to be a drama."

WW: (gray eyes fill with sympathy). "I'm sorry, didn't anyone tell you? We've filled our quota for new dramas, but we could use one more sitcom to round out the fall schedule. Naturally, if you want to take a pass, and try again next year, we'll understand."

BW: (panicking). "Oh, no, I'm definitely interested! I'll need a few days to make the changes—"

WW: (picks up the phone and pushes some buttons). "Don't bother. Our writers will polish up the script, then we'll shoot the pilot and take it from there." With the phone pressed to her ear, the WW EXEC stands up and extends her hand over the desk to another BAMBOOZLED black-Hollywood-wannabe to signal that the meeting was *over*.

THE END

Black Males Are The Main Targets Of The Media's "Jungle Fever"

The latest trend in Hollywood and television is the (token) black actor in otherwise lily-white movies, TV shows, and commercials. The list is too long for this book, but includes TV shows like "Sex in the City," "Desperate Housewives," the remake of "Beverly Hills 90210," and dozens of major motion pictures. There is one more equally disturbing trend: ***the black actor co-starring with white and non-black females.***

Racial Progress Or Divide And Conquer?

Some viewers see these interracial pairings as racial progress. Others see it as a clever strategy to increase the "crossover appeal" of black actors. If this was the intent, why isn't the "cross-over potential" of the largest minority in the US (Hispanics) being tapped by pairing Hispanic actors with white actresses?

If ***black females outnumber black males*** in the US, why are black actresses becoming an endangered species, and why are the majority of on-screen interracial relationships ***between black males and white females?***

"In the animal kingdom, the predator searches for the weakest animal in the herd, and drives it away from the safety of its numbers (unity). The human animal in the role of predator wisely uses the same killing strategy."
-- Anon

A Hollywood Reality Check

"I was part of a writer's panel where a white writer -- who pretended to be this super-liberal -- made a statement that nearly knocked me off my chair. He said they needed more scripts where black males are romantically involved with white females. I was sitting there with two other black women. He was looking right at us when he said it." – Noelle, 30, black female writer at a major television network.

Hollywood Casting Call: Black Females Need Not Apply

The popularity of black actors in primetime TV dramas and Hollywood films is a stark contrast to the increasing LACK of roles for black actresses in movies, television shows, and TV commercials. With the exception of independent black films and (buffoonish) black sitcoms, it is rare to see a black man and black woman holding hands, kissing, or making love in prime-time TV shows, or in major motion pictures.

"I asked a white casting director why there weren't more roles for black women to play the love interest of a black man. Do you know she had the nerve to say, 'America is not ready to see love between black men and women.'"

At first, I was shocked, but I shouldn't have been. Most TV programs, commercials, and ads pair the black man with anybody but a black woman. The black woman is always alone; that is, if we can be found at all.

I guess they're trying to tell us (black women) something but we're just not getting it. I'm not against interracial relationships, but black actresses are catching hell in Hollywood." -- Melody, 27, unemployed actress.

Black Woman: Part Whore; Part Mammy; Part Beast

"Several years ago, I was a summer intern for one of those trash talk shows. That day's show was about out-of-control teen girls. I was backstage, watching this black girl, about 13 or 14, in short-shorts and a halter-top, acting all ghetto, and dropping it like it's hot. After we went to commercial, I heard the girl's mother ask her why she was acting so crazy, and the girl said, "That's how the producers told me to act."

That was the first time I was aware of how these black girls were being exploited. The media wants these ugly images of black females to go out all over the world." -- Diane, 26, aspiring filmmaker.

Top Six Roles For Black Actresses (With A Few Exceptions)

1. The light-skinned or biracial female who lusts after white men, aka the "white man's whore." The "provocative mulatto wench" is a carryover from the early 1900s minstrel shows.
2. The long-haired, light-skinned, or biracial female who plays the love interest of the main black male character.
3. The brown-skinned, hostile, immoral female who can't get or keep a man.
4. The brown- or dark-skinned, mannish, tough, ghetto female.
5. The dark-skinned obese female as a single desperate female, mammy figure, or demonic character.
6. A black actress who does not fit any of the above five categories defaults to the largest category of black actresses: the UNEMPLOYED.

Truth Is Stranger Than Fiction

Who are the people (behind the scenes) who create, script, cast, direct, and produce most of the TV shows, commercials, music videos, and movies? The **Women in Entertainment Power List** -- published yearly by the *Hollywood Reporter* -- ranks the most powerful women in the entertainment industry.

For obvious reasons, their names are not listed in this book, but their titles are impressive, nonetheless: Chairman, Co-Chairman, President, Chief Operating Officer (COO), Co-President, Executive Vice-President, Producer, Senior Executive Vice-President, Managing Director, Literary Agent, Head and Co-Head, Founder, Partner, and Senior Vice-President. Predictably, with a few exceptions, ***the vast majority (over 95%) are white women.***

Fact Or Urban Fiction?

CONFIDENTIAL MEMO: OPERATION JUNGLE FEVER

Our goal: to promote interracial relationships between white females and black males as a superior alternative to black male/female relationships. By doing so, we are making significant inroads against the stability of the black family. It is imperative to destroy the concept of black male/black female love since this controversial (and perverted) form of love represents the greatest danger to continued white domination and white genetic survival.

Until further notice, all TV networks, cable stations, movie studios, record companies, media distribution, movie theaters, radio stations, newspapers, and magazines must meet our "Wholesome Entertainment Standards (WES)." Attached is the most current copy of the WES. Each network must submit their fall season schedules for formal review ASAP.

Ms. A. Bergman, President of Entertainment, XYZ Group
(Please initial and return the enclosed document)

Wholesome Entertainment Standards (WES)

Destroy the natural bond between the black male and black female by creating programming that:

1. degrades the black male and black female
2. shows black females as the enemy of black males
3. shows black males as the enemy of black females
4. shows black females as undeserving of the love, support, and respect of black males via talk shows
5. shows black females and males as baby-mommas and daddies
6. shows attractive black females as whorish and immoral (music video hos)
7. shows a positive bond between the black male and white female
8. shows white females supporting black males
9. shows black males risking their lives to save (and assist) white females
10. shows dark-skinned blacks as less educated and less intelligent than light-skinned blacks.

WARNING: Any positive sexual expression or affection between the black male and black female ***is strictly forbidden.***

WES Objectives

1. To program the black male to reject the black female in favor of the white female so he will breed himself out of existence and reduce the number of black offspring.
2. Pair the black male with the disposable white female population to neutralize the black male's will to oppose white domination and his own destruction.
3. Reward black entertainers with fame and financial enticements if they demean blacks; in particular, the black female. This is a highly effective strategy since black males seldom defend black females.
4. Once the abandoned black female becomes completely demoralized, she will produce dysfunctional black offspring that can be easily disposed of. The added benefit is an increase of homosexual black females – a predictable reaction to their devaluation by black males and as well as a critical shortage of available black males.
5. An overall breakdown of the black family will cause significant declines in future stable black populations.
6. Based on our present rate of success, "Operation: Jungle Fever," assures we will exceed our stated goal: **The extermination of the 'Dark Nation.'**

Is the **WES (Wholesome Entertainment Standards)** an urban legend or urban fact? We confess, it is a work of fiction. Regardless, it appears someone's plan is working just fine...

> *"Nearly three quarters of the 403,000 black-white couples in 2006 involved black husbands."*
>
> *45 percent of black women in America have never been married, compared with 23 percent of white women, according to the U.S. Census Bureau's American Community Survey in 2006.*
>
> *"This country is in an interracial marriage boom," Dr. Hare says. "One out of 10 Black men will marry White women; that's 10 percent of our men gone."*
>
> *"Now they aren't 'hos,' but there were some nappy-headed women on that team. Those are some of the ugliest women I've ever seen in my whole life." -- Black comic D.L. Hughley, on Jay Leno's "Tonight Show," on Don Imus and the Rutgers University Basketball team (May 2007).*
>
> *[6 months later: D.L. Hughley hosts 'The 13th Annual Critics' Choice Awards' on VH1 (Nov 2007), the 39TH NAACP IMAGE AWARDS (Feb 2008), the BET AWARDS (June 2008), and was the host of a short-lived CNN comedy/ news (?) show "D.L. Hughley Breaks the News" (Oct 2008)].*

Five Reasons Black Males Are Encouraged To Date Interracially

1. To destroy the concept of the strong black family.
2. To encourage the black male to commit genetic self-genocide.
3. To destroy the black male's self-respect and neutralize his will to oppose white supremacy.
4. To emotionally demoralize the black female, who is now raising 70% of the next black generation alone. The more unstable the frustrated black female becomes, the more likely she is to raise dysfunctional black children who will be no threat to white supremacy.
5. To focus the growing rage and frustration of the white male collective onto black males. It is NO coincidence that the increasing numbers of black males who are dating white females is followed by an increase in black male unemployment, incarceration, police abuses, and police murders *by* white males.

The Zebra and the Lions Revisited

> *"The lioness hunts for the lion. She finds a zebra that is weak enough to take down then the lion joins in to finish off their prey. Without the lioness, the male lion would not be such an efficient hunter. Without the lion, the lioness would lose her protection. Together, they make a formidable team, thus ensuring their GENETIC SURVIVAL." -- Anon*

CHAPTER 27

THE BALLOON AND THE BASKET

She was a beautiful mahogany-brown Balloon who loved soaring high in the blue skies. Attached to the Balloon was a handsome, sturdy brown Basket who provided stability and kept the Balloon from getting too close to the sun. The strong brown tethers (cords) that had held them together for the last thousand years had endured a thousand terrible storms.

One day, the Balloon and the Basket passed over a traveling circus where hundreds of shiny red, blue, green, and purple balloons floated on long, silky strings above the striped tents. The Basket was awestruck. They were the most beautiful balloons he had ever seen -- mainly because they weren't *brown*. It didn't matter that they were too small and puny to lift a basket his size; he was still impressed.

The winds picked up and carried the Balloon and the Basket away from the circus. Heartbroken, the Basket watched as the brightly colored balloons shrank in the distance.

The Basket blamed the Balloon for being too big to steer against such a strong wind. If only he could be free of the Balloon, his life would be perfect! When the Balloon heard the Basket grumbling below, she decided *she* was tired of being controlled by the Basket. If only she could be free of the Basket, her life would be complete!

Below them, the huge, jagged white rocks and swirling waters beckoned to the Balloon and the Basket. "Come on, take a swim," the waters coaxed the pair. "We promise we won't let you drown."

The Balloon and the Basket paid the deceptive waters no mind. They had survived more than a thousand years together by avoiding the dangers of the jagged white rocks and raging waters.

Tragically, their dependence on each other was now the main thing driving them apart. They had been a team for so long that they took each other for granted. Secretly, each believed he or she would be better off apart, and each made plans for their escape.

The next afternoon, the westerly winds blew the Balloon and the Basket toward the circus tents and the brightly colored balloons. This time, the Basket came prepared. He took a long sharp stick from the bottom of his basket and started poking holes in the Balloon until he heard sharp hisses of air.

The Basket was so intent on being free; he didn't notice that the Balloon was sawing away at the strong brown tethers that held them together with a saw she'd hidden away.

With each poke of the Basket's stick, they descended another 50 feet. Now, they were only 200 feet above the jagged white rocks and swirling waters. The Balloon frantically sawed faster and faster.

When the last tether was completely severed, the sturdy brown Basket went into a free fall, tumbling over and over toward the jagged white rocks. When the Basket realized his fatal mistake, he called out for the Balloon to save him but she was too busy plugging up the holes he'd made.

With a loud crash and a terrifying scream, the Basket hit the jagged white rocks and broke into a thousand pieces. The swirling waters pulled what was left of the once sturdy brown Basket beneath the rolling white foam. The Balloon shouted with joy! She was finally free! Without the weight of the Basket and his controlling ways, she was soaring higher than ever before!

Then the Balloon noticed her smooth, slick surface was melting. She was too close to the sun! With a cry of dismay, she tried to descend to a safer altitude but the torn brown tethers were of no use in steering.

Frightened, and in agony, the Balloon cried out for her beloved brown Basket! Like the Basket, she realized her fatal mistake too late. The Basket had allowed her to soar, but he had also kept her safe.

When the Balloon bounced off the sun, she exploded into a thousand shiny-brown pieces! What was once a magnificent brown Balloon floated down to the jagged white rocks and was consumed by the swirling white waters.

Then something happened that had never happened in the history of time. The swirling waters rose until they completely covered the jagged white rocks, and for the first time in a thousand years, the raging waters were calm and peaceful.

Without the Basket, the Balloon could not steer clear of the dangerous sun. Without the Balloon, the Basket could not rise above the dangerous white rocks. Together they made a formidable team. Apart, they were doomed.

THE END

"The lion cannot survive alone; without the lioness, he will perish."
-- Umoja

"Look at the parts that make up the whole. By separating the parts, sowing dissension and division, you can bring down even the most formidable foe."

Robert Greene,
"The 33 Strategies of War"

WEÂPON #7

ENTERTÂINMENT

(DEGRÂDE)

Bling Bling
Rap Videos & Video Hos
Glorified Violence
Pants Hanging Off Ass
50% High School Dropouts
Comedy
Black Sitcoms
Black Buffoons
Who Yo Baby Momma?
Yo Momma So Black Jokes

Chapter 28

ENTERTAINMENT: THE NEW CRACK FOR BLACKS

"Black people didn't start acting crazy until we began seeing ourselves on the TV screen." – Umoja

A Crackhead Fairy Tale

Once upon a time, people relied on other people for conversation and entertainment. They visited friends, went on picnics, took long walks, played cards and board games, worked in the garden, or spent afternoons at the museum. People listened to the radio, read books, magazines, and even the backs of cereal boxes. Strangely enough, without knowing it, their brains grew because reading stimulated their minds, and listening to the radio stimulated their imaginations.

Staying indoors was punishment for children back in the day. They preferred spending time outdoors, breathing fresh air, and creating sport out of the natural world, like mud pies in the summer and snowmen in the winter; playing hide-and-seek, jumping jacks, double-dutch, softball, and hopscotch. Children developed the muscles in their brains and their little limbs because they were using them.

Then someone named Philo T. Farnsworth invented the television. Soon, every American home, rich and poor, had one. There was only one set per household, so the entire family watched TV together, and the children watched whatever their parents watched in full view of their parents. Families still ate dinner together at the dinner table, and most households only had one phone, so no family member could spend the entire evening talking into a piece of plastic.

When televisions became more affordable, everyone demanded their own set. Family members spent more time apart under the same roof, watching more TV and talking to each other less. Children didn't have to compromise or share to watch the program of their choice. With the introduction of 24-hour programming, cable channels, video rentals, pay-per-view, DVD, hi-def, surround-sound, projection, and flat-screen TVs, television turned the home into a private entertainment center.

The most popular book in the American home became the *"TV Guide,"* for the few who bothered to read at all. The 21st century brought increasingly dismal news for publishers, bookstores, and authors: (links found on website)

- 42% of college graduates never read another book.
- 80% of US families did not buy or read a book last year.
- Only 32% of the US population has ever been in a bookstore.

For too many Americans, reading has become a lost art. For others, it was an art never found. A young black man appeared in court for some recent parking tickets on a car he'd sold over a year ago. When the judge asked, *"Did the light bulb come on after you realized the car was still registered in your name?"*

The young black man's response: *"What light bulb?"*

This Is Not A Joke; It's A National Tragedy

Reading was not the only casualty of the TV age. Childhood obesity shot through the roof. Dinner time meant grabbing a wing from the KFC bucket on the way to somewhere else. Kids stopped ripping and running and riding bikes outdoors. It was easier—and safer – to ride the universal remote that controlled the TV, DVD player, & stereo CD player. Kids could have hours of fun without interacting with a single human being—and some grew to prefer it that way.

Millions of children (and adults) fired up their Play Stations, X-boxes, and DVD players to see the life-like blood and guts that would desensitize them to the REAL thing just outside their doors.

Neighbors stopped being neighbors because they'd rather watch the tube, instead of watching out for their neighbors' kids. The streets became more dangerous because it was easier for predators to slip in and slip out among the strangers who lived next door.

TV became the entertainer, the educator, the baby-sitter, and the child-rearer. TV started doing all our thinking, too. It told us which fads were in; which were out, and what kind of house, car, liquor, clothing, job, and spouse would validate us as worthwhile human beings.

TV commercials over-stimulated our tastebuds and drove us off our couches to do a Taco Bell or Seven-Eleven midnight drive-by. The glowing tube told us that anything we wanted was only a pill-popping second away. All we had to do was sit on our asses, armed with our remote control, and get richer, skinnier, sexier, more popular, and stay young forever by sending six payments of $19.95 to the address shown on the screen.

After black folks began appearing on the movie and TV screens, some of us began to redefine who we were based on fools and buffoons. The TV show *"Good Times"* taught poor black folks – between laughs – that no matter how hard we tried, or how promising things looked, we couldn't escape the ghetto, but, at least we could be a "cool fool" like J.J. "Dynomite" Evans!

Temporary layoffs and easy credit rip-offs were as good as it got for poor black folks in the projects, according to the TV show *"Good Times"* theme song. Today's "good times" means endless entertainment, movies, videos, cable, Blockbuster, Netflix, pay-per-view, and Play Stations under one roof.

Good times means snotnosed kids really *are* smarter than the average adult (*Are You Smarter than a Fifth-Grader?*). And let's not forget all those trash-talk TV shows that broadcast the message that it was NORMAL to be ABNORMAL -- and NORMAL to be cruel and ridicule people in distress.

Good times meant poor black, brown, and white folks got their 15 minutes of fame for being dishonest, whorish, foolish, or unfit parents. If they didn't know who 'they baby daddy' was, they could always go on *"Maury"* for a second, third, or sixth paternity test, and another all-expense-paid trip to New York City.

The studios could afford it because profit margins exploded through the roof after the entertainment industry sharpened its laser focus on the thousands of single-parented black youth, already primed by missing fathers, stressed-out single mothers, and rap music with its violent, black and black female-hating lyrics. It was the perfect opportunity to deepen the psychological destruction of the descendants of former slaves:

> *"We can kill the minds of two (million-plus) black kids with one CD or DVD, and get them to pay for the privilege!"*

The television taught black boys that pretty black girls were "hos," and that being an "authentic" black man meant being uneducated and poor -- unless he was a rapper, ballplayer, or drug-dealer. The black boys learned they better *"Save the Last Dance"* for a white girl if they wanted to be *"In the Mix"* like Usher.

Black girls learned it was normal to be a "bitch" or a "ho" since the rich rap stars sang the praises of those gorgeous black "video hos." What poor, little black girl doesn't want to be sexy -- even if she had to be a "ho" to do it? She better shake that brown rump roast or the black boys would *"leave her ass for a white girl,"* just like Kwayne West sang in his platinum *"Golddigger"* song.

The new breed of black female superstars with their colored contact lens, and honey-blond weaves (that clashed unnaturally with their beautiful caramel and chocolate skin) represented the new "black beauty", so what black girl in her right mind wanted to look "authentically black?" The only time an "authentically-black" black woman came on TV, she was always fat, sassy and ***man-less***.

With rap songs that demeaned black men and women playing 24-7 on TV, radio, and car stereos, the mainstream media moved in for the kill, ***playing up interracial relationships and playing down black-on-black love.***

Self-esteem-starved black males began to look for (white) validation as full human beings in the arms of white (or non-black) females. Black girls decided they better look "less black" if they wanted a black man. After all, having a piece of man was more important than loving themselves, because...

Real love between a black man and black woman was too much to ask for because black love was DEAD. It must be dead, because they never saw it on a TV or movie screen.

Love must be a white, Hispanic, or Asian thing because whenever black girls saw a black man kissing, hugging, or loving a woman on a TV or movie screen, the woman was never black. Even when a black female wound up with a man, they didn't get along because everybody knows black women don't know how to treat a man right.

Everybody knew black women, love, and marriage didn't go together. Even on the black sitcoms, a romance between black men and women was hard to take seriously because a laugh track followed every kiss or hug, so it was easy to come to the conclusion that:

BLACK LOVE WAS DEAD.

Even rescuing black females seemed fake because all the famous black actors (MAMMY MEN), only befriended, rescued, or protected white females and little white girls. Black girls and women finally got the message: they'd better learn to protect their damn selves because black males were too busy protecting and providing for white women and little white girls. So, it had to be true:

BLACK LOVE WAS DEAD.

Where did (our) black love go? It can't be found in the gang-banging movies, gangster rump-shaking rap videos, the endless stream of mind-numbing, buffoonish sitcoms, vulgar comedy shows, or sexually explicit music that talked about sex but never mentioned real love or respect.

We were so thrilled to see black folks on the screen, dancing, prancing, joke-telling, clowning, shucking and jiving, we never stopped and asked ourselves what these black entertainers were doing TO us -- and to our children.

Fortunately, a growing number of self-respecting black viewers began asking why there were NO black TV dramas and movies that told our love and life stories? And they were catching on and tuning OUT. Unfortunately, it was too late for most of the TV-hooked generation. The damage had already been done.

The ABNORMAL had become the NORM. An entire generation of black folks were stone-cold-hooked on Entertainment Crack.

What Is "Entertainment Crack"?

"Entertainment Crack" aka "EC" is the most addictive legal substance on the planet. Also known as "crack entertainment" because of the cracking sounds it makes inside your skull. EC is such a powerful drug that it kills millions of brain cells on contact without leaving any traces (of an intellect). It is hard to predict when the EC user will become completely brain-dead, but after 12 months of continuous TV, video-viewing, and music-listening crack, the user is HOOKED.

Common Street Names For Entertainment Crack (EC)

Prime-time, reality shows, soap operas, trash-talk TV, sitcoms, comedy shows, prime-time dramas, rap videos, brain candy, electric kool-aid, white girl/black boy, black boy saving white girl, black girl saving her damn self, black female misfit, white man's whore, black mammy men, "urban" entertainment, black sellouts, blaxploitation, bootleg videos, and boob tube.

Common Street Names For Entertainment Crack Users

Couch Potato, Reality Show Junkie, Brain Dead, Numb Skull, Snow White, Coal Black, Sneezey, Grumpy, Dopey, Dumbed-Down, Illiterate, Wigger, Powder Puff, Ho, Pimp, Dawg, Bitch, Nigga, Baby-Daddy, Baby Momma, Sperm Donor, Thing, It, Thug, Player, Dead Head, Drop Out, Neuro-Brain, Rock Head, and Crack Head.

Physical Descriptions Of Entertainment Crack (EC)

White flakes with an occasional black speck thrown in for "diversity." The most popular EC among hard-core users is the "zebra" (black and white) or the "Jungle-Fever-Wet-Dreams" brand. Chronic use results in a brown residue around the lips.

Who Are The Biggest Users Of Entertainment Crack?

Entertainment crack respects no socioeconomic, racial, ethnic, religious, or age boundaries, but is more common among the young, the poor, the homebound, and the unemployed. Unfortunately, the low cost of today's electronics has made entertainment crack affordable to virtually everyone.

Due to the breakdown of the extended black family, entertainment crack use has risen to epidemic proportions among elementary, and high school "latch-key" children who come home to empty houses where there is no parental supervision. Entertainment crack is a stimulant and a depressant, depending on what is being viewed (ingested) at that moment. After the effect of EC wears off, the user frantically seeks another hit, by changing channels or DVDs.

Where Does Entertainment Crack Come From?

The main sources of "Entertainment Crack" are the corporate boardrooms high above Hollywood Hills, Wall Street, and restricted country clubs and golf courses, where the most powerful media conglomerates in the country decide what the public will be allowed to see and hear.

A few minor black and brown players are allowed to sit outside the door, as long as they were willing to collect their paychecks, cosign whatever decisions are made, not make any waves, and keep their mouths shut.

Symptoms Of Entertainment Crack Addiction

- Diminished vocabulary due to low brain activity
- Short attention span and inability to focus without pictures & sound
- Loss of interest in reading, math, or anything that resembles brainwork
- Setting unrealistic goals, like shooting for rap stardom at age 40
- Uncontrollable impulses that drive users out at night to cop a Taco Grande or Big Mac
- Chronic dissatisfaction with one's material status or possessions
- Increased feelings of inadequacy

- Low impulse control
- Confused thinking
- Violent behavior (imitating movies and videos)
- Damaged self-image and self-esteem
- Weight gain due to steady diet of pizza, pies, cakes, hotdogs, hamburgers, polish sausages, potato chips, microwave popcorn, french fries, pork rinds, barbecue ribs, fried chicken, & diet colas
- Unplanned pregnancies and single parenting without ability to parent
- Chronic boredom, which leads to higher dosages of entertainment crack
- Feeling of weightlessness in the upper cranium area. (The overall effects of the entertainment crack can last for decades after the first hit)
- Unwashed dishes in kitchen sink for days
- Pizza stains on bed sheets, pillowcases, and sofa cushions
- Dust a mile thick on everything but the TV screen
- Kids running wild in the street (or unsupervised at home)
- Empty potato chips, microwave popcorn, and beer nuts packages in trash can
- Stacks of unpaid bills under a light covering of dust
- Electricity "abruptly" turned off in the middle of favorite TV program
- Unexplained periods of unemployment (got fired)
- Males wearing earrings as big as (crack) rocks in both ears (like a female)
- Males wearing pants hanging below their butts (like a prison sex trick)
- Females appearing on *"Maury"* (talk show) to learn "who they baby daddy is"
- Males calling young females "dude" and "man"
- Females calling other females "ho" and "bitch"
- Males calling other males "bitch"
- Females calling males "bitch"
- Greets family members, friends, casual acquaintances, coworkers (white and black), the boss, and the police with, *"What up, my nigga?"*

The Cure

Unfortunately, there is no quick or easy cure for entertainment crack addiction. Only after years of therapy, the elimination of entertainment crack, and mandatory black history courses, will addicts regain their common sense, self-respect, and sanity.

The most difficult part of recovery is getting the crack addict to admit they have a crack problem, or that they have been programmed. The sad irony is even the television bigwigs call their product "*television programming.*"

For more updates, be sure to tune in next week, same time, same station...

CHAPTER 29

BLACK FOLKS LAUGHING TO THE GRAVE

By the end of slavery, joke-cracking, grinning, subservient, and buck-wing-dancing **'Rastus'** was the most popular black man in the South. Rastus was so popular they wrote books about him like, '*Adventures of Rufus Rastus Brown in Darktown,*' and '*Rastus Comes to the Point: A Negro Farce.*' Rastus was so popular they sang songs about that old rascal, Rastus, like '*Rastus, Take Me Back,*' and '*Rufus Rastus Johnson Brown, What You Going to Do When the Rent Comes 'Round?*'

That old rascal, Rastus, was so popular in the South that they immortalized him in films like '*Rastus Runs Amuck*' (1917); '*How Rastus Got His Chicken*' (1911); '*Rastus Loses His Elephant*' (1913); '*Rastus in Zululand*' (1910); and '*Rastus And Chicken*' (1911); and '*Rastus' Rabid Rabbit Hunt*' (1914).

Why are grinning, joking, and clowning negroes so popular in American culture? Because a grinning negro is a SAFE negro.

The real appeal of the clown-like, smiling, cowardly, and never angry black man is NOT that he is entertaining, but he is REASSURING. A grinning negro is like a pacifier to a white supremacist. A grinning negro wouldn't think of plotting revenge against white folks because a grinning negro ain't mad at nobody about nothing, including that big foot called **racism** pressing down on his black neck.

How Minstrel Shows Perpetuated Black Stereotypes

Thanks to the popularity of minstrel shows in the early 1900s, black people became synonymous with ignorant, lazy, buffoonish, and superstitious. We were still good to have around because we were so musical and carefree; even if we were simple-minded, lazy, and conniving.

Typical Minstrel Show Characters

- The old darky who was more loyal to the master than he was to himself
- The provocative mulatto wench (who combined light skin and white features with the perceived sexual promiscuity of a black woman)
- The dandy (pretty boy)
- The trickster (con artist)
- The shiftless, shifty-eyed buck
- The fat, sassy, and happy (dark-skinned) mammy
- The lazy, dim-witted brown female

Singing And Dancing Darkies Are Cheerful Darkies

The characters in minstrel shows (usually white males in blackface) portrayed blacks as cheerful, simple-minded darkies who loved to sing and dance for the "white folks." Songs about slaves yearning to return to their slave masters were common in minstrel shows. The message to the white audience was clear: ***Don't feel bad for these niggers; they are happy with their lot in life.***

Roasting, Fishing, Smoking, Peeling, And Planting Niggers

There were comic songs in which blacks were "roasted, fished for, smoked like tobacco, peeled like potatoes, planted in the soil, or dried up and hung as advertisements. There were multiple songs in which a black man accidentally put out a black woman's eyes. A script might call for the white masters to break up black lovers in the act of sex, or the script may call for the white masters to sexually assault the black women, themselves.

Not surprisingly, racism made the minstrel business a dangerous profession for black performers. When playing in Southern towns, black performers had to stay in character. Even when offstage, they had to wear ragged "slave clothes" and keep a big smile on their faces around whites.

1906 postcard advertisement featuring dandy-type characters

The white actors who portrayed black characters spoke an exaggerated form of 'black English'. The illustrations on the show programs depicted pictures of blacks with huge eyeballs, overly wide noses, and thick-lipped mouths that hung open or grinned foolishly. One character expressed his love for a black woman with "lips so large a lover could not kiss them all at once." Other descriptions of blacks included huge feet, and a preference for "possum" and "coon" to more civilized (white) fare.

Black characters were often described in animalistic terms, with "wool" instead of hair; "bleating" like sheep; having "darky cubs" instead of children; drinking ink when they got sick "to restore their color;" and filing their hair instead of cutting it.

Everybody Loves A Coon!

Coon songs were little more than racist lyrics set to ragtime music, like "Every Race Has a Flag but the Coon," "A Trip to Coontown," and "All Coons Look Alike to Me" were the latest national craze in post-slavery America. Over 600 coon songs were published from 1880 to the 1920s and some sold millions of copies.

"Last night I did go to a big Crap game,
How dem coons did gamble wuz a sin and a shame...
I'm gambling for my Sadie,
Cause she's my lady,
I'm a hustling coon, ... dat's just what I am."
(From "Gimme Ma Money" by Nathan Bivins)

Coon songs perpetuated the most common (and ugly) stereotypes of black people, which was the main reason they were so popular. Blacks were pictured as dishonest, unambitious, lazy, trifling, whorish, gambling, alcoholic, immoral, violent, buffoonish, watermelon-and-fried-chicken-eating COONS.

For example, "Ma Honey Gal" reinforced the false notion that blacks were more likely to cohabit that to marry, when in fact, the marriage rate for blacks during the early 1900s ***was higher than it was for whites.*** Whites wrote most coon songs, but there were black "coon" songwriters, like Bob Cole, author of, *"A Trip to Coontown,"* and Ernest Hogan's *"All Coons Look Alike to Me."*

Yesterday's Minstrel Shows Are Today's Black Entertainment

It's hard to tell the difference between yesterday's minstrel shows, and today's black sitcoms, comedy routines, and movies. Our nothing-is-off-limits approach ensures hours of wholesome fun as we degrade ourselves, our skin, hair, features, religion, ancestors, culture, and yes – even our black mommas. And the fatter and blacker our mommas are, the bigger our belly laughs.

Mentacide Soup For The (Black) Soul

(An updated version of a time-tested recipe from the early 1900s)

INGREDIENTS

- 50 pounds of starving black comedians/actors/actresses, soaking wet
- 50 pounds of chitling-network sitcoms with meaty laugh-tracks
- 30 pounds of *"Yo momma's so black"* jokes
- 30 pounds of pee-pee, wee-wee, and doo-doo jokes
- 30 40-oz jars of chocolate syrup
- 50 boxes of instant vanilla pudding mix
- 1000 pounds of teeth-whitener
- 100 cups of ground-up dignity and self-respect
- 50 pounds of sweet potato pie spice – (to disguise bitter flavor)

DIRECTIONS

1. Place black comedians/actors/actresses on a greasy baking sheet.
2. Mix sitcoms, yo-momma, pee-pee, wee-wee, and doo-doo jokes together.
3. Add sweet potato spice and teeth whitener until fully blended.
4. In separate bowl add vanilla pudding and chocolate syrup, apply mixture to comedians/actors/actresses' ribs, and let the dish set for 45 minutes.
5. Pre-heat industrial sized gas oven to 1500 degrees.
6. Stuff the jokes, sweet potato spice, and teeth whitener mix into entertainer's ears and mouths.
7. Cook dish for 200 years, adding chipped niggers to maintain steady choking black smoke.
8. Dish is done when completely self-hating inside and out.
9. Hang upside down and stick a fork up the ass (a cooking tip from Kramer)
10. Sprinkle ground-up dignity and self-respect on the smoldering, blackened meat while still red-hot.
11. Chill at the "crib" until ready to broadcast worldwide.

Feeds a half-million black folks per serving! Enjoy!

CHAPTER 30

WHY THERE ARE NO BLACK DRAMAS ON NETWORK TV

Let's Examine The Difference Between A Drama And A Sitcom:

1. **Drama** – an hour-long television program where the characters face serious, real-life issues and relationships. The characters are so realistic many viewers identify with them.

2. **Sitcom** -- short for "situation comedy." Even serious situations and dramatic moments are comical. A laughtrack is always present to make sure the audience doesn't take the story OR the characters too seriously. The characters in many sitcoms are caricatures. According to Webster's dictionary, a **"caricature"** is a comic, or ***grotesque*** (ugly) **imitation** or exaggeration of a person or human being.

For example, in the animated sitcom, *The Simpsons,* the cartoon characters may deal with real-life problems but no viewer would ever mistake the Simpsons for HUMAN BEINGS, no matter how entertaining they may be.

The Simpsons" are CARICATURES based on human beings – not REAL HUMAN BEINGS. If the image of a race is based on television "caricatures," NOT human beings, the humanity of that race is deformed and diminished. Let's examine the average black sitcom:

Typical Black Sitcom Caricatures

Most black sitcoms (with a few exceptions) usually involve a random mix of the following (dysfunctional) caricatures:

- a foolish dark-skinned black male (clown)
- an emotionally unstable black female
- an obese, dark-skinned black momma (mammy) with a heart of gold
- a dark-skinned black male ex-con
- a successful, light-skinned black male
- an uneducated, ghetto, brown- or dark-skinned black female
- a single, desperate, man-hungry brown- or dark-skinned black female
- a sexually promiscuous black female
- a materialistic, dark-skinned female from humble beginnings
- a stuck-up, light-skinned female from the black upper-class
- a disagreeable, dysfunctional baby's momma
- a token white female from central casting

Add to this potent mix, a whole lot of eye-bucking, neck-rolling, trash-talking, white-teeth-grinning, foot-hopping, hip-popping, nappy-hair-and-weave-joke-cracking, dancing, clowning, shucking, and jiving, and the end result is the typical black TV sitcom.

This bizarre but predictable cast of (clown) characters makes it impossible for any (intelligent) viewer to take blacks seriously – ***which is exactly why over 95% of black TV shows are sitcoms.***

The Difference Between Comedy And Buffoonery

There are white comics, comedies, and sitcoms where the characters may be silly, goofy, or foolish, but the object of ridicule is NEVER the real or exaggerated racial characteristics of whites, like jokes about pasty-white skin, thin lips, stringy hair, or flat asses.

Buffoonery is black males making fun of black women's "buckshot" (the hair at the nape of the neck). Buffoonery is blacks ridiculing black churches and preachers. Buffoonery is creating demeaning images of blacks that are seen all over the world. Buffoonery is portraying brown and dark-skinned black women (our mothers, sisters, daughters, wives, and lovers) as "ghetto" and "unattractive."

Buffoonery is the bamboozled black masses rewarding black entertainers who degrade black people, only to wonder, after the laughter is over, why so many non-blacks think black people deserve no respect. ***THAT is the definition of buffoonery.***

With a few exceptions, the majority of black sitcoms pick up where the early minstrel shows left off. Both leave the same impression on their black and white audiences: ***blacks do not deserve respect because they do not respect themselves.***

To Be Serious And Black (On Network TV) Is No Joke

Dramas are about ***real people*** and ***real problems***. Dramas HUMANIZE fictional characters. Only after the NAACP threatened to boycott the major TV networks in 1999, were a few token black actors sprinkled into otherwise lily-white primetime dramas.

The lives of these token black actors usually revolved around their jobs, and the personal problems of their white (or Asian) co-workers. The black characters interactions with other blacks (outside of his or her occupation) was usually of a negative nature. What is the message in this "programming?"

If a black person wants to be taken seriously (be fully human), they MUST BE surrounded (validated) by WHITE people.

This is NOT about right and wrong. Those standards don't apply here. There is no point in blaming the white media. Their job is to maintain the white status quo and white supremacy/black inferiority. They are doing their jobs.

When we will do ours?

CHAPTER 31

TALES OF THE BACKSIDE: FLIPPING THE HOLLYWOOD SCRIPT

Disclaimer: The following is entertainment satire and a work of fiction. All names, characters, places, and incidents are the product of the authors' imagination and used fictitiously. Any resemblance to actual persons, living or dead, business establishments, events, or locales is entirely coincidental.

SCENE: Rufus Smurf, the black superstar singer/entertainer/actor, walked into the oak-paneled boardroom where studio execs were waiting to hear his latest brainstorm.

"How about this?" Rufus said, wide-eyed with excitement. "A sequel to 'Great Big Whale of a Black Momma,' called -- 'Great Big Whale of a White Momma!"

The icy silence that followed made big balls of sweat pop out on Rufus's brown forehead. "Don't you get it?" Rufus continued hastily. "Instead of a fat, nasty, ignorant black momma, she'll be a big, fat, nasty, ignorant white momma!"

"Mr. Smurf." The silver-haired Chairman of the Board fixed his steely blue gaze on the quivering black man standing before him.

"Yassuh?"

"Do you want to work in this town again?"

"Oh, yassuh!" Rufus's lips stretched as wide as the white-toothed grin on the black statue of Rastus that the Chairman kept on his desk.

He felt like kicking his own black butt! He shoulda known better than to mess with white women when he got one of his brainstorms! He'd better stick with the nigga females from now on!

"Then stick to the program," the Chairman ordered, sliding a fat white envelope across the desk. "And do the job you were hired to do."

"Sho nuff, boss!" Rufus glanced inside the envelope stuffed with large-denomination bills.

"Just a little bonus for your 'Great Big Whale of a Black Momma,'" the Chairman said. "And we're submitting your name to the Academy for your portrayal of nigg -- black women."

"Yippee!" Rufus flashed a big white grin as he jumped up and clicked his heels in the air to punctuate his glee.

The white men in the room chuckled and shook their heads. One murmured low to another, "Niggers sure can jump."

"Can I go now, boss?" Rufus giggled, pretending not to hear.

"What's your hurry, boy?" The Chairman asked sternly.

Rufus cocked his head to one side and hunched his shoulders, like a puppy caught peeing on the new rug. "Got a court date with my new baby's momma," he said, feigning embarrassment, but secretly proud that these white men knew he was a baby-making stud.

"You colored boys sure love the pootang."

"Yassum, we sho do!"

The Chairman waved an imperial hand. "Go ahead. Don't spend all that cheddar on too much black booty, boy."

"I won't, nassum," Rufus said, as he backed out of the room.

After the door closed, the Chairman's cold smile evaporated. He reached under the table and opened a cardboard box filled with white robes and pointy white hoods. "Time to get rid of these damn things once and for all," he said. "The blacks are doing all our dirty work for us."

"The nerve of that nigger, thinking we'd demean our white race with a movie like that," The redheaded VP of programming finally spoke.

"My grandfather, bless his dear, departed soul, used to talk fondly about the good old days," the Chairman said, with a nostalgic smile. "He loved those old minstrel shows with darkies singing, dancing, and making fools of themselves."

"What good old days?" the redheaded man sneered. "What's changed?" His question was met with derisive laughter from the men in the room.

"Blacks are animals. They respect nothing, not their own women, mothers, churches, or themselves," said a blond man, shaking his head in disgust.

"Of course, they're animals. That's their nature. Personally, I thank God every day for making niggers." The Chairman patted the backs of the men as they filed out the door. "That 'Great Big Whale of a Black Momma' just paid for my new 80-foot yacht."

THE END

CHAPTER 32

HOW BLACK COMEDY DIMINISHES BLACK LIFE

In 2006, Comedian Dave Chappelle appeared on the Oprah Winfrey show to discuss his reasons for turning down a $50-million dollar deal with the Comedy Central Network.

Chappelle explained, during the taping of a particular sketch, after a white crew member laughed, he was struck by the thought that people were laughing at him, not with him. He confessed that some of his sketches made him feel "socially irresponsible," making him question the kind of messages his comedy was sending to the millions of viewers who tuned in each week. Which brings to mind a different question: ***Why would any comic be worth $50 million dollars, and what would be the return on such an investment?***

Millions of broken-spirited, self-hating black people

Any black comedian willing to use authentic civil rights footage of black marchers being fire-hosed, beaten, and bitten by police dogs as the backdrop for a "comedy" sketch is certainly worth TWICE his weight in gold to the white supremacists. Try to imagine a Jewish comedian using footage of Jews being bulldozed into mass graves as the backdrop for his comedy sketch. Would the Jewish audience be rolling in the aisles with laughter? Or would that comic be looking for a new career -- and a new identity -- in the morning?

Who Is Most To Blame? Black Comics Or The Black Audience?

If we did not support black entertainers who degrade black people, they could not make money doing it. When our "comedy" ridicules our heroes, like Martin Luther King and Rosa Parks, our religion, churches, pastors, our beautiful black mommas, and our skin, noses, lips, and hair, WE make it harder for every black man, woman, and child to get respect at home, at work, on the street, in the courts, at the mortgage company, and at the hands of law enforcement.

By supporting and defending black "entertainers" who degrade black people for profit, WE are making life harder for every black male who applies for a job and is denied one because he has been stereotyped as an irresponsible fool before he opens his mouth. WE are making life harder for our black mothers, daughters, wives, and lovers to get the respect they deserve, when they are publicly referred to as "bitches" and "hos" by ***us***. Yet we -- black people -- demand respect as "black people" even when it is obvious we DO NOT RESPECT ourselves?

Degrading Images Of Black People Diminish The Value Of Black Life

"You see if we go back to Nazi Germany and Joseph Gerbels, who understood if we keep putting out negative images of semites and the Jewish religion, we can train the population to say: 'Look, they're animals, they're not human. And so the sooner we get rid of them, the better.' -- Dr. Frances Cress Welsing, author of the "Isis Papers," during an appearance on Tony Brown's Journal.

Try to imagine white females dying from AIDS at the same rate that black females are dying. Would the response from the larger (white) society be SILENCE? Try to imagine unarmed whites being slaughtered by police at the rate that unarmed blacks are being slaughtered. Would the response from the larger (white) society be SILENCE? Try to imagine young white males dying at the rate that young black males are dying. Would the response from the larger (white) society be SILENCE?

Our answer: The Columbine killings (of white children) became a "national tragedy" and "an emergency wake-up call" to the nation even though black and brown youth had been dying in the streets for decades.

Dead Black Children Have Become The Norm In America

Dr. Carl Bell, a prominent black psychiatrist in Chicago, recalled a strange encounter he had while attending a conference during the 1980s. He was wearing one of the T-shirts he had created that read, *"Stop black-on-black violence,"* when he was approached by a white woman who said that the slogan on his shirt frightened her.

Surprised by her admission, Dr. Bell asked why stopping black-on-black violence would frighten anyone.

"If you stop killing each other, you'll start killing us," the woman said.

The white woman's response explains why the first wave of black youth killing black youth wasn't seen as a "national emergency" for white America." It is more desirable for black people to take out our understandable rage and pent-up frustration on other blacks (victims) than to direct our energies (and power) where they belong: ***the system of racism/white supremacy.***

The slaughter of black children did not happen overnight. After crack cocaine, automatic weapons, and rampant unemployment was "introduced" into poor black communities, they became battlegrounds between warring drug gangs, law enforcement, and poor, trapped residents.

The real question is: why didn't Black America declare black children dying as OUR NATIONAL EMERGENCY two decades ago?

One answer: ***"People who do not respect themselves will not defend themselves." -- Dr. Frances Cress Welsing***

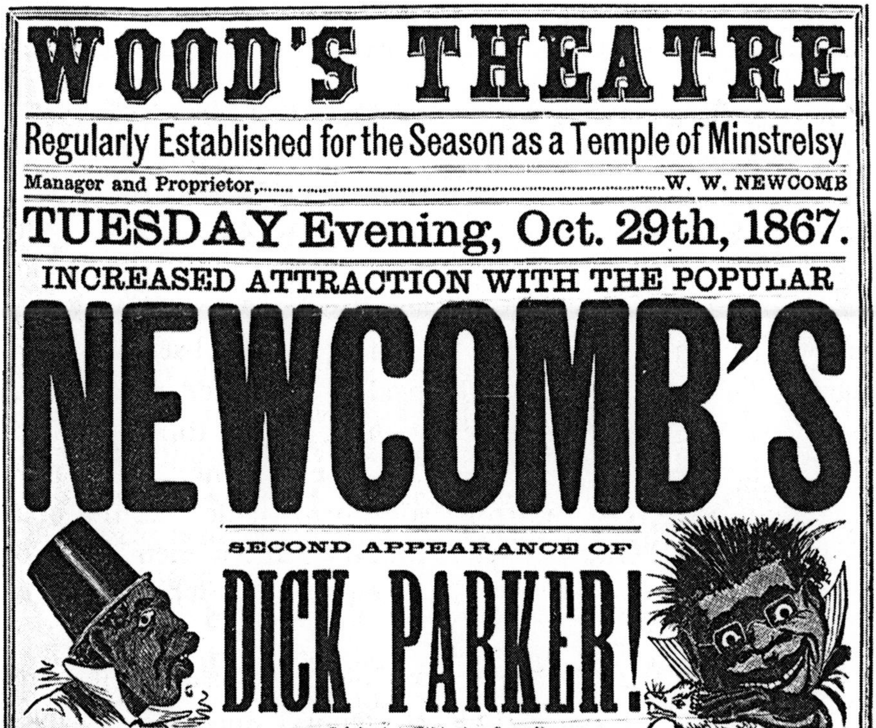

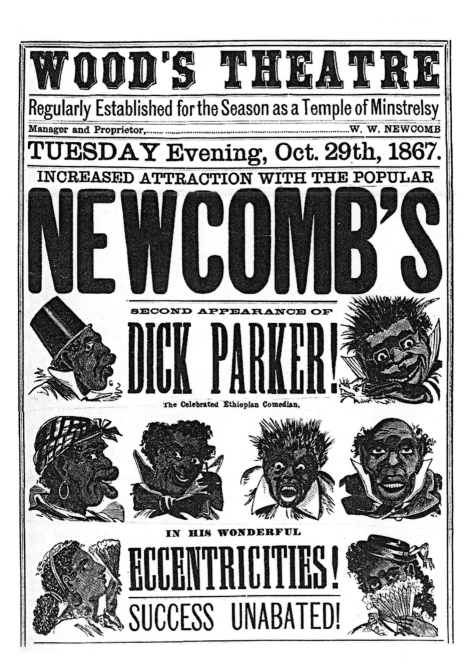

"Convince your enemies to wage war on themselves and you win the war by default." -- Anon

WEÂPON #8

MÂTERIÂLISM (CORRUPT)

"No, there is plenty wrong with Negroes. They have no society. They're robots, automatons. No minds of their own.

I hate to say that about us, but it's the truth. They are a black body with a white brain. Like the monster Frankenstein. The top part is your bourgeois Negro. He's your integrator. He's not interested in his poor black brothers.

He's usually so deep in debt from trying to copy the white man's social habits that he doesn't have time to worry about nothing else. They buy the most expensive clothes and cars and eat the cheapest food. They act more like the white man than the white man does himself."

Malcolm X

CHAPTER 33

MATERIALISM: THE NEW BLACK RELIGION

"Black folks are hypnotized by money." – Neely Fuller, Jr.

It's hard to deny it. Black folks are blinded, bamboozled, baffled, bewildered, bedazzled, beguiled, and bewitched by money; no matter how great or how small the amount...

Malinda's Misfortunes

After spending the night with Wendell, her new man of three weeks, Malinda, 22, returns to the apartment she shares with her mother and her three-year-old son, Malik. She immediately phones her home girl, Delores, with the good news: *"Yeah, girl, he works for the Post Office. That's right, Uncle Sam don't play when it come to child support."*

Malinda is so thrilled with the idea of getting MONEY – no matter how small the amount – that she refuses to consider the huge cost and responsibility of raising another child. She gets no child support from her son's father, who's in prison, but this small detail doesn't faze Malinda. Her plan is to find a man with a good job, get pregnant, get on Section 8, and collect child support from at least one of her baby's fathers.

Three months later, one of Malinda's wishes comes true. She's pregnant, which isn't surprising, since she doesn't believe in birth control or condoms. She has the baby – against Wendell's and her mother's wishes – both of whom beg Malinda to have an abortion.

Malinda says she's grown and knows exactly what she's doing. Three days after giving birth, she files for child support. On the way home from the courthouse, Malinda can't stop thinking about the check she'll get for the next 18 years. She'll be able to move into her own place and get away from her mother's constant nagging to get her GED.

Malinda is ecstatic when she receives her first $300 check, despite the total lack of involvement of her "baby's daddy." Shortly after, she moves into her first apartment; a tiny one-bedroom.

Unfortunately, Malinda's crafty financial scheme hits a brick wall a year after her youngest son is born. Wendell's temp job is abruptly terminated and the support checks stop coming. He has disappeared, leaving no forwarding address and a disconnected cell phone number. Malinda is shocked and bitter about her sudden decline in fortune, and disparages Wendell every chance she gets.

Malinda needs more money to support herself and her two children. She dropped out of high school during her first pregnancy; has no GED, no marketable job skills, and is struggling to make it on her minimum wage job. She occasionally "dates" older, married men, who are willing to pay for a few hours of her time.

She swears she'll stop but then the light bill or the rent comes due. Every man she likes runs for the border as soon as he finds out she has two hungry mouths from two different daddies to feed. After one man found out she had lied about having any children, he stopped returning her phone calls.

Within two years of moving out of her mother's apartment, Malinda is three months behind in the rent and the landlord evicts her. With nowhere else to go, she and her two kids move back into her furious mother's cramped, one-bedroom apartment.

Let's Do The Math:

- $300/mo child support = $3600 for ONE year of child support
- $3600 divided by 18 years = $200/year (minus the cost of clothing, feeding, educating, and providing for one child for the next 18 years.

Turning Back The Ancestral Clock

Two young black males loiter in front of a closed liquor store, watching the cab at the corner discharge its passenger. It's one am and the streets are deserted. The cabdriver is writing his last trip in his log, unaware that he's being watched. Tony nods toward the idling cab and says to his homie, Dante, "Yo, check that out." He jams his hand into a pocket and whips out a small handgun. "Let's jack that bitch."

Tony is so excited about getting (somebody else's) MONEY that he's willing to risk decades in prison for it. Gun in hand, Tony and his homie, Dante, sprint toward the cab. They intend to rob the cabdriver and disappear into the night, but things don't go like they planned (or didn't plan).

The cabdriver, who has been robbed twice, retrieves a pipe from beneath his seat and takes a hard swing at Dante's head. Dante goes down for the count. Tony panics and starts shooting. He grabs the dead cabdriver's wallet and the cab medallion from the dashboard, and leaves his unconscious "homie" at the scene of the crime.

The cops come. A semi-conscious Dante is taken by paddy wagon to the county hospital and is cuffed to a hospital bed. Two white detectives grill him for a solid two minutes and thirty-five seconds before he cracks, fingers Tony, and pins the entire robbery and murder on him. At three am the police swarm the projects, kick in Tony's mother's front door, and find Tony hiding in his closet. After ransacking his mother's apartment, they find the cab's medallion in the refrigerator freezer.

Tony is booked on first-degree murder charges; no bail. His mother is evicted due to a clause in her lease about harboring fugitive felons. It takes an all-white jury only 30 minutes to reach a unanimous verdict: *guilty*.

On his nineteenth birthday, Tony's gift is a 36-years-to-life sentence. His pal, Dante, gets five years as part of a plea deal with the prosecutors. Tony will spend the next four decades behind bars for killing another black man over $200.

Let's Do The Math:

- $200 divided by 36 years = **a whopping $5.55 per year.**
- If Tony worked for $5.85 (minimum wage) at McDonalds, he would have made MORE in one hour than he makes in prison in ONE YEAR. It gets better. Tony is assigned to kitchen detail, scrubbing pots and pans for eight hours a day for **80 cents an hour**.

Let's Do The Math – Again:

- Tony scrubs pots and pans for 36 years for 80¢/hr = **$59,904**
- Tony works for McDonald for 36 years for $5.85/hr =**$438,048**

One More Thing:

As a free man, Tony could continue his education, learn a skill or a trade, start his own business, become a rap star, win a lawsuit, marry a rich woman, win the lottery, or get a job that pays more than $5.85 an hour. Tony could spend his money anyway he wanted, go anywhere he wanted, and have sex anytime he wanted (with a woman).

He could eat his momma's fried chicken, collard greens, and cornbread, a bowl of gumbo, or an order of fresh fried catfish, crab legs, or jumbo shrimp. He could check out a movie, go night-clubbing until four am, get drunk, rent videos, play a video game, take his best girl clothes-shopping, buy a car, go skating, bowling, dancing, smoke a blunt, have a cocktail, take a vacation, or fly in an airplane (something Tony has never done). He could rent an apartment; buy a big screen TV, buy his own home, have children, and do all the wonderful and fun things that FREE men – even black men – are able to do.

For the HUGE sum of $200 (he never got a chance to spend), Tony turned his ancestral clock back 200 years: one year for every dollar he stole.

Now, Tony will live out the rest of his life – or, at least the next 36 years -- as the "property" of the state, aka a "number," aka a **21st CENTURY SLAVE.** Tony will be told what to do, when to do it, how to do it, and where to do it by the prison "overseers" (his new slave masters). The truth is, Tony has it worse than his SLAVE ANCESTORS because they were never imprisoned within a steel box for 24-7.

Unfortunately, a life sentence isn't the only price Tony will pay for killing the cabdriver. He's the youngest and newest inmate in his cellblock (fresh meat). Within three days of landing in state prison, Tony is gang-raped in the showers, and becomes an older, much tougher inmate's "jacked bitch."

Living The Good Life

David, 30, and Benita, 32, consider themselves the ideal married couple. Both are college graduates, have good jobs, and a combined income of $130,000. They live in a spacious, rent-controlled, two-bedroom, two-bath high-rise apartment that is close to work and very affordable for their income. Since neither have any children, they decided to wait a few years before starting a family.

One evening they attend a house-warming party of one of the black managers in David's company. At first, they are thrilled because this is the first time David has socialized with management. As they toured the mini-mansion with the other guests, they felt an uneasy mixture of awe, envy, and resentment. David thought his wife had a good time, but when they got home, her mood abruptly soured. She said that the only reason they were invited was to have the house rubbed in their faces.

After thinking it over, David reluctantly agrees. They ignore the fact that the black manager has been with the company longer, makes twice what David makes, and is 20 years David's senior. The apartment Benita had decorated with so much pride seems dark and cramped now. Every evening, armed with the real estate section of the paper, Benita starts pressuring David to buy a house.

Interest rates are low, she says, and while their credit isn't perfect, it's good enough to qualify for a mortgage. Benita paints glorious pictures of how much better life could be as homeowners, and how David could practice his saxophone as much and as often as he liked; something he couldn't do now without disturbing their neighbors.

The following weekend, they go to an open house event sponsored by a local realtor. After running their incomes, outstanding debt and credit history, the bubbly blonde realtor reassured them that $190,000 was a ballpark figure, based on a 30-year fixed mortgage, which almost nobody "bothered with anymore."

David really got into the spirit of things after viewing a 15-year-old tri-level with a big backyard, and a full basement for $239,000. The realtor said they could do better; that the house was on the lower end of what they could really afford. David only half-listened to that. The woman worked on commission. She wouldn't be the one struggling to pay a mortgage, two car notes, two student loans, and several credit cards.

David hinted at looking at some less expensive houses, but Benita had different ideas. Before he knew it, they were driving into the parking lot adjacent to a new homes subdivision. Benita and the agent exchanged a look then Benita asked, what was the harm in looking. They spent an hour going from one model to the next; each one more impressive than the last. The almost three-story homes were huge; with cathedral ceilings, sweeping staircases, and gourmet kitchens.

They were really too big for two people but Benita reminded him that it wouldn't always be just two of them; that they'd have enough room to start a family; plus the house was an investment that would appreciate in value.

Benita finally steered her husband down the stairs to the finished basement, with oak wall paneling, recessed lighting, Berber carpeting, a full bath, and plenty of storage closets.

David had the strangest feeling his wife had been there before but then his imagination took flight, as he imagined making the basement his domain, where he could play his saxophone to his heart's content and get away from Benita when she had one of her "attitudes."

Before he had a chance to object, Benita was filling out an application and writing a check for the "Oxford" model—one of the few homes still unsold--with a hefty price tag of $425,000. The $5,000 deposit wiped out all but a few hundred dollars of their small joint savings account.

David felt queasy on the drive home but didn't say much. As soon as they walked into the door of their apartment, Benita was all over him. As they made frantic love, David was trying to remember the last time his wife had been so passionate in bed. Maybe, this move would mean a fresh, new start for their marriage.

He was still in shock a few days later when they were approved for a no-money-down, interest-only mortgage from XYZ Mortgage. According to the loan broker, their "2-28" loan was the most popular mortgage on the market. They would pay $900 a month for two years and then the rate would adjust up OR they could simply refinance and get another adjustable or interest-only loan and their payments would stay the same. The BIG advantage, the broker said with a broad smile, is on the day they sign the final papers, their house would have already appreciated 15 percent!

After the closing, David carried Benita over the threshold, still in shock. They couldn't believe they owned such a big, beautiful home that cost $300 LESS per month than their old apartment! They swore right then that they would save the extra money to pay off their outstanding debts.

Then the credit card offers started flooding their mailbox. It seemed too good to be true. Their savings plan would have to wait. They needed new furniture, bedding, towels, and window treatments for every room; Oriental carpets, cookware, dishes, gardening equipment, a riding lawnmower, a riding snowblower, ladders, hedge clippers, and a new double door freezer, which they kept stocked to the max on their almost daily shopping trips.

David used one of the new Master Cards for a new computer, a computer desk, and laser printer for the room he claimed as his new office. Armed with her new Visa, Benita turned "her room" into a reading room, and hired a carpenter to build a wall of matching bookcases.

When they were physically and financially exhausted, they threw their first house-warming party. The party was catered by one of their favorite seafood restaurants, courtesy of another new Visa card. David invited the black manager who had started the ball rolling. It was gratifying to see the surprise on their guests' faces as they feasted on champagne, shrimp cocktails, and prime rib. It was a stark reminder of how far they had come. Their new mantra: *"Living better than the boss was the best revenge."*

They relied on cash advances to pay their delinquent accounts, which seemed to be growing by the day. It didn't make sense. Not only were they not saving a dime, they were in more debt than before! Things got so bad they were afraid to answer the phone because the student loan people were calling day and night.

Then, the letter came. The one that offered a home equity line of credit. They were shocked at the ease in which they were approved for a $50,000 loan after being in their home for only five months!

The loan broker, a well-groomed black man with a beautiful baritone, reassured them that their home had appreciated significantly and not to worry about payments. They could refinance in 12 months, roll over the second into the first, and their payments would only be $50 more a month.

Elated, Benita and David signed the papers. They threw another party in celebration, serving expensive liquor and seafood to their guests. A few weeks after that they took $7,500 of the money and took a two-week Caribbean cruise. They were living proof that the GOOD LIFE was available for anyone gutsy enough to go after it. Why shouldn't they have everything they wanted right now? Didn't they deserve it?

Two weeks before their mortgage was due to reset, the subprime mortgage industry collapsed. Frantic, Benita and David made dozens of calls but couldn't find a single bank or mortgage company willing to refinance their home. They owed $95,000 more than their home was worth; were in debt up to their proverbial eyeballs; and their credit was WORSE now than before they bought the home because every credit card and loan was delinquent more than 60 days.

The only bill they were current on was their first mortgage and both car payments. That wouldn't last because the new terms of their reset mortgage made their payments shoot up from $900 a month to $2400 a month, plus the $875 for their second mortgage.

More bad news followed. The transmission went out on David's BMW, and Benita's Lexus needed a complete engine overhaul, new tires, brakes, drums, & rotors. They had been so busy "living the good life," their cars hadn't been serviced in over a year.

Two years after moving into their first house, David was loading up the last of their personal possessions into a U-Haul truck, while Benita cried in the front seat. He was crushed, too, that they had lost the house to foreclosure, but also strangely relieved. It had been a great ride while it lasted.

Let's Do The Math:

- **Net worth (before house) = negative $55,000**
- **Net worth (after foreclosure) = negative $158,800**

Benita and David ruined their good credit; are currently homeless (until they find a landlord who will accept their terrible credit); lost a great rent-controlled apartment; and have almost TRIPLED their debt with only some depreciating household items to show for it.

That's not the end of the bad news. A year after the foreclosure, they received a tax bill from the IRS for $34,603. The IRS had declared the forgiven mortgage debt as "income."

Not only does money drive us mad, it stops us from doing the math. When a person is hypnotized by money, it doesn't take much to put them into a complete, skull-cracking, brain-numbing trance.

Why are so many black folks so money-hungry? The childhood years form the foundation of our attitudes about money. Kids watch their parent(s) struggling, fighting, worrying, fussing, arguing, and always wishing for more money, and bigger and better things.

Newspapers and news programs are filled with stories of people who scheme, rob, lie, cheat, and kill to get money. We are taught to elevate, envy, and admire rich people. We are taught that money is the quick fix for everything that ails us.

Money becomes a safe, secure haven in a tumultuous and dangerous world. Money (or the lack of it) determines which people are respected and protected, and which ones are disrespected and left without protection.

Television and movies are constant reminders of what working and poor people don't have -- and how much happier they would be if they had it. The something-for-nothing mentality also distorts our sexual and romantic expectations.

The Man Of Her Dreams

Nellie, an attractive, single, black professional in her mid-thirties, was posed at her usual spot at her favorite upscale bar, wearing her best after-five designer finery. The evening so far had been a total bust. None of the men at the club measured up looks-wise to her high standards.

Then her dream man walked in the door. As the tall, dark, and handsome stranger came her way, Nellie swiveled in his direction and crossed her legs, exposing a provocative length of thigh. Nellie checked out the new arrival as he stood at the bar and ordered an expensive brandy.

She was savvy about men's clothes. His tailored suit looked like Armani, and the tasseled loafers had to be Gucci. When the man lifted his glass, his gold and diamond watch glittered under the bar lights. Rolex! So far, the man was batting a thousand!

Nellie tried to think of an icebreaker. Something clever that would let him know he was dealing with a quality sister. To her delight, the stranger beat her to the punch and introduced himself. As they talked, she discovered they had everything in common.

They liked the same movies, sports teams, and shared the same views on politics and religion. Talking to Tim was like talking to herself. Everything she liked; he liked. She was flattered that the best-looking man in the club had focused all his attention on her, ignoring his female (and male) admirers. *Tim was just too good to be true.*

Then Tim lowered the boom and completely blew Nellie's mind. He took her hand and said God had finally answered his prayers. He was tired of running from woman to woman and was just about to give up on finding his soul mate because few women met his high standards. Now that he was independently wealthy, owned a multi-million-dollar company, and several rental properties, he didn't have to work anymore, and was ready to start a family. What sweet music that was to Nellie's ears!

Tim said he had everything a man could want: two Mercedes 500SL sedans, a country club membership, and a three-car garage, six-bedroom Colonial home in an upscale suburb. The only thing missing from his life was a good black woman to share it with.

Nellie had to grab the bar with both hands as the words, "Mercedes 500SL" rang in her tender ears. God had finally answered her prayers! Which was surprising, since she hadn't stepped foot inside a church since her grandmother's funeral five years ago. As a matter of fact, she couldn't recall the last time she got down on her knees and asked God for anything, including forgiveness. That was cool. She didn't have to ask because God already knew what kind of man she wanted. He *was* God, wasn't he?

When Tim asked if he could drive her home, Nellie said yes, even though her car was outside in the parking lot. He led her to a black Toyota Corolla and opened her door. Before Nellie could ask the obvious question, Tim explained the Corolla was one of several company cars he used during the week for tax purposes. Nellie liked the sound of "one of several company cars" and let it slide after she saw a stack of manila folders on the back seat.

When his car stopped in front of her apartment building, Nellie invited Tim (a total stranger) inside for a nightcap. She wasn't about to let him go before the deal was sealed. One glass of Jack and Coke led to two, then three. She was blasted now; talking gibberish, and tempting Tim with an impromptu striptease, but what did that matter since he had already declared his intentions?

The next morning, Nellie woke up in an empty bed with a pounding head. She recalled the primo loving she'd laid on Tim. She'd used everything in her little black bag of sexual tricks. At the sound of running water, Nellie closed her eyes and smiled. Her future husband was in the bathroom, handling his morning business.

When she opened her eyes again an hour later, the water was still running. The jacket and pants draped over the chair were gone. So were the tasseled loafers and gold watch. Nellie jumped off the bed like the mattress was on fire and ran into the bathroom. The only sign of life was the tub's cold faucet running full blast.

Frantic, she ran out of the bathroom, screaming Tim's name, searching her apartment for a note or scrap of paper with his phone number on it. Then she remembered: Tim never asked for hers. She chased away the panic by recalling the evening of romantic and sexual bliss. No man could fake that kind of passion – could he? When they had sex – no, when they made love -- Tim's exact words had been: "*The moment I saw you, it was love at first sight.*"

Maybe Tim had an emergency and was too considerate to wake her up. Maybe he got scared because they'd gotten too close too quick. But the little voice in her head said there was no excuse for a man to leave like a thief in the night, without a word, a goodbye, or even a "thanks for the booty call, ma'am." *What the hell was up with that?*

Nellie remembered how lucky she'd felt when the women at the club had stared at her and Tim with envy. *Tim had to call.* He'd be back. *He had to come back!* He knew where she lived. She couldn't believe he didn't want to see her again after he got her primo goodies!

Every day for a week, Nellie rushed home from work and checked her mailbox for a note or card. Finally, reality sunk in. How could Tim do this to her after making all those promises to love, honor, and always provide for her?

The following Saturday night, Nellie and three of her single girlfriends headed out for their usual night of partying. When Nellie suggested they check out one of the white clubs, her surprised friends asked why. *"I'm through with these trifling ass black men,"* Nellie snapped. *"A white man knows how to treat a good black woman."*

THE END

Instant Gratification + Romance = Disappointment & Heartbreak

Tim wasn't rich. He didn't own a business, a home, or any rental properties. Tim's gold Rolex, Gucci shoes, and designer clothing were cleverly designed fakes from the local flea market. Tim worked as a sales clerk at a discount shoe store and lived in his mother's basement.

In today's society, it is the norm to expect instant gratification. If we want something, we want it NOW, whether we can afford it or not. If we don't get what we want when we want it (like right now), we become frustrated and hostile toward that person or thing that is denying us what we (think we) deserve.

Nellie expected a perfect relationship from a total stranger because her desire for instant gratification and romance overwhelmed her instincts and common sense. This self-centered sense of entitlement is one of the major reasons so many marriages fail within the first five years. Our collective poisonous individualism is creating thousands of broken, dysfunctional black families and crippling future black generations to come. Our desire for something for nothing also means we refuse to take responsibility when something doesn't go our way.

A White Woman's Got A Brotha's Back

Melvin, a never-married, 41-year-old postal supervisor, enjoyed the lifestyle of a single, self-proclaimed ladies man. He was handsome, fit, and well-dressed. He spent most of his disposable income on himself, buying designer-label clothing, topshelf liquor, and weekly entertainment. Regarding marriage, he used to joke, *"Why should I buy the milk when the cows are giving it away for free?"*

Then Melvin met Loretta, a registered nurse five years his senior, at the Christmas party of a friend. She was everything he wanted in a woman: She was a professional, educated, mature, kept a clean house, and was financially secure.

Her kids were grown and out of the house, and most of all, Loretta knew how to treat her man. She was generous and often treated Melvin to fancy dinners, theater tickets, and extravagant gifts. Melvin accepted without hesitation; she could afford it.

Loretta had significant savings and investments and owned her own home, a split-level, four-bedroom home in an affluent black area. After dating for three months, Melvin proposed. Since this was Loretta's second time down the aisle, she wanted to forgo the big formal wedding and reception and have a simple, private ceremony at her church.

However, this was Melvin's first marriage and he insisted on a big church wedding. The fact that Melvin didn't belong to a church and had less than $2,500 in savings wasn't a deterrent to spending tens of thousands of dollars on a wedding he couldn't afford to pay for. It was their first major disagreement.

Finally, after weeks of haggling, Loretta suggested a compromise. A small church wedding and reception, a one-week honeymoon cruise, and she would make the down payment on the new Lexus Melvin had been eyeing for weeks. Melvin agreed, since he wouldn't be paying for any of it. He secretly congratulated himself for choosing a woman who understood the art of compromise.

When they returned from their cruise, the honeymoon continued. Loretta made sure his clothes were laid out in the morning and his food was hot by the time he came home.

Anything Melvin wanted – within reason – like a hot bubble bath or a new Italian leather jacket, Loretta did her best to accommodate him. She wasn't a pushover; she just liked pleasing her man.

There was only one problem. Melvin wasn't in love with Loretta. He didn't even find her that sexually appealing. It wasn't that she was unattractive; it was just that she was so pleasant he found her boring. But Loretta was too good a deal to pass up.

And it wasn't like he was coming to the table empty-handed. Loretta was lucky to have a husband and a handsome escort to take to parties and spend the holidays with. If he had to fantasize that his wife was the tender, 22-year-old temp, Tenishia, whom he was sexing on the side, at least Melvin was able to perform his husbandly duties in the bedroom.

Melvin bragged to all his buddies that he had the perfect life: a beautiful home, a generous, good-natured wife, and hot, young ass on the side. Perry, a coworker, warned Melvin not to blow his good thing. He said Tenishia was spreading Melvin's business all over the post office, bragging that she had Melvin's nose wide open. She said, it was only a matter of time before Melvin left his wife. Perry said he'd seen it happen a thousand times. Black men and women destroying their marriages for a few minutes of pleasure.

Melvin dismissed the older man's advice as a jealous, old, player-hating nigga. A few minutes, his ass. Just ask Tenishia!

Once Melvin asked Perry if he ever cheated on his wife, and the old wimp said, *"Only a fool shits in the same nest he gotta sleep in every night."*

All Melvin could do was shake his head. That old nigga was a pussy-whipped, henpecked fool. Perry was so busy wearing his wife's panties, his old lady didn't have no choice but to wear the pants.

Damn that, Melvin wore the pants in *his* house, even if his wife paid for them. It never occurred to Melvin to be grateful for what he had, because he felt he deserved to have whatever he could get.

Nine months later, the inevitable happened. Tenishia announced she was pregnant. Melvin didn't panic right away since abortions were cheap and legal. Then Tenishia lowered the hammer right down on his tender skull. She told him not only was she planning to keep her baby, she was filing for child support asap.

Melvin went ballistic! Had she lost her damn mind? The bitch got pregnant on purpose then had the nerve to sue him for child support? Melvin was so busy blaming Tenishia, he conveniently forgot that he refused to use condoms because he couldn't *"feel anything"* when they had sex. He also conveniently ignored that it was his -- not Tenishia's responsibility -- to honor his marriage vows by staying faithful to his wife.

When Melvin accused Tenishia of trying to ruin his marriage, she said his marriage was *his* problem – and now he had to pay. And pay is exactly what Melvin did. He did his best to keep the news from his wife, but shortly after the baby girl was born, someone – probably that bitch Tenishia – sent Loretta a copy of the birth certificate, the child support papers, a photo of him and Tenishia kissing at a party, and a detailed description of the bedroom he shared with his wife.

His once generous and loving wife turned vicious, threw him out of the house, and stopped paying the note on his Lexus. Melvin had no choice. He moved in with Tenishia but that didn't last more than a few months.

Her place was always a mess, the baby was always crying, which drove him crazy, and the damn girl was too damn lazy. She didn't cook, clean, or take care of her kid – *their kid* -- like he thought she should have. The endless arguing over bills and a million other things finally drove Melvin up the wall and out of her house.

Six months after his divorce, Melvin struggles to make it on what's left after paying his rent and utilities, his $800 Lexus car note, car insurance, and $500 a month in child support. A very bitter and very broke Melvin hates all women, especially black women, and tells everyone his ex-wife was a low-down, disloyal black bitch who kicked her black man when he was down.

Melvin doesn't hesitate to drop some knowledge on the younger black men he supervises. *"Get yourself a white woman, cause she got a black man's back when some shit goes down."*

THE END

The Millionaire Mind

Most millionaires do not "invest" in designer clothing, 12-cylinder, high-powered automobiles, or mansions that cost a fortune to heat, cool, and finance. Millionaires don't "invest" in the lottery, racetracks, casino riverboats, or get-rich-quick schemes. They make their millions by investing in "assets" that increase in value (appreciate), instead of cars, clothing, shoes, etc. that lose value (depreciate).

Black and White America could learn a lot from immigrant entrepreneurs. Their children are introduced to business (and money) at an early age. Instead of running the streets after school, many immigrant children are stocking shelves, mopping floors, busting suds, chopping vegetables, polishing precious stones, and operating cash registers.

While American children are spending hours sitting in front of the boob tube, hanging out in the streets or in the malls, and playing video games, immigrant children are learning how to run a business that will put food on the table.

By the time these children leave high school, they know more about money, finance, and business than the top-of-his-class Harvard MBA graduate after five years at an Ivy League university.

Money doesn't faze them because they're used to handling money, and understand -- firsthand – how money is made, and how it should be spent if they want to make more. The children of immigrant entrepreneurs understand that a college education is just a means to an end — the end meaning they will choose entrepreneurship over getting of a "good job," and working to make someone else rich. Unfortunately, the American educational system is designed to create workers, not entrepreneurs, ensuring financial slaves for generations to come.

It is no accident that the typical high school graduate in the US will spend 13 years in school without being taught how to read a credit card or mortgage application.

People who are used to handling money know money is NOT magical, and doesn't appear out of thin air or from wishful thinking. They know getting rich has nothing to do with luck, or "investing" money in the lottery, casinos, and riverboats. And they know there's a world of difference between being "financially secure" and being "ghetto rich."

Showcasing, Styling, And Profiling

This is NOT a condemnation of the black community. When a race of people has been systematically degraded and dehumanized, "showcasing" becomes a quick fix to repair damaged self-esteem. In other words – *"If I look like I'm somebody, I stand a better chance of being TREATED like I'm somebody."*

If we stopped wasting our time and money on quick fixes that don't work, we would have the time (and the will) to build real financial wealth for ourselves, our families, and our communities.

For I hungered, and ye gave me to eat; I thirsted, and ye gave me to drink; I was a stranger, and ye took me in; I was naked, and ye clothed me; I was ill, and ye visited me; I was in prison, and ye came to me.

Then shall the righteous answer him saying, Lord, when saw we thee hungering, and nourished thee; or thirsting, and gave thee to drink?

And when saw we thee a stranger, and took thee in; or naked, and clothed thee? and when saw we thee ill, or in prison, and came to thee?

And the King answering shall say to them, Verily, I say to you, Inasmuch as ye have done it to one of the least of these my brethren, ye have done it to me.

Matthew, Chapter 25
King James Bible

WEAPON #9

ECONOMIC WARFARE (IMPOVERISH)

"...a living wage...must include enough to secure the elements of a normal standard of living -- a standard high enough to make morality possible..."

Theodore Roosevelt, 26th President, giving his address at the Convention of the National Progressive Party in Chicago, (August 1912)

CHAPTER 34

THE BLACK TAX

What is the **"black tax?"** It's the hidden cost of **being black** in a white supremacist society. For those who claim the "black tax" does not exist, a small sample of the mountains of evidence is presented in the following pages:

Black Tax #1: Stolen Black Inventions

A tiny sample of the thousands of black inventors who helped to modernize and enrich the lives of Americans as well as much of the world:

- *John Christian* -- inventor of the new lubricants used in aircraft and NASA space missions.
- *Donald Cotton* -- invented propellants for nuclear reactors.
- *Dr. Charles R. Drew* -- inventor of the first blood bank.
- *Philip Emeagwali* -- developed the fastest supercomputer software in the world.
- *Frederick Jones* -- invented the first automatic refrigeration system for long-haul trucks.
- *Joseph Winters* - patented the fire escape ladder.
- *Lewis Latimer* -- invented an important part of the light bulb -- the carbon filament.
- Tom J. Marshal -- invented the fire extinguisher
- *Otis Boykin* -- invented electronic control devices for guided missiles, IBM computers, and the pacemaker.
- *Dr. Paticia Bath* -- invented an eye surgery technique that helped many blind people to see.

Modern life -- as we know it -- would not be the same had it not been for the creative genius of black (and brown, red, yellow, and white) people. What is not known is who benefited financially from these black inventions, since it was rare for black inventors prior to the late 20th century to get the credit ***or the profits*** they deserved. The following story is typical:

Garrett Morgan, a black man, was the inventor of the first traffic light and the first commercially used gas mask. After a heroic rescue by Garrett, wearing his then untested gas mask during a tunnel explosion, orders for his gas mask poured in from police and fire departments all across the country.

Unfortunately, after it was discovered that Garrett was black, most of the orders were cancelled. Garrett's gas mask was later utilized by the U.S. Army, but Garrett did not reap the potential millions of profits. It was later rumored that his wife died penniless, and on welfare.

Black Tax #2: Stolen Black Labor

It is impossible to calculate the value of 400 years of forced labor – whether as a slave or as a black man or woman who was not paid a fair wage. We will not attempt that here but it can be stated with ABSOLUTE CERTAINTY, that there is NO PRICE TOO HIGH to compensate black people for the cultural, economic, educational, and psychological damage that has been done to us.

Professor Joe R. Feagin, of the University of Florida at Gainesville, made a brave attempt to calculate the amount of reparations that are due to blacks from slavery to present day discrimination:

"Clearly, the sum total of the worth of all the black labor stolen by whites through the means of slavery, segregation, and contemporary discrimination is staggering – many trillions of dollars. The worth of all that labor, taking into account lost interest over time and putting it in today's dollars, is perhaps in the ***range of $5 to $24 trillion****."*

Black Tax #3: No 40 Acres And A Mule

According to economist Dr. William Darity, a Professor at Duke University, **40 acres today would be worth about $1.6 million** – not counting the mule. Black tax dollars have helped to pay reparations for Jews and Japanese, yet our claim that we are still owed our 40 acres for 400 YEARS OF FREE LABOR is met with ridicule and resistance from the government and the white collective.

Black Tax #4: Real Estate Swindles

1. Black Homeowners Pay A Hidden Tax

In most racially changing (white to black) neighborhoods, it is common for real estate professionals, mortgage companies, appraisers, and banks to conspire against black homebuyers by selling homes at inflated prices. To make matters worse, after whites move out, the area usually changes for the worst. City services, police protection, and school funding are cut back, and local businesses and employers abandon the area, causing a decline in property values.

Local real estate industry, mortgage companies, local government, and businesses make property values *whatever they want to them to be*. Even in affluent black areas, comparable homes in white areas are always worth more, simply because the residents are white.

2. Red-Lining

The widespread practice of lenders refusing to make loans in black residential areas reduces the individual and collective wealth of black people. The home is the average American's biggest investment. When blacks are unable to make improvements to property, it is difficult to increase or even maintain its value.

3. Gentrification & Urban Property Tax Schemes

Gentrification occurs when more affluent (usually white) people move into a poor (usually black) neighborhood, and force them out by (1) raising property taxes, (2) reducing city services (like street cleanings, public transportation, police protection, etc.) until residents leave in frustration, or (3) declaring imminent domain under the guise of "necessary" projects, like an expressway, or an Olympics bid.

It is common for city officials and real estate developers to conspire against poor black residents in order to reclaim valuable areas previously abandoned by whites (who fled to the suburbs to get away from blacks). Due to longer commutes and higher gas prices, many affluent whites are running back to the cities where there is a surplus of cultural events and attractions, museums, restaurants, lakefront property, business and financial districts, universities, and public transportation.

By "taxing" poor black residents out of their homes and communities, city and state officials and real estate developers are spared the legal costs of declaring eminent domain and avoid paying black homeowners a fair price for their increasingly valuable property.

The triple "black tax" whammy occurs when poor blacks, displaced by gentrification, are given vouchers to relocate to middle-class black suburbs. The influx of low-income renters and Section 8 tenants usually causes an erosion of the property tax base, decreased funding of public schools, lower property values, deteriorating city services, more crime, and more businesses fleeing the area, devastating the net worth of black suburban homeowners.

4. Reverse Red-Lining & Subprime Mortgages

In 2002, President George W. Bush pledged to "increase the number of minority homeowners by at least 5.5 million families." On cue, a bloodthirsty mob of banks, mortgage companies, finance companies, and various predatory lenders descended upon the same black and Hispanic communities they had previously shunned, and began targeting residents and the elderly with subprime mortgages that were designed (from the start) to self-destruct.

Even when blacks and Hispanics qualified for cheaper prime mortgages, they were steered into expensive loans loaded with higher interest rates, penalties, and hidden pitfalls.

- *"If you're white they overlook the fact that your credit score is a little too low, or you have one extra late payment," said Barbara Rice, a community organizer at the Massachusetts Affordable Housing Alliance, a nonprofit advocacy group.*
- *According to the Center for Responsible Lending, African-American borrowers with prepayment penalties on their subprime home loans were 6 percent to 34 percent more likely to receive a higher-rate loan than if they had been white borrowers with similar qualifications." (SOURCE: Racial disparities with subprime mortgages: A Study by Center for Responsible Lending (June 2006)*

5. Stolen Black Land

After the Civil War up to around 1910, blacks owned around 15 million acres of land, an amazing feat for a people just a few decades away from being "property" themselves. Since blacks had no civil or legal rights after slavery that the white man "was bound to respect," they had no legal right to claim their property.

According to Dr. William Darity, a Professor at Duke University, most of the land *"was systematically taken away through terror, taxes, and fraud. There were instances of the wholesale destruction of black deeds by arson."*

Today, blacks own around one million acres, even though our population have tripled from just under 10 million in 1910, to over 35 million today. Blacks have lost 80 percent of the 5.5 million acres of farmland they owned in the South 32 years ago, according to the U.S. Agricultural Census.

6. Katrina's Land Grab

After insurance companies refused to pay the damage claims of Ninth Ward homeowners, thousands of blacks lost their land and homes. Four years after Katrina, the horrific injustices continue. Black Katrina survivors who attempt to return to New Orleans to reclaim their land are finding they are no longer welcome. The real question is: *who will claim their land, once the plight of New Orleans Lower Ninth Ward blacks completely falls from the national radar?*

Black Tax #5: Stolen Business Opportunities

Black Wall Street

The Greenwood neighborhood of Tulsa, Oklahoma in the 1920s was a prosperous, all-black town with its own bus line, hospital, theater, library, and many successful businesses. It all came to an end after a young black male bumped into a white female on an elevator, and she was pressured to accuse him of a rape that never happened.

Whites went on a bloody rampage, looting Greenwood businesses and attacking blacks randomly on the street. Gun battles broke out. Whites firebombed black homes and businesses from above using planes loaded with kerosene.

The "Tulsa Race Riot" in 1921 left dozens of blacks and whites wounded and killed, and the once prosperous Greenwood community was burned to the ground.

Every black man, woman, and child was arrested, but NO whites were ever charged with a crime. Blacks claimed it was jealousy of the phenomenal success of Greenwood compared to nearby white towns that sparked the race riot, not the fictitious rape of a white girl.

Tulsa, OK aka "Black Wall Street" was one of the more than 50 all-black towns created by former slaves between 1865 to 1920, to escape the brutal racism of that era. Like Tulsa, many all-black towns were prosperous and self-sufficient. Most were destroyed by white sabotage, Jim Crow laws, and the Depression.

Whites, who were obviously threatened by black progress and independence, tried to force blacks to live in racially mixed, racially segregated communities, where they could continue to control and oppress blacks.

Blacks who were economically successful faced reprisals or sanctions. When author Richard Wright tried to train to become an optometrist and lens-grinder in the 1930s, the other men in the shop threatened him until he was forced to leave. In 1911, blacks were barred from participating in the Kentucky Derby because African-Americans won more than half of the first 28 races.

Those who (falsely) believe that blacks are incapable of governing themselves, need only study the history of those all-black towns in Oklahoma and Florida. Every attempt blacks made after slavery up to the present day to be self-sufficient has been met with extreme violence and resistance from whites.

In light of the historical FACTS, it should be no mystery why Black America is so dependent on White America. The real question is: ***why do whites find the idea of black independence and prosperity so threatening?***

There's no way to estimate the massive wealth that could have been generated had free blacks, slaves, and their descendants been allowed to participate in the "American Dream." The potential wealth from lost business and professional opportunities was literally "black-taxed" (stolen) into nonexistence.

Black Tax #6: Stolen Life Insurance And Investment Opportunities

Life insurance is designed to: (1) to replace the lost income of a deceased parent or spouse, (2) pay funeral costs, and (3) to leave a financial legacy for future generations. Up until the late 1970s, blacks were not allowed to buy policies or freely invest in the stock market.

- *"As late as the 1960s...company rate books unabashedly warned 'Negroes and Indians need not apply' for coverage." ("What's Wrong with Your Life Insurance" by Norman F. Dacey)*
- *"At one time, life insurance in the African-American community became known as 'burial insurance.' African-Americans were allowed only to buy a small policy for burial expenses, and this is how it was marketed to them. Yet many times, their Caucasian counterparts, who had the same type of insurance policy, paid less, and were offered more coverage."* ***(African Americans and Life Insurance, Dereck L. Smith JR, LUTCF Secure Heights Financial, Inc. Financial Advisor.***
- *"The practice of charging African Americans as much as 35% more for life insurance than white policyholders is not a new one." (Black Enterprise, June 2002 by LeAnna Jackson)*

Black Tax #7: Predatory Lenders & Fraudulent Credit Scoring

A car is the second biggest purchase for most Americans. Black and Hispanic consumers pay thousands more in higher interest rates and other hidden costs when financing a car than whites, making this one of the biggest "black taxes."

> ***"Car buyers' suits charge racial bias in lending.*** *Rogers, who is black, is among 15 local plaintiffs who claim that auto-financing companies discriminate against car buyers based on race.*
>
> *"Their five lawsuits, filed against the financing companies of Ford, General Motors, Toyota, Honda and Nissan allege that the lenders allow dealerships to inflate interest rates without telling consumers. "If you compare blacks and whites with the same credit risk, blacks pay more," says Gary Klein, one of a team of attorneys representing black car buyers in the lawsuits.*
>
> *"It is standard practice, unfortunately, at many dealerships and many financing companies that they can make more money on blacks and other minorities," says Remar Sutton, author of "Don't Get Taken Every Time: the Insider's Guide to Buying or Leasing Your Next Car or Truck."*
>
> *"The markup usually is higher for black customers than for white customers, according to a Nashville lawsuit. Debby Lindsey, a business professor at Howard University, analyzed thousands of loans from GMAC and NMAC and concluded that blacks paid more in dealer markup than whites paid."*

Discriminatory Lending Practices Not Limited To Car Loans

- *Blacks and Latinos are denied access to **credit and financial services** at a much higher rate because of their credit scores, according to a recent study by the University of Denver Center for African American Policy.*
- *Credit card companies offer residents of black communities a lower credit limit than residents with the same profile from white neighborhoods, an economist at the Federal Reserve Bank of Boston has found.*
- *In his report, "Credit Card Red-lining," Ethan Cohen-Cole studied the **credit reports** of 285,780 individuals. Blacks moving from an 80%-majority white neighborhood to an 80%-majority black neighborhood reduced their credit by an average of $7,357 – even when their employment, incomes, and payment history remained the same.*
- *Seattle Post-Intelligencer newspaper found **payday loan companies** target black areas and the military, charging as much as **400 percent on a two-week loan.** In addition, payday lenders are exempt from most state usury laws that limit what the maximum interest rate on loans."*

The difficulty blacks and Hispanics experience in obtaining bank loans – even when their credit history is comparable to whites – makes the short-term payday, car title, or finance company loan the only alternative in a financial emergency.

Cooking Up Credit Scores

Credit scoring is nothing more than a black box that takes our information and spits out a number. Since this process cannot be monitored, or verified as to its accuracy or fairness, we are left to assume the worst.

If American financial institutions systematically practice racism against non-whites, it is logical to assume that "skin color" and "ethnicity" are some of the prime ingredients that go into "cooking up" our credit scores.

Black Tax #8: WWB (Working While Black)

- Prior to the 1970s, the American Medical Association barred black physicians, from membership, professional support, and advancement.
- US school districts excluded trained black professionals, and black teachers from working as public school teachers until the 1950s.
- Historically, blacks have been barred from many high-paying occupations even when they had the educational requirements.
- Black men earn 78 cents for every dollar white men earn, even when education is comparable. Black women earn 68 cents for every dollar whites earn even when education is comparable.
- Black employees generally make less than whites for the same work.
- Blacks are more likely to be fired than whites for committing same offenses.
- Blacks are disproportionately laid off during corporate downsizings.
- ***White women, not blacks***, benefited the most from affirmative action.
- Blacks are not privy to "it's-who-you-know" job opportunities. For example, whites are more likely to live next door to someone who has the clout to give a son-in-law, daughter, nephew, etc., an internship or job at their firm.
- The construction trades, police, and fire departments are notorious for discriminating against non-whites, to reserve blue-collar, good paying jobs for white males who are not college or "executive" material.
- Unemployment is significantly higher among college-educated blacks than college-educated whites.
- A recent study found it is easier for a white man with a criminal record to get a job than a black man with no criminal record and a college degree.

Real News Tells The Real Story

> *A lawsuit filed by former employees of Chicago's R.R. Donnelly alleged that the company fired nearly all 575 black employees at the Chicago plant when it closed in 1994, while a third of the white employees were transferred to other locations in the suburbs.*

Black Tax #9: Unjust Incarceration

The effect on the lifetime earnings of black men and women who have been falsely imprisoned; given longer sentences than whites for the same crimes; or who are serving mandatory five and 10-year sentences for ***non-violent*** drug sentences, ***is impossible to calculate.***

After release from prison, ex-offenders -- the innocent and the guilty -- are handicapped by felony convictions, barred from getting college grants and loans, are unable to join the military, work for the government, or get professional licenses.

Inmates Aren't The Only Ones Doing Time

Inmates' families -- among the poorest Americans -- are penalized financially and emotionally by a corrupt penal system.

> ***County jail inmates pay more for phone calls***
> *SAN FRANCISCO -- Telephone companies and California counties have made hundreds of millions of dollars from some of the state's poorest people through high, unregulated phone rates for calls from local jails, an Associated Press investigation has found.*
>
> *The average California county jail inmate's local call home costs more than seven times as much as a 50-cent pay-phone call. It adds up to more than $120 million a year in phone bills for families and friends of county inmates statewide. (SOURCE: Staff and Wire Reports).*

Black Tax #10: The Generational Curse Of Poverty

Money can be earned by anyone. REAL WEALTH is created by passing it from one generation to the next.

Parents who are able to pass along intellectual and real property, real estate, investments, insurance proceeds, businesses, quality educational opportunities, social and professional contacts, access and exposure to a higher standard of living, better medical care, and all those things that create emotional, social, and professional confidence and quality of life are creating **GENERATIONAL WEALTH.**

Black mothers and fathers who have been systematically and historically blocked from accumulating or retaining businesses, intellectual property, land, and money are creating a **GENERATIONAL CURSE OF POVERTY** that will be passed from one generation to the next.

To compare whites -- who have had financial, legal, educational, and occupational advantages for over 500 years -- to blacks and other non-whites is as logical as comparing apples to elephants.

The "Black Tax" Bottom Line

Blacks -- collectively -- make less money, get less for their money, and pay more for everything they get in America. The ***"black tax"*** is the emotional, financial, and professional burden that blacks (and other non-whites) carry from generation to generation, from the cradle to the grave.

CHAPTER 35

DO BLACKS DESERVE REPARATIONS?

"The fact is, you can't brutalize a people massively and then just tell them to get over it. That will never work -- just as it would never work in our personal lives." – Donna Lamb, C.U.R.E. (Caucasians United for Reparations and Emancipation)

The idea of reparations for slavery is nothing new. Neither is the outrage against racist injustice and oppression.

Walker's Appeal (Published September, 1829)

David Walker, a black slave, published "Walker's Appeal" in 1829; a 76-page pamphlet that condemned white Christians for not opposing racism and slavery. Walker encouraged slaves to rebel by any means necessary, including violence, in order to win their freedom. In his "Appeal," Walker stated that blacks suffered more than any other people in the history of the world did:

"The whites have had us under them for more than three centuries, murdering, and treating us like brutes..."

"Walker's Appeal" Identified Four Causes For The "Wretchedness" Of Slaves:

1. Slavery,
2. A submissive and cringing attitude towards whites (even amongst free blacks),
3. Indifference by Christian ministers, and
4. False help by groups such as the American Colonization Society, which promised freedom from slavery only on the condition that freed blacks would be forced to leave America for colonies in West Africa.

Walker vigorously opposed the idea of leaving a country that had been built on the backs of slaves:

"Let no man of us budge one step, and let slave-holders come to beat us from our country. America is more our country, than it is the whites — we have enriched it with our blood and tears. The greatest riches in all America have arisen from our blood and tears: — and will they drive us from our property and homes, which we have earned with our blood?"

Unfortunately, Walker didn't live long enough to see slavery abolished. He was mysteriously poisoned, allegedly by whites.

Black Manifesto (1969)

"If we can't sit at the table [of democracy], let's knock the fucking legs off!" -- James Forman, black civil rights leader and author of the "Black Manifesto" (1969)

As a part of his Black Manifesto, James Forman demanded $500 million in reparations and a percentage of the assets from white churches and other racist institutions to make up for injustices blacks had suffered over the centuries. The original ten-point "program demands" outlined in the Black Manifesto:

"We call for the establishment of a southern land bank to help our brothers and sisters who have to leave their land because of racist pressure and for people who want to establish cooperative farms but who have no funds. We have seen too many farmers evicted from their homes because they have dared to defy the white racism of this country. We need money for land. We must fight for massive sums of money for this southern land bank. We call for $200,000,000 to implement this program."

"Why We Owe Them" By Carol Chehade, C.U.R.E. (Caucasians United for Reparations and Emancipation)

"Stop living in the past and move on after slavery!" This is what we often tell African Americans. Well we certainly forced them to move on. We moved on to Black Codes, Jim Crow, lynching, de facto segregation. We moved on to White knights hiding behind ghosts of themselves while religiously lighting crosses in praise of a Satan they were fooled into thinking was God.

We moved on to the cities of Tulsa, St. Louis, and Rosewood where we, apparently, were unaffected by the burned and seared flesh of Black people. We moved on to laws that upheld racial oppression over and over again. We moved on to the many Black men placed on death row because they fit the description.

We moved on and made sure that Emmett Till would not be the last fourteen-year-old Black child whose unrecognizable corpse was the price paid for supposedly whistling at a White woman. We moved on to exclude African Americans from rights of democracy by blocking avenues to employment, education, housing, and civil rights.

In the final decade of the last century the slow, consistent racial apocalypse started showing signs of even more things to come when a Black man's head was seen rolling behind a pick up truck in Jasper, Texas. By the time we racially profiled our way from Texas to New York, we find a city plagued with plungers and forty-one bullets. Every time Black people have tried leaving the shackles of slavery behind, we find that we were the ones that couldn't stop living in the past."

Let No Man Budge One Step

Ray W., 48, was having his usual lunch; sitting alone, reading, and eating a sandwich he'd brought from home. He always sat in a corner of the company cafeteria at the smallest table to discourage company. He was known as a loner, a strange black man who worked in the solitary confinement of the copier room and always had his nose buried in a book.

Ray found it hard to relate to his coworkers, even the black ones. Most people lived in their small boxes and had little interest in anything that did not affect them personally.

He learned to keep his thoughts to himself, do his job, be cordial to all comers, and then go home to his wife and three kids. Ray was so engrossed in his newest literary acquisition, a copy of *"Walker's Appeal,"* he didn't notice O'Brien, a payroll clerk from accounting, peering over his shoulder.

"You're always reading," said the forty-something red-haired man.

Ray slowly closed his book. This white man made reading sound like a crime. Maybe it was for a black man. Ray knew some of his coworkers were puzzled by a black man who didn't chase tail, cheat on his wife, talk a lot of jive, or constantly grin like a damn fool.

Ray assumed his strange ways were responsible for his failure to be promoted out of the copier room, despite a bachelor's degree in accounting. After a decade of working for corporate America, Ray had lost his taste for ambition, and had settled for earning enough of a living to keep a roof over his family's head and some food on the table.

He glanced at his watch, annoyed. In fifteen minutes, his lunch would be over. He didn't relish wasting it, talking about nothing with a man who didn't speak when they passed in the hallway.

"What's that you're you reading?" O'Brien asked, eyes reaching across the table.

"Walker's Appeal."

"Appeal? You studying to be a paralegal?"

"Walker's Appeal was written almost two hundred years ago by a slave." Ray stopped short. He knew from experience that whites weren't interested in any history but their own – and only the parts that painted them in a flattering light.

"I thought slaves couldn't read and write." O'Brien looked skeptical.

"David Walker," Ray repeated firmly. "Wrote an appeal condemning slavery. He said slaves should fight for their freedom by any means necessary, and that slaves deserved their share of the wealth they helped create."

"You're one of those." O'Brien folded his arms across his chest.

"Those who?" Ray frowned.

"You think blacks should get reparations."

"I *know* we should," Ray said without hesitation.

"Why should I pay? My family didn't own slaves. "

"Blacks didn't put Jews or Japanese in concentration camps, but we paid."

"That's different."

"How?"

"Why don't you ask the African chiefs who sold you for reparations."

"Because slavery didn't make Africa the richest nation on earth."

"You think slaves made America rich?" O'Brien's eyes widened in disbelief.

"Do you know how much wealth was generated by millions of people working for free for 400 years?" Ray asked. "All the work back then had to be done by hand. You didn't have no machines to do it. That's why slaves was so valuable. We never got our 40 acres and a mule. You know how much 40 acres is worth today?"

"What's that got to do with you? Were you a slave?"

Ray almost said he still was. If he had any doubts, all he had to do was think back a week ago when two white cops pulled him over and frisked him in broad daylight, while the other drivers slowed down to watch. After no drugs or guns were found, they let him go. Without one word of apology.

"Maybe some plantation owners got rich from picking cotton," O'Brien conceded. "That didn't make America rich."

Ray couldn't resist the opportunity to educate this ignorant white man. A lot of people -- blacks and whites -- thought all slaves did was pick cotton, when in reality, slaves were the biggest pool of skilled workers, ironworkers, carpenters, planters, inventors, cooks, and baby-raisers in the South. Hell, slaves built the damn White House!

"Say you started a small company that made widgets," Ray continued, ignoring the tight-lipped expression on O'Brien's face. "Somehow -- it doesn't matter how -- you got ten million people to work for your company for free. They didn't get any salaries, no medical benefits, no pensions, nothing. They worked from sunup to sundown, never took a day off, never took off sick, and worked until the day they literally dropped dead. Then their kids and grandkids took their place--"

"I know where --"

"Let me finish," Ray said. "You got all the credit for the work they did, even the inventions they created to make their work easier, since they were doing all the work, anyway. Four hundred years later your company's the biggest widget maker in the world. Nobody could compete with you because nobody else had free labor. Your kids, granddaddies, and great grandkids are super rich because they inherited the company and all the inventions. How in the world could you fix your mouth to say 400 years of free labor didn't make your family rich?" The question hung unanswered as the two men stared at each other in silence.

"You act like we never did nothing for the blacks." O'Brien finally said, in a tone ringing with resentment.

"We who?" Ray's laugh was harsh. "*We* did everything for you."

"What about civil rights, affirmative action, welfare—"

"Who's talking about welfare?" A small voice in the back of Ray's head warned him to let it go. He'd noticed the curious looks they were getting as people passed by the table, pretending not to eavesdrop, but he couldn't stop himself. He was sick and tired of eating Jim Crow and choking down white denial.

"I never been on welfare a day in my life, I pay taxes the same as you. Didn't nobody give black people civil rights, we died fighting for those rights, the same way me, my daddy and my granddaddy fought overseas for this country. You ever been in the military?"

"You got all the answers, you tell me."

"You asked a question, I answered it," Ray said. That's right, he was a smart nigger. The kind of nigger O'Brien's kind had no use for.

"You people need get over yourselves." O'Brien's chair scraped the floor as he shoved it back. "Nobody's gonna pay for something that happened before you was born. It's ridiculous."

"*You people* ?"

"That's right, you poor black people, we're so sorry we kidnapped you from Africa where you were starving and brought you to America so you could live in the greatest country on earth, and here's the key to the U.S. Treasury. Just take what you think we owe you.'"

"Don't worry, we plan to." Ray didn't know how but he was working on it.

"You want reparations?" O'Brien jammed a hand in his pocket. "Start with this."

Ray sat as still as a statue as the quarter rolled across the table and bounced off his book. Everything in him wanted to reach out and choke the shit out of that white man for all the David Walkers who had come before him – and for all the black men who were still treated like dirt. He opened his book, and tried to focus, but the words swam in his blurred vision. O'Brien stood up, and leaned on the table, palms flat, eye-to-eye with Ray.

"If you hate America so much," O'Brien said quietly. "Why don't you leave?"

"Because we earned the right to be here." Ray stared into the hard blue eyes without blinking. "More than you and anyone else in this room."

After O'Brien left, Ray couldn't help wondering if he would be looking for a new job soon. He uncapped the neon yellow highlighter with a trembling hand and swept it across a passage:

> *"Let no man of us budge one step, and let slave-holders come to beat us from our country. America is more our country, than it is the whites — we have enriched it with our blood and tears. The greatest riches in all America have arisen from our blood and tears..."*

THE END OF STORY

FACT: America would NOT be the nation it is today without 500 years of free slave labor, economic exploitation, and the cultural, medical, and scientific contributions, and ingenuity of black people.

For those who claim that slavery only enriched the South, here's a short list of American corporations that profited from slavery:

1. North American Continent
2. Aetna, Inc.
3. American International Group (AIG)
4. Lloyd's of London
5. New York Life Insurance Company
6. FleetBoston Financial Corporation
7. JP Morgan Chase Manhattan Bank
8. Lehman Brothers
9. RJ Reynolds Tobacco Company
10. Loews Corporation (Lorrilard)
11. Canadian National Railway
12. CSX Corporation
13. Norfolk Southern
14. Union Pacific Railroad

Reparations Paid By The U.S. Government

1971	$1 Billion + 44 acres	Alaska Native Land
1980	$81 Million	Klamaths of Oregon
1985	$105 Million	Sioux of South Dakota
1985	$31 Million	Chippewas of Wisconsin
1985	$12.3 Million	Seminoles of Florida
1986	$32 Million	Ottawas of Michigan
1990	$1.2 Million	Japanese Americans
2001	$56 Million	Seminoles of Oklahoma

Reparations Paid By Other Governments

1952	German	$822 Million to German Jewish survivors
1988	Austria	$25 Million to Holocaust survivors
1990	Canada	$230 Million to Japanese

Do Blacks deserve reparations for 400 hundred years of slavery, and over 140 YEARS of post-slavery racism and discrimination?

Hell yes -- and we should keep on demanding them until we get what is OWED us.

CHAPTER 36

A TALE OF TWO CITIES

A Tale Of Two Cities: One Black, One White

A black neighborhood on the southeast side of a large city is plagued by frequent drive-by shootings and gang violence. Young and old men loiter outside the 24-hour liquor stores, while police cars cruise by the open drug markets on every street corner.

The schools are rundown, and on most blocks the streetlights and sidewalks are broken. Parents make their children play indoors because it is too dangerous outside. Most of the residents avoid going out after dark for fear of being a victim of crime.

Things have gotten so out of control, the police don't bother coming until the disturbance has ended. Their callous attitude has emboldened the gangbangers, robbers, rapists, burglars, and drug dealers to commit crimes in broad daylight. After a drug dealer shot an elderly man, and firebombed a woman's apartment for reporting neighborhood drug dealing to the police, one dealer was overheard boasting, *"The police be telling us what niggas got diarrhea of the mouth."*

The black residents know not only does it not pay to "snitch;" it can cost them their lives. They know they can't trust the police, so they live in bitter resignation; seething with rage every time the media paints them as ignorant savages who refuse to "cooperate with the police for their own good." A few people move away only to find the same problems in the only neighborhoods they can afford.

Six months later, the city receives an urban renewal grant from the federal government, and chooses their rundown neighborhood to "revitalize" (gentrify). The residents know the city has been scheming for years to get the area back because it is close to the lakefront, a major university and hospital, expressways, and reliable public transportation.

Three years later, their old neighborhood has undergone a remarkable transformation. The 24-hour corner liquor storeowners lose their licenses, and in their place are quaint coffee shops, boutiques, and French bakeries. The streets and sidewalks are repaved; flowers are planted; and the streetlights are replaced.

Four adjoining vacant lots are turned into a small park and playground with swings and park benches. A new school is being built near the newly rehabbed brownstones and duplexes because the old school was too small and its facilities were too outdated.

In order to attract the kinds of residents that can afford the sky-high rents and exorbitant housing prices, everything – especially the schools -- must be of the best quality, the major proudly explains to the press.

The old trailers that once substituted for classrooms have been hauled away. Construction is almost complete on a state-of-the-art police and fire station even though nightly police sirens are now a thing of the past.

The drug dealers, with a little "encouragement" from the police, have already relocated to another distressed (black) neighborhood to terrorize the residents and operate without police interference. The garbage pickup and street cleanings have been increased to twice a week; and the police response to calls of distress are swift and competent.

The traffic cameras installed at every intersection have been removed, after an influential donor to the mayor's re-election campaign receives a ticket for running a yellow light a block from his luxury townhouse.

The mayor justifies his decision by reporting that crime is down significantly due to his police chief's *"innovative crime-fighting techniques."* He announces that the traffic cameras will be relocated to more "distressed" (black) areas, and plans on doubling the fines to *"discourage lawbreakers."*

Former residents who drive through their old neighborhood shake their heads in disbelief when they see white people walking their dogs after dark on the same streets where gunfire was a nightly occurrence.

There is one small drawback. The drug dealers' best customers have to drive further south to "cop" their heroin and crack before returning to their picture-perfect, crime-free suburban communities.

"A man who tosses worms in the river isn't necessarily a friend of the fish. All the fish who take him for a friend, who think the worm got no hook in it, usually end up in the frying pan.

All of these things dangled before us by the white liberal posing as a friend and benefactor have turned out to be nothing but bait to make us think we're making progress.

The Supreme Court decisions have never been enforced. Desegregation has never taken place. The promises have never been fulfilled. We have received only tokens, substitutes, trickery, and deceit."

Malcolm X

WEÂPON #10

DOMESTIC TERRORISM

(INTIMIDÂTE)

"The seizing and shooting and beating reminds me of when there were lynchings all over the country. We've got to start saying, `No further. This must stop."'

Actress Ruby Dee, who along with her husband Ossie Davis, was arrested when they participated in the protests against police brutality.

CHAPTER 37

DOMESTIC TERRORISM

If ***"terrorism"*** is the systematic use of terror against a "civilian or non-combatant" population to achieve political or ideological objectives, and ***"domestic"*** refers to government policies and laws that occur inside a country, then the term, ***"Domestic Terrorism,"*** is the most accurate description of what is happening to black people all over the United States...

> *"I had an uncle...and they hung him... They hung him down there because they say he was crazy and he might ruin the other Negroes... See, and that is why they hung him, see, because he was a man, and he had a good education as some of the white — better than some of the white people down there..." -- Big Bill Broonzy, blues singer*

Domestic Terrorism Is...

1. **Economic...**

- Blacks who were economically successful faced reprisals or sanctions. When Richard Wright tried to train to become an optometrist and lens-grinder, the white men in the shop threatened him until he was forced to leave.
- In 1911, blacks were barred from participating in the Kentucky Derby because African-Americans won more than half of the first 28 races."
- Black Ohio town denied use of public water supply for over 100 years (2008)

2. **Legal...**

- In the Midwest and West, many towns posted "sundown" warnings, threatening to kill any African-Americans who remained overnight.
- Black housing was segregated in the North, and, in many regions, blacks could not serve on juries.
- The Supreme Court — made up almost entirely of **Northerners** -- gutted the 14th and 15th Amendments, which legalized segregation.
- In 1924, the Klan's 4 million members controlled the governorship and a majority of the state legislature in Indiana, and much of Arkansas, Oklahoma, California, Georgia, Oregon, and Texas.
- Historical evidence suggests that US President Warren G. Harding (1921-1923) was inducted into the Klan in a ***White House ceremony***.

3. **Psychological...**

- Whites often reacted violently to black efforts at migration; for instance, in his autobiography *Black Boy*, Richard Wright notes that he concealed his intention to move North because he was afraid of being beaten. The constant threat of terror was used to keep blacks "in their place."

4. **Violence And Murder...**

- *"Blacks were lynched for anything or nothing -- for wife-beating, stealing hogs, being "saucy" to white people, sleeping with a consenting white woman, or for being in the wrong place at the wrong time."* – Ida B. Wells-Barnett (1862-1931)

- There were mob attacks on blacks (called race riots) in Houston, Philadelphia, and East St. Louis in 1917. The most famous occurred in 1919 in Chicago. White mob violence raged for a week, leaving 15 whites and 23 blacks dead, over 500 injured, and more than 1,000 homeless. Later estimates of the dead were much higher.

- The 1921 Tulsa Race Riot in Tulsa, Oklahoma was even more deadly after white mobs invaded and burned the Greenwood district of Tulsa (Black Wall Street). Witnesses reported seeing whites in airplanes dropping dynamite on the city's black neighborhoods. 1,256 homes were destroyed and 39 people (26 black, 13 white) people were confirmed killed, although recent investigations suggest that the number of black deaths were considerably higher than reported.

5. **The Police...**

"INSIDE the locker of a narcotics cop in Philadelphia: A cartoon of a man, half as an officer in uniform and half as a Klansman with the words: 'Blue By Day - White by Night. White Power.'"

Good Police Officers Should Be Recognized And Rewarded

Most police officers are men and women who do a difficult, dangerous, and often thankless, job. There are (white) police officers like Jim Coursey and Rodney Watt, who along with several white Highland Park, Illinois police officers, filed a federal lawsuit in 2000 against their police chief and his commanders for racially profiling minorities.

"This is a case like no other where current police officers are willing to testify. Usually it is the victims who come forward," said Reverend Jesse Jackson, who met with the officers and Assistant Attorney General in Washington, D.C. "These are courageous men and women who've decided to let their conscience be their guide."

Over 300 people attended a rally at a nearby church to show support for the white officers. The black community, more than any other, should defend and support the police officers who do the right thing by ***all*** citizens. Otherwise, we're left with the deadly alternative: ***the Rogue Police Officer.***

The Rogue Police Officer AKA The Domestic Terrorist

Rogue police officers steal, rob, deal dope, take bribes, abuse, beat, rape, sodomize, torture, and murder unarmed citizens. Rogue officers operate within poor and minority communities like sociopathic outlaws armed with a badge and a gun -- with the blessing of police and city administrators.

It is difficult in poor black communities to tell the difference between the rogue officer and the criminal since BOTH operate outside the law. The irony is the people who need the most police protection also have the MOST to fear from the (rogue) police.

The "Blue Code Of Silence" AKA "Don't Snitch" On Fellow Officers

By remaining silent while their fellow rogue officers break the law, abuse and murder citizens, good police officers must accept some of the blame. It's easy to understand why good police officers are reluctant – even afraid – to report the illegal activities of their fellow (rogue) officers. Their careers – and in many cases their lives – would be in jeopardy, especially when illegal drugs are involved.

What is hard to understand is why anyone expects the most vulnerable and least protected people in America -- poor black men, women, and children -- to ***SNITCH*** on dangerous criminals when armed and trained police officers are unwilling (and afraid) to ***SNITCH*** on rogue officers?

It is common knowledge in the poorest communities that rogue officers and rogue police departments are COOPERATING with neighborhood drug dealers instead of arresting them. The proof? If crack and heroin users from the suburbs know where to "cop" their drugs, it is ludicrous (and point-blank-idiotic) to think the police don't know where drugs are being sold.

It is also common knowledge that rogue officers pass along the names of complaining citizens and witnesses TO drug dealers and gang members. If poor black residents are afraid to complain to the police, it doesn't take a genius to understand why they are not "dying" to testify:

> *"19-year-old Fred Morton was questioned by the response team's detectives about a murder he had witnessed. Twelve days later, he was found dead in a city park. He had been strangled, and his throat was slit."*

> *"In Jefferson County, two witnesses were murdered after repeated threats from drug dealers. In both cases, prosecutors knew their witnesses had been threatened."*

> *A Towson, MD witness is gunned down, and police say a hit was ordered because he was going to testify in a murder trial. Six people are now charged with the witness' murder.*

Domestic Terrorism Is Driving While Black (DWB)

"Racial profiling" is a police officer or a person in authority who uses his or her authority to harass, intimidate, or arrest non-whites (practice racism). In many cases, racial profiling is condoned by city officials to send a message that non-whites are not welcome to live, work, shop, or even drive through certain white areas. Racial profiling is also used as a ***psychological tool of intimidation*** to remind non-whites that they are NOT due the same rights and respect that whites take for granted in a white supremacy society.

Even "Powerful" Blacks Are Not Immune To DWB

In 2007, US Representative Danny Davis was pulled over for a traffic stop by Chicago police. When Congressman Davis asked why, he was told, *"You swerved. You were driving left of center."*

Davis, who had a clean driving record – only five tickets in 50 years – had been stopped the week before for a "routine" seat belt check. Davis had been buckled up. After the latest incident, Davis filed a complaint with the Office of Independent Review, accusing the white officer of racial profiling. He concluded that, *"...the only reason I was stopped was because I was black."*

Unfortunately, some (black) drivers are not as "lucky" as Rep. Davis, to drive away with just a ticket. In 1999, LaTanya Haggerty, an unarmed 26-yr-old black female, was shot to death by Chicago police as she reached for her cell phone during a traffic stop.

Within the same seven-day period, Robert Russ, an unarmed 22-yr-old black male, was shot and killed by Chicago police after being stopped for "driving erratically." Russ was an honor student and star football player at Northwestern University, who was due to graduate the week he was killed (murdered).

Domestic Terrorism And Torture In America's Jails

Documented torture methods used against black men in Philadelphia (PA) police headquarters:

- Beating a suspect's feet and ankles
- Twisting or kicking testicles
- Pummeling the back, ribs, and kidneys
- Beaten with lead pipes, blackjacks, brass knuckles, chairs, and table legs
- One suspect was stabbed in the groin with a sword-like instrument
- Suspects and witnesses testified that they were forced to watch beatings through one-way windows, and were told they would receive the same treatment unless they cooperated.

From 1972 to 1991, over 200 black men were tortured by Chicago Police Commander Jon G. Burge and other Chicago detectives to coerce confessions. In 2008, Burge, who was living in Florida on a Chicago police pension, was arrested -- NOT for torture -- but for false written answers to questions in a civil lawsuit!

Documented Torture Methods By Chicago Police:

- Suffocation with the plastic cover of a typewriter
- Being battered with telephone books
- Burned with cigarettes and radiators
- Threatened with handguns
- Electrically shocked with a telephone generator
- Cattle prod applied to men's nipples, genitals, and rectal interiors

Let's Compare Torture In America's Jails and Police Precincts To Wartime Torture Of Alleged Terrorists

> *"Three Iraquis and a Jordanian alleged that they were tortured by US defense contractors during their detainment at the Abu Ghraib prison in Iraq from 2003 to 2004. The torture included electrical shocks, forced nudity, and sexual humiliations."*

The Abu Ghraib prisoners should be thankful they were NOT black males in America or they would have suffered a far worse fate.

In spite of overwhelming physical evidence, the police abuse and torture of black men is largely ignored and easily dismissed:

> *Court overturns three convictions in Abner Louima police torture case Abner Louima, a Haitian immigrant, was sodomized with a broomstick handle inside a New York (70th Precinct) police station by two white police officers. Abner Louima suffered severe internal injuries after being assaulted in a precinct bathroom. Police Officer Schwarz held him down while Police Officer Volpe shoved a wooden stick into his rectum. (1997)*

Abner Louima, Rodney King, and Sean Bell are a confirmation of:

AXIOM #6: "THE BLACK VICTIM = A VICTIMLESS CRIME" THEORY. A BLACK PERSON IN A CONFLICT WITH A WHITE PERSON (OR WHITE SYSTEM) CANNOT BE THE VICTIM IN A WHITE SUPREMACY SOCIETY. THE BLACK INDIVIDUAL IS ALWAYS AT FAULT, REGARDLESS OF WHO INITIATED THE CONFLICT, OR WHAT FACTS OR EVIDENCE ARE PRESENT.

The Most Dangerous Black Person On The Planet: The Self-Hating Black Authority Figure

When 26-year-old Latonya Haggerty was shot and killed during a traffic stop in 1999, the black female officer who fired the fatal shots, claimed Ms Haggerty's cell phone, *"...looked like a handgun."*

It is extremely unlikely that Haggerty, the passenger, would have pulled a handgun during a traffic stop. A college graduate with no criminal record, Ms Haggerty did not fit the profile of a dangerous cop-killer.

It is also extremely unlikely that the black officer would have shot an unarmed white female during a minor traffic stop -- ***unless the black officer was willing to spend decades in prison.***

Like many blacks in positions of authority, black Rogue Officers who abuse and murder black people ***are expressing their own self-hatred, and are MORE likely to abuse blacks than white officers***.

However, black Rogue Officers ***never*** make the fatal mistake of abusing, murdering, or "accidentally shooting" white people. Most black officers are secretly terrified of the day they may be forced to take the life of a dangerous, violent, or armed white person. They know it's a lose-lose situation since they will either lose their lives, their careers, OR their freedom (will go to prison).

Which explains why there has NEVER been a single instance of a black police officer unloading his or her weapons into an unarmed white person in the history of modern law enforcement. ***Why?***

A black police officer killing whites contradicts the purpose of having a police force in the first place: to protect property AND white life -- in that order.

By limiting their abuse to black people, black rogue officers ***foolishly*** believe they are guaranteeing their own safety within a racist police department that despises all black people—including those that wear a badge and a uniform.

They believe that being a "team player" (abusing other blacks), somehow, erases the "stigma" of being black. The sad irony is by abusing black people, black rogue officers are ENCOURAGING the abuse and murder of ALL black people – including black police officers:

- *"White officer who shot Black undercover cop in New York found guilty."*
- *"Black officer was shot (by white officers) several times in the back while he was falling or already lying face down."*
- *"Black undercover officers face a disproportionate risk of being injured by mistake by other (white) police officers."*
- *"Black undercover cops, particularly those posing as drug dealers, run a high risk of being shot, or beaten by their white officer counterparts."*
- *"Sometimes black officers are not given an opportunity to identify themselves; in other instances they are attacked after announcing that they are cops."*
- *"According to retired NYPD detective, Roger Abel, who is writing a book on this subject, not one white officer has ever been shot by a black officer."*

Role Call: Murder-By-Rogue-Cop Victims

"They're just covering up. They've done it again. They've done it again. I've talked to the police and the way they were talking, I could tell they were thinking: We just got another black man off the street." – Beverly Hunt, speaking about the shooting death of James E. Alexander, a 62-year-old black man by Roanoke, VA police.

- *James E. Alexander* – 62-yr-old black male shot and killed by a Virginia State police officer during a drug investigation at a neighbor's house. (2004)
- *Donta Dawson* – unarmed black male shot in the head and killed by Philadelphia, PA police who claimed he was "blocking traffic." (1998)
- *Stephen "Kuado" Opaku* – unarmed Ghana-born black male died after a car wreck in which a Philadelphia, PA police officer shot out the window in an "attempt" to rescue Opaku. The bullet set the car on fire. Opaku was killed in the blaze. (1998)
- *LaTanya Haggerty* – Unarmed 26-yr-old black female college graduate shot to death by Chicago police as she reached for her cell phone during a traffic stop. (1999)
- *Robert Russ* – Unarmed 22-yr-old, shot and killed by Chicago police after being stopped for "driving erratically." Russ, an honor student and star football player at Northwestern University, was supposed to graduate the week he was killed (murdered). (1999)
- *Charles Matthews* – unarmed black male shot 23 times and killed by eight New York police officers. (1992)
- *Moses DeJesus* – unarmed black male beat to death by New York police officers. (1994)
- *Joseph Gould* – unarmed homeless man shot and killed by off-duty police officer, Gregory Becker. A passer-by testified that Becker grabbed Gould around the neck while Gould did nothing. (1995)
- *Tyisha Miller* – unarmed 19-year-old black girl killed by four Riverside, CA police officers who found her sitting unresponsively in a parked car. Police smashed her car window and fired into the car 24 times, striking her 12 times. (1999)
- *Michael Byoune* – unarmed 19 yr-old black male shot and killed by Inglewood, CA police officer. (2008)
- *Amadou Diallo* -- unarmed West African immigrant street vendor living in the Bronx unarmed African living in Bronx shot 41 times by four white New York City police officers while attempting to show identification. (2000)
- *Nathaniel Jones* – unarmed 41-yr-old black male beat to death by six Cincinnati police officers using metal batons even though his arms were cuffed behind his back. The beating was captured by camera mounted on police squad car. (2001)
- *Timothy Thomas* – unarmed 19-year old black man shot and killed by a Cincinnati police officer in 2001. Thomas was the fifteenth black man killed by the Cincinnati Police Department in five years, and his death led to outrage in the black community that culminated with the 2001 Cincinnati Riots.

- *Ousmane Zongo* – unarmed Burkinabè (African male) arts trader living in New York City shot and killed by New York City Police Department officers during a warehouse raid (2003)
- *Unidentified homeless black woman* -- killed by Los Angeles police for suspected theft of shopping cart. (1999)
- *Newby* – unarmed black male shot in the back and killed by Louisville, KY police officers. He was the seventh black man to be fatally shot by Louisville police in the past five years (2004).
- *Roy Pettaway III* – unarmed 27-yr-old black male shot in the back of the head outside nightclub by Fulton County, GA police. His 26-yr-old brother, Ron, was shot in the back but survived. (2007)
- *Kathryn Johnston* – 92-yr-old woman shot and killed by Atlanta police after they break through a burglar bar entry door and wooden door, to conduct a "drug raid" at her home. (2006)
- *Devin Brown* – unarmed 13-year-old gunned down by Los Angeles Police for running from police. (2005)
- *Sean Bell* – unarmed 23-yr-old black male shot fifty times by five New York police officers on the day before his wedding. (2006)
- *Tarika Wilson* – unarmed 26-yr-old black female shot and killed by Lima, OH police officers while holding 14-month-old infant in her arms. Officers on suspicion of drug dealing by a boyfriend, break down the door and open fire on mother and child. Ms. Wilson was not armed nor was she or her baby a suspect. (2008)
- *Oscar Grant* -- 22-yr-old black male shot in back while lying face down on a rapid transit platform (BART) in California by white transit cop. (2009)

"Rogue Cops Caught on Videotape" Is Psychological Terrorism

Why would a white supremacist justice system that ***condone***s (and ***denies***) the widespread police brutality against blacks allow the mainstream media to broadcast the VIDEOTAPED evidence that these (racist) abuses actually exist?

One Possible Reason:

To remind (terrorize) the black collective that ANY black person at ANY time at ANY place for NO reason can be victimized by law enforcement. This psychological tool of terror actually reinforces the black inferiority complex (niggerization) by allowing law enforcement to show a blatant disregard for black life, because black life has no value in a white supremacy society.

In fact, this was the LAW over 150 years ago when the US Supreme Court ruled in 1856 that blacks had *"no rights which the white man was bound to respect."* (The Dred Scott v. Sandford Decision). Obviously, little has changed.

Role Call: Police Brutality Victims

- *Rodney Glen King* – unarmed 26-yr-old cab driver stopped and beaten by several Los Angeles police officers. The beating was captured on videotape. The acquittal of the police officers by an all-white jury sparked the 1991 Los Angeles riot. (1991)
- *Yvette Hayes* – unarmed 33-yr-old black female forced to lie facedown alongside the freeway by Milwaukee police officers investigating "stolen vehicles". The former elementary school principal was five months pregnant. The officer's squad car dash-camera captured the incident. (2007)
- *Beverly Wilson Ellison Sr.* – was dragged from her vehicle and slammed repeatedly against her SUV by a white Chicago police officer for "staring" at him. The incident occurred in front of her 10- and 11-year-old daughters who were inside the car. She received a traffic citation for "failure to stop at a stop sign." (2007)
- *Carlos McLoud* – unarmed Jamaican immigrant shot by a Philadelphia police officer. McLoud attempted to help a robbery victim when shot by plainclothes officer. The bullet injuries left McLoud paralyzed from the waist down. (1994)
- *Coprez Coffie* -- unarmed black male sodomized by officers with a screwdriver in an alley after being pulled over by Chicago police officers. Though police denied his allegations, the jury was convinced by the evidence presented, including doctors reports of tears to Coffie's rectum and a screwdriver found in the police car's glove compartment with fecal matter on it. (2007)
- *Stanley Miller* – unarmed black male kicked in the head and brutally beaten with a metal flashlight by LAPD cops (2005)
- *Aaron Harrison* – unarmed 18-year-old shot in the back by Chicago Police (2007)
- *Lillian Fletcher* -- 82-year-old black grandmother suffering from dementia and schizophrenia is tasered by Chicago Police and spends five days in hospital recovering. (2007)
- *Haitian immigrant Abner Louima* -- sodomized by a broomstick handle inside a New York (70th Precinct) police station by two white police officers. Louima suffered severe internal injuries after being assaulted in a precinct bathroom, where he was held down by Police Officer Schwarz while Police Officer Volpe shoved a wooden stick into his rectum. (1997)
- *Seven African Immigrant Van Drivers* – accused a Queens, N.Y. police officer of raping and sodomizing them in separate incidents. The District Attorney Richard A. Brown dismissed the charges. (1993)

The obvious question must be asked: If black people are still being assaulted, sodomized, and murdered by police in the 21st century, what is OUR definition of "black progress?"

Jeremiah Mearday VS Chicago Police

> *"I didn't know my son," Jeremiah's father said when he went to the hospital on September 26, 1997. "He was a bloody mess. He had two holes knocked in the top of his head, his five front upper teeth along with the gum, severed, and a broken jaw. They stomped him in his stomach and there was trauma to his back." -- Revolutionary Worker #934, November 30, 1997.*

Jeremiah Mearday – unarmed 18-year-old black male kicked and beaten with flashlights by two white Chicago police officers for no apparent reason. After the beating, Mearday was hospitalized with a broken jaw and head injuries. (1997).

On November 7, nearly 200 white police officers forced Jeremiah Mearday and his attorneys to walk a gauntlet of intimidation in a Chicago courtroom. This gestapo display -- which was tolerated by the presiding judge -- was met by protest and outrage. Five years later, the city of Chicago agreed to pay Jeremiah Mearday $1.75 million to settle the police brutality case if Mearday drops his lawsuit.

Why Blacks Are The Biggest Targets Of Domestic Terrorism

Reason #1: The African man and woman -- the first man and woman on earth -- possess the MOST MELANIN, which makes them, genetically and biologically speaking, ***the most powerful people on the planet*** -- and the ***greatest genetic threat to white survival.*** (See pp 49-52)

Reason #2: When one group oppresses another group, the oppressed group ***correctly views their oppressors as their enemy. The reverse is ALSO true.*** The oppressors know it is foolish (and illogical) to trust the same people they are oppressing (mistreating).

A white supremacist system **logically** assumes that all non-whites are "enemies of the state" and potential threats to the white status quo, which is why non-whites are ALWAYS assumed to be secretly plotting against whites.

The ***police and court systems*** are used to intimidate and terrorize the oppressed to keep them from rebelling against an unfair (racist) system. This explains why law enforcement is allowed to abuse and murder blacks at will.

It also explains why blacks and non-whites (in general) are not perceived by the white collective as "patriotic," and in some cases, NOT citizens at all. The oppressor class knows it is ILLOGICAL (and insane!) for the oppressed "minorities" to be loyal to the same system that is oppressing them. Sadly, some blacks do not understand how illogical (and self-disrespecting) their "loyalty" is.

Reason #3: The abuse/murder of blacks by the police provides visible "proof" to the white collective that whites are more privileged than (superior to) blacks, thus ensuring the loyalty of whites to a system that is also exploiting them, but still allows even poor whites to feel superior to blacks. This divide-and-conquer strategy by the white elites allows the continued economic and political exploitation of BOTH whites and non-whites.

CHAPTER 38

THE TRUTH ABOUT BLACK CRIME AND POVERTY

"To be a Negro in this country and to be relatively conscious is to be in a rage almost all the time." -- James A. Baldwin

When the first wave of European immigrants landed on American shores during the 1800s and 1900s, most were poor and illiterate. Because of ethnic and economic discrimination, some immigrants turned to crime to feed their families.

Economic hardship, poverty, and widespread illiteracy became the breeding ground for the first urban gangs, gangbangers, ghettos, juvenile prisons, and America's first "drive-by shootings" during the Al Capone era.

Due to selective amnesia, ghettos, gangs, and drive-by shootings are now synonymous with black people. The obvious link between crime and poverty for Europeans is conveniently ignored when it comes to analyzing black crime and poverty.

Some whites (and sadly, some blacks) arrogantly claim that, *"America is the land of opportunity. There is no excuse to be poor unless you want to be poor. If other people (European immigrants) pulled themselves up by their bootstraps, why can't poor blacks do the same?"*

Reason #1: Most Whites Have Not Pulled Themselves Up

It is illogical to claim whites have "pulled themselves up by their bootstraps," if they didn't start out at the bottom. Despite the advantages (all) whites have in a white supremacist society, 90% of white (and non-white) Americans make less than $60,000 a year and live from paycheck to paycheck.

Obviously, these Americans have not "pulled themselves up" above that. In fact, many formerly "middle-class" Americans are now discovering just how difficult it is to actually ***pull themselves up after a financial setback*** -- especially if they can't afford any bootstraps.

Reason #2: Black Poverty Is Different From White Poverty

If a poor white boy gets an education, or a marketable skill, he will be easily absorbed into the white mainstream (middle-class). Regardless of his humble beginnings, he will always be "white" in a white supremacist society.

No matter how much education, skill, or talent a poor black boy has, he will always be black in a white supremacist society. This does not mean every poor black boy will stay on the bottom, but most will not rise much higher than that.

Reason #3: Capitalism Is An Economic Pyramid

Capitalism, in its purest form, is an ***economic pyramid***. That means the bottom -- the ***foundation*** -- will be the largest (and widest) part because ***everything*** else must rest on top of it.

A capitalist system cannot exist without the poor because the poor are the ***foundation***. To maintain a capitalist system, there must be an economic (class) system ***that guarantees that most of the people remains poor.***

This cannot be disputed logically. The false (and naive) notion that everyone in a capitalist system can rise to the middle (class) is illogical and goes against the laws of physics, economics, and common sense.

Reason #4: Racism Is The Foundation Of American Capitalism

For one person to move up from the bottom of an economic pyramid, someone else must take his or her place. Otherwise, the entire foundation collapses. An example is a new widgets factory that hires 150 workers (to fill the bottom). This creates jobs for supervisors and managers (the middle). Five years later, the widgets factory goes bankrupt and lays off all the workers. Without the bottom workers, there is NO NEED for supervisors or managers (the middle). In other words, without the bottom (the poor), there would be no middle (class).

Following this logic, for a poor European immigrant to move up the economic pyramid, someone else has to take his or her place at the bottom. In a white supremacy system, it is logical to assume that the people MOST likely to become a permanent fixture at the bottom will always be the ***darkest people*** (blacks).

To guarantee that the "right" (black) people ***willingly*** stay on the bottom, an inferiority complex must be instilled in the black collective. In theory, once blacks are convinced they are ***inferior*** and cannot achieve (or rise from the bottom), they will spend a lifetime living down to society's (false) expectations.

Why Do So Many Blacks Kill Blacks?

For the same reasons whites kill whites, yellow people kill yellow people, red people kill red people, and brown people kill brown people. Despite the urban legends of black criminals targeting mostly white people, FBI statistics indicate that the majority of crimes in the US are INTRA-RACIAL, meaning the victim and the criminal ***are of the same race***. One only has to view the crime statistics in poor black neighborhoods to know most black criminals victimize black people.

Adding fuel to poverty and racism is the massive inferiority complex that is systematically bred into the black population via the white supremacist educational, social, economic, political, and criminal justice systems. The end result -- violence and self-destructive behaviors -- is predictable.

Johnny's Story

Johnny is a little black boy who lives in one of the most crime and drug-infested neighborhoods in a large Midwestern city. By the tender age of seven, Johnny has already seen several stabbings, shootings, and six murders.

The police regularly harass and abuse the black boys and men in Johnny's neighborhood. Once, they even made Mr. Brown, a deacon at his momma's church, lay facedown on the dirty sidewalk when he was just coming home from work.

Another time Johnny saw a white policeman stomp on a teenaged boy who had his hands cuffed behind his back. Johnny wondered why the boy didn't get up, even after the ambulance came. Later, he heard some grown-ups talking about how another black boy got killed by the police, and how nobody did nothing to stop them.

He didn't understand why the grown-ups were always mad, or drinking, or cursing. He didn't understand why the white men in the blue uniforms hated black people so much. Johnny didn't understand the power of hate – yet.

Everybody on Johnny's block has a relative -- a brother, sister, mother, father, uncle, son, or daughter -- in prison. A lot of the men are unemployed, in prison, or dead. The ones who were left standing, stood on corners, drinking out of brown paper bags, cussing, or fighting. Without realizing it, these men were the role models for fatherless boys like Johnny.

Johnny's mother is a single parent who works two jobs to make ends meet, so he's alone most evenings. He hears noises all the time, especially after a strange man tried to break into their house last summer when Johnny was home alone. As soon as it turns dark outside, Johnny goes from room to room and turns on all the lights even though he gets a spanking for wasting money.

Johnny has two older brothers, George, 14, and Tommy, 19. George runs with a street gang. Tommy is the smart one, who always has his head in a book. Tommy attends night school after his shift at a fast food restaurant.

Tommy is the closest thing Johnny has to a father, and is always telling Johnny he's going to go to college, get a good job, and buy them a real nice house in a nice neighborhood where Johnny can ride a bike and play outside without worrying about being shot.

That summer, tragedy strikes Johnny's family. On his way home from night school Tommy is shot and killed by the police. The two officers -- one black, one white -- swear Tommy pointed a gun at them and they had to defend themselves.

One of the witnesses -- Mrs. Johnson, an elderly black lady -- said she saw the police plant a gun on Tommy's body after they shot him, but the police investigating the crime scene refuse to take her statement. The TV news crews decline to interview Mrs. Jones even after she got up in their faces.

When Johnny's mother heard the news, she screamed so loud and long, Johnny thought she had gone mad. That was the first time Johnny wet himself before he could make it to the bathroom. It wouldn't be the last time.

Tommy had a closed casket at the funeral. His mother fell out during the service and had to be carried out of the funeral home. Johnny heard some people saying, no wonder, because the police shot Tommy so many times – 28 times – that the bullets had literally ripped his face apart.

Johnny is psychologically shattered but no one knows enough to recognize the signs. He is nine years old and is still wetting the bed. His traumatized mother takes out her frustration on Johnny by whipping him every time he has an "accident." She does not understand that she and both her sons are in need of counseling, nor does she have the time or the money for such "luxuries."

Johnny is ten now. He likes to break things, like glass bottles, park swings, and park benches. He picks fights with smaller kids and has been known to steal their bikes and toys.

Sometimes, when no one is looking, Johnny throws bricks at the windshields of parked cars just to see if they'll break. The neighbors shake their heads, wondering what happened to the sweet little boy with the bright smile.

Johnny prefers the streets to staying home alone. He likes to hang around the men on the corner, who boast, brag, and complain about the white man between sips from the bottles hidden in brown paper bags. Johnny's ears perk up when they say things like, *"Killing niggas just like killing cockroaches to the white man. All he think is, just one less roach in the world."*

Johnny believes the men because he once overheard a white policeman at a crime scene say in a nasty tone, *"Let them kill each other. The only good nigger is a dead nigger."*

The men on the corner were nice to Johnny, sometimes slipping him some loose change to buy some candy. One time, one of them let him take a sip from a brown bottle, but Johnny didn't like the taste and spit it out.

It never occurs to anyone that Johnny and his brother, George, needed counseling, and even if it had, there was no free mental health counseling in their poor neighborhood. Maybe, if the boys had gotten help, Johnny's only brother, George, wouldn't have committed an armed robbery at 18 and been sentenced to eight years in prison.

By age 11, Johnny is running drugs for his brother's gang. There were no jobs, so a lot of the young men in his neighborhood sold drugs. Some spent their money on girls, cars, and $4,000 rims. Other boys were helping out at home because so many grown-ups were unemployed.

Not Johnny. He didn't run drugs for the money, the girls, or the bling-bling. Johnny did it because he hated the police. When Johnny turned twelve, the gang invited him to be a bonafide member. Johnny jumped at the chance -- and got jumped in. It was the next best thing to having his brothers back.

Black Crime And Poverty Is By Design

If the most powerful people in the nation, who control America's educational and financial resources, wanted to eliminate crime and poverty, little boys like Johnny would be the rare exception instead of the tragic rule.

CHAPTER 39

KATRINA SHOULD HAVE BEEN A WAKE-UP CALL

On August 29, 2005, a massive, category-five hurricane slammed into the Gulf Coast. Hurricane Katrina went down on record as the costliest natural disaster in US history at $81.2 billion. To put this number into perspective, the cost of replacing the destroyed buildings and infrastructure in NYC after 9-11 was estimated at "only" $21.8 billion.

The most severe loss of life and property damage occurred in the Lower Ninth Ward in New Orleans' after the levees broke. More than 2,000 people perished. An untold number are still missing and feared dead. There is one more statistic that is rarely mentioned: ***Katrina was the largest single displacement of blacks since the Civil War.***

Was Katrina Preventable?

In the Netherlands, more than 15 million people live below sea level. Hydraulic sea walls were installed to prevent the kind of devastating floods seen in New Orleans.

> *"I don't want to sound overly critical, but it's hard to imagine that (the damage caused by Katrina) could happen in a Western country," said Ted Sluijter, spokesman for a Netherlands park where the sea walls are exhibited. "It seemed like plans for protection and evacuation weren't really in place, and once it happened, the coordination was on loose hinges."*

Mr. Sluijter is right. It is hard to imagine the technology used in the Netherlands was NOT known to the US Army Corps of Engineers. Many long-time New Orleans residents give a more sinister explanation for the failed levee system. They claim city officials have blown up levees in the past to prevent flooding in the more affluent, predominantly white French Quarter area.

Katrina Survivors Lack Credibility With Congress

> *Tuesday, December 06, 2005: Black Witnesses Testify Racism Influenced Katrina Response. A government hearing was held by a special House committee investigating the Bush Administration's slow response to Katrina.*

Only five white and ***two*** black lawmakers attended the hearing requested by Rep. Cynthia McKinney, a Democrat from Georgia and a member of the Congressional Black Caucus. She has since been "voted" out of office.

After a (black) grandmother testified that military troops focused machine gun laser targets on her granddaughter's forehead, Rep. Christopher Shays, R-Conn said, *"I don't want to be offensive when you've gone though such incredible challenges...I just don't frankly believe it."*

AXIOM #10: A BLACK EYEWITNESS IN A WHITE SUPREMACY SYSTEM CANNOT BE CREDIBLE IF HIS OR HER TESTIMONY CONTRADICTS THE OFFICIAL (OR DESIRED) VERSION OF EVENTS.

When survivors compared the Superdome in New Orleans -- where they were being held at gunpoint against their will without food or water or adequate toilets -- to Nazi concentration camps, they were chastised by officials for making such an inappropriate (?) comparison.

August 2005 Was Not The First Time The New Orleans Levees Broke And Flooded The Predominantly Black Ninth Ward.

In 1965, Hurricane Betsy flooded the Ninth Ward. Residents believed the city officials blew up part of the levee so the water would flood the Ninth Ward instead of the more affluent, white French Quarter. Similar rumors followed the wake of Hurricane Katrina, as well as eyewitnesses who claimed they heard explosions after the storm was over. There were also rumors of a gunfight between federal agents and New Orleans police at the levees.

US Government Refused Katrina Aid From Other Nations

Offers poured in from Russia, Japan, Belgium, Canada, France, Honduras, Germany, Venezuela, Jamaica, Australia, the United Kingdom, the Netherlands, Switzerland, Cuba, Africa, Greece, Hungary, Colombia, the Dominican Republic, El Salvador, Mexico, China, South Korea, Israel, the United Arab Emirates, and NATO and included boats, aircraft, tents, blankets, medical equipment, doctors, combat troops, generators, water purification equipment, engineers specializing in repairing dams, levees, roads, bridges, and transportation systems, cash assistance, and medical teams.

France offered 600 tents, 1000 camp beds, 60 generators, three portable water treatment plants, two planes, two naval ships, and a hospital ship. The US did not accept France's offer. Cuba offered to send 1100 doctors despite US sanctions. Israel offered hundreds of doctors, nurses, and experts in trauma and natural disasters. Prime Minister Sharon has also offered field hospitals and medical kits as well as temporary housing and other help that could be deployed within 24 hours. The Netherlands offered a dike inspection team.

PRESIDENT GEORGE W. BUSH'S RESPONSE:

Headline: "Bush rejects/ignores foreign offers of disaster aid." – Bloomberg, September 2, 2005. "I'm not expecting much from foreign nations because we hadn't asked for it. I do expect a lot of sympathy and perhaps some will send cash dollars. But this country's going to rise up and take care of it."

Why would the US refuse help from a Dike Inspection Team? Perhaps, Katrina's levees could not withstand the light of international scrutiny...

Contrast The US Government Response To Katrina With The US Response To The Thailand Tsunami In 2004 – *One Year Earlier*

"Within hours of the Dec. 26, 2004, earthquake and tsunami that devastated large swaths of the Indian Ocean region, the US response was massive, immediate, and comprehensive. USS Abraham Lincoln Carrier Strike Group's 17 helicopters and aircrews flew relief supplies to survivors. The USS Bonhomme Richard Expeditionary Strike Group, with support ships, 25 helicopters, and pre-positioned ships full of supplies left Japan, Guam, and Diego Garcia en route to the region.

Within days, more than 15,000 US military members were in Southeast Asia assisting relief and recovery efforts under Operation Unified Assistance, the name given the post-tsunami relief efforts focused on Indonesia, Sri Lanka, and Thailand. At least 17 Navy ships and a Coast Guard cutter were in the region or en route within a week.

"If you look at the front pages of many papers, you'll see pictures of the US military rescuing people, delivering food and water, assisting with emergency medical types of assistance," Defense Secretary Donald Rumsfield said in a Jan. 4 radio interview. Hundreds of Marine Corps engineers and Navy Seabees helped Sri Lankans repair infrastructure and reconstruct a sea wall.

Army engineers deployed to Thailand to help rebuild roads, bridges, and power infrastructure. Several teams of military forensics experts; including anthropologists, dentists, and mortuary affairs specialists helped manage the overwhelming number of bodies. More than 1,300 fixed-wing aircraft flights, resulting in more than 4,635 hours flying time. More than 2,200 helicopter flights, resulting in more than 4,870 hours flying time. In all, US Pacific Command assets delivered or coordinated delivery of more than 24 million pounds of relief supplies, food, clothing, water, and equipment into the region.

"One thing the Indonesians are never going to forget is who was there first," US Ambassador to Indonesia B. Lynn Pascoe said a few weeks later during a visit to the Lincoln." (Department of Defense, 2005 Year in Review)

Katrina survivors will never forget, either.

"Bush Doesn't Care About Black People."

In a promotional TV appearance for an NBC telethon to raise money for Katrina victims, black singer, Kanye West diverted from the canned speech on the teleprompter and said, "George Bush doesn't care about black people."

Was Kanye Right?

While black people drowned in their attics, President Bush was on vacation; Dick Cheney went fly-fishing; and Condoleeza Rice was buying shoes. Neither Bush nor anyone in his cabinet showed up in New Orleans for a full week.

Seems Like The Rest Of The World Agrees With Kanye West

"Already the finger of racism is being pointed at official Washington for the slowness of federal agencies in responding to the disaster. Especially in New Orleans, the city hardest hit by the hurricane, which is 67 percent black."
-- Manila Standard Today, Philippines

"America's old racial demons have been reawakened by the crisis unfolding in a city that is 67 percent black, and where almost a third of the population already lived below the poverty level." -- The Independent, UK

"That government had no evacuation plan, it is incredible, the first power in the world that is so involved in Iraq ... and left its own population adrift." -- Venezuelan President Hugo Chavez said in a live television interview.

"Washington, in a bizarre display of uncaring aloofness in their hour of need, appeared unable to respond to the crisis until days later. The disaster also revealed the racial fissures in American society. Most of the hapless survivors who filled New Orleans Superdome were black, with the more affluent white residents able to flee in their sports utility vehicles..." -- The Star, South Africa

"Many things about the United States are wonderful, but it has a vile underbelly which is usually kept well out of sight. Now in New Orleans it has been exposed to the world."— The Mirror, UK

"The ever-sensitive question of race in the United States has exploded into the furious debate over the government's handling of the disaster unfolding in New Orleans." — Aljazeera.net, Middle East

"When I see poor blacks, whites, Latinos, and other ethnic groups crying out for help in an undignified manner...something is wrong with the social and ethnic fabric of the United States."-- The Bahama Journal, Bahamas

"The fact that New Orleans is a southern town predominantly populated by African Americans ... explains why President George W. Bush did not see the need to cut short his holiday.... Being in America does not make a black man an American." — The Herald, Zimbabwe

"Hurricane Katrina has come and gone — leaving behind one strong message — Racism still exists in America." -- Hindustan Times, India

The rest of the world got it. Why haven't we?

CHAPTER 40

THE VICTIMIZATION OF KATRINA SURVIVORS BEGAN BEFORE KATRINA

The Facts Of Life For Poor Blacks In New Orleans BEFORE Katrina:

- *Louisiana had the highest incarceration rate of any state in the US.*
- *The Orleans Parish Prison, a city jail, was the eighth largest jail in the US.*
- *If Louisiana were a country, it would have the highest incarceration rate in the world.*
- *95% of the detained youth in 1999 were black.*
- *Louisiana spent $4,724 to educate a child in the public schools and $96,713 to incarcerate each child in detention. (2004)*

"Indigent defense in New Orleans is unbelievable, unconstitutional, totally lacking the basic professional standards of legal representation, and a mockery of what a criminal justice system should be in a Western civilized nation." -- Orleans Parish Criminal District Court Judge Arthur Hunter

"We've suffered under a policy where the city builds a huge jail that is then required to be filled with human beings, or else it's a waste of money."
-- Civil rights attorney Mary Howell.

The Demonization Of Katrina Victims

The "victim" status of black Katrina's survivors was cut short as the mainstream media geared up to do what it does best: ***demonize black people***. Some of the headlines that appeared in major media only days after Katrina struck:

- *Half Katrina Refugees Have Records*
- *Katrina Evacuees - Crime Surge Continues in Katrina's Wake*
- *Did Katrina evacuees bring more crime to Houston?*
- *After Katrina, New Orleans Crime Moves to Other Cities*
- *Houston Cops Link Crime to Katrina*
- *Crime Wave Katrina (Sometimes I'm ashamed to be an American)*
- *Katrina Residents Shooting at Rescuers*
- *Lawless Mobs Shooting at Rescue Helicopters*
- *Substance Use Patterns among Hurricane Katrina Evacuees*

From Victims to Villains

The coverage was so damning that Houston Mayor Bill White delivered a stern warning to (black) Katrina evacuees as they arrived in Houston: ***a jail cell was waiting for anyone who crossed the line.***

While it is understandable that any mayor would be concerned about absorbing thousands of homeless, traumatized people, it is highly doubtful that a group of white evacuees would have received such a cold-blooded and judgmental welcome.

Post-Katrina Crime Greatly Exaggerated

The police chief of New Orleans, Eddie Compass, later admitted he had *"exaggerated post-Katrina crime."*

> *"There were reports of rapes and children being raped. And I even got one report ... that my daughter was raped," said Mr. Compass in the Spike Lee documentary, "When the Levees Broke: A Requiem in Four Acts."*

Local Officials Admitted Reports Of Rampant Crime Were False

> *"I'm going to tell you that during that storm, the national media reported rampant rumors that have now turned out not to be true," said Louisiana's lieutenant governor, Mitch Landrieu.*

Regardless of the facts, the media continued their racist criminalization of the predominantly blacks survivors of the worst "natural" disaster in US history. Major media outlets published photos of black Katrina survivors scavenging for food and called them "looters" (criminals), while white survivors scavenging for food were sympathetically referred to as "scavengers" (victims).

The mainstream media (falsely) reported incidents of blacks stranded for days on rooftops shooting at their rescuers, when in FACT these distraught survivors were shooting in the air to attract the attention of helicopters that flew past without stopping to rescue them. Some survivors (eyewitnesses) testified that helicopter crews were laughing and waving as they flew past, without stopping to rescue a single survivor.

One year after Katrina, black survivors were being prosecuted for stealing a few thousand (after losing their homes, jobs, land, and every possession they owned) while the government ignored the ***hundreds of millions of dollars*** that were stolen by con artists and white charitable organizations.

As of May, 2009, FEMA has announced plans to "repossess" trailers from homeless survivors, and plans to scrap the trailers or sell them for a fraction of what they're worth, leaving thousands of survivors homeless.

Katrina survivors, many of whom never received a trailer, were accused of vandalizing trailers, as the government and the mainstream media continued to demonize survivors (victims) as criminals who didn't deserve the public's sympathy or the government's help, once again confirming:

AXIOM #6: "THE BLACK VICTIM = A VICTIMLESS CRIME" THEORY. A BLACK PERSON IN A CONFLICT WITH A WHITE PERSON (OR WHITE SYSTEM) CANNOT BE THE VICTIM IN A WHITE SUPREMACY SOCIETY. THE BLACK INDIVIDUAL IS ALWAYS AT FAULT, REGARDLESS OF WHO INITIATED THE CONFLICT, OR WHAT FACTS OR EVIDENCE ARE PRESENT.

The mainstream media was a tool used to JUSTIFY the US government's inhumane handling of Katrina. However, there may have been an added benefit to demonizing black survivors: ***the permanent removal of black people from New Orleans aka another black land grab.***

Four Years Later The Devastation Continues

Empty trailers still sit in vacant lots scattered across several states. Four years after Katrina, the survivors continue to fight with insurance companies for money to rebuild their homes, businesses, and lives.

Missing family members are now counted among the unconfirmed dead. Empty houses with "for sale" signs out front are ringed by overgrown weeds. Some survivors who have returned home are unable to find work or affordable housing for their families.

Skyrocketing rents in New Orleans and scarce job offers are forcing many former residents to relocate and abandon their claims on their land and property.

Public housing units are being torn down, reducing low-income housing by more than 50%, and doubling the homeless population. Displaced New Orleanians who return to New Orleans often discover they have no homes OR jobs to return to.

The message to black Katrina survivors:

NOW THAT YOU'RE GONE, STAY GONE.

Headlines Reveal the (Real) Aftermath of Katrina

"Without access to affordable housing, thousands of working class New Orleanians will be denied their human right to return." Kali Akuno, director of the Stop the Demolition Coalition

Many evacuees still await financial assistance. The millions raised by organizations, fundraisers, entertainers, and well-meaning citizens all over the world has disappeared God knows where.

A flyer reads, "Add Mexican workers as part of your long-term workforce planning. Supply limited. Order now."

All 4,900 New Orleans teachers fired, days after the storm. Charity Hospital and many key health facilities remain closed.

After "winning" a no-bid contract to rebuild New Orleans, Haliburton (a company associated with then Vice-President Dick Cheney) trucked in illegal workers ***instead*** *of hiring out-of-work Katrina survivors. Many illegal workers later complained that they were not being paid at all.*

"In the aftermath of Hurricane Katrina what happened was that hundreds of thousands of black workers were systematically excluded from the reconstruction and hundreds of thousands of immigrants were systematically exploited". -- Saket Soni, Lead Organizer New Orleans Center for Racial Justice.

"These are American citizens who are being displaced, who cannot pull themselves up by their bootstraps because the federal government is promoting illegal activity, promoting the hiring of people who are in this country illegally." -- Minuteman leader, Simcox

ARE WE FINALLY GETTING WHAT THE REST OF THE WORLD ALREADY GOT?

Who Profited From Katrina? (Always Follow The Money)

On September 13th, two weeks after hurricane Katrina made landfall, the Heritage Foundation held a meeting. Representatives of all the big right wing think tanks like Cato, Hoover, and the Republican Study Group in Congress -- the most ideological Republican congressmen and women were present. At the end of the all-night meeting, a list of 32 free market solutions was created for hurricane Katrina.

"The first one was to roll back labor standards in the region so you could hire whoever you wanted at whatever wage you wanted. That was the first on the list. Roll back environmental standards. Turn the gulf coast into a 'free market enterprise zone' is what they called it.

Basically tax holidays. Within days, (President) Bush is championing every single one on the list. New Orleans became an opportunity for people who had been pushing forward neo-liberal policies. To do it in the blink of an eye and get away with murder." -- Saket Soni Lead Organizer, New Orleans Center for Racial Justice.

Katrina should have been a wake-up call for Black America.

"Brownie, you're doing a heck of a job."
– President Bush, to FEMA director Michael Brown, while touring hurricane-ravaged Mississippi, Sept. 2, 2005

"Now tell me the truth boys, is this kind of fun?" – House Majority Leader Tom Delay (R-TX), to three young hurricane evacuees from New Orleans at the Astrodome in Houston, Sept. 9, 2005

"We finally cleaned up public housing in New Orleans. We couldn't do it, but God did." –Rep. Richard Baker (R-LA) to lobbyists, as quoted in the Wall Street Journal

WEÂPON #11

RELIGION (BRÂINWÂSH)

"Christ wasn't white. Christ was a black man. Only the poor, brainwashed American Negro has been made to believe that Christ was white, to maneuver him into worshiping the white man. After becoming a Muslim in prison, I read almost everything I could put my hands on in the prison library.

I began to think back on everything I had read and especially with the histories. I realized that nearly all of them read by the general public have been made into white histories. I found out that the history-whitening process either had left out great things that black men had done, or some of the great black men had gotten whitened."

Malcolm X

CHAPTER 41

SEARCHING FOR THE HOLY WHITE GRAIL

In spite of our exceptionally painful and oppressive history in America, Black America is still searching (in vain) for a Holy White Grail. Former US president Bill Clinton is a perfect example. Even before the election of the first black president, Barack Obama, some blacks had already honored Clinton with the title.

The Holy White Grail doesn't have to perform extraordinary or even ordinary feats. Something as trivial as playing a sax in front of a black audience was enough to convince (some of) us that our White Savior (rescuer) had finally arrived.

If we took off our emotional hats and put on our ***logical thinking hats***, we would understand that it is more important to pay attention to the kind of legislation passed by the Clinton administration than whether Bill played a mean saxophone.

Where does this (mindless) need for a Holy White Grail come from?

Suspect #1: White Jesus And The Black Church

It is an all-too-common sight in many black Christian homes: **a framed picture of a blond-haired, blue-eyed Jesus.** What is the psychological impact on a people who pray to a human image that NOT ONLY DOES NOT RESEMBLE THEM, but is identical to the (white) face of oppression?

Try to imagine Africa one thousand years ago. Would our African ancestors have conjured up a blue-eyed man as their creator and savior – or would their god have been made in their own image?

Where did the image of the "white Jesus" displayed in most black churches and homes come from? ***The European colonization of Africa.*** Europeans slave traders ***used religion and their own images*** to convince (con) the colonized and enslaved Africans to accept total white domination and black subjugation (submission) as the natural order of things.

Our worship of our true God was replaced by a worship of a white "God" and a white "Jesus" to program us to worship (and submit to) a physical manifestation of "God" in human form: ***the white male.***

The fraudulent images of white Jesus completely contradict Bible passages that describe Jesus with hair like lamb's wool and feet the color of burnt brass. Despite the alleged birthplace in the middle east (once part of Africa), all too many blacks still prefer to worship a white image and reject the black one.

Once blacks kneel down to the image of a white Jesus, they won't have much further to lay down to total white domination.

If whites dominate blacks in the present life, it seems right and natural for whites to continue dominating blacks in the afterlife. Some blacks will passionately – even violently – defend their "white Jesus." What difference does it make what color Jesus is?" they might ask impatiently.

The best answer: ask them what would happen if they went into a white Christian church and replaced the picture of a white Jesus with a black one. Would the white church members shrug their shoulders and say, "*What difference does it make?*" Or would they DEMAND the picture of black Jesus be taken down?

Any people who willingly worship their oppressor's images instead of their own do not respect themselves.

People who have been colonized and brainwashed will accept any image their oppressors give them, even if that image does not reflect their own humanity OR reality. Regardless, no more time will be spent here trying to prove the skin color of Jesus. What's important is understanding that our slave-like, messiah-worshipping ***acceptance*** of white domination **starts in the black church and in the black home**.

Suspect #2: The White Doll Vs The Black Doll

Black children are already programmed by the age of three or four by the TV, media, educational system, black adults, white adults, and the black church, to believe white is superior and black is inferior. This lays a foundation for the kind of inferiority complex that requires the validation of a "Holy White Grail."

Suspect #3: The Holy White Grail In Africa

The image of the "white savior" is a common fixture in Africa. Even today, Africa is portrayed as the domain of the European male or female "wildlife expert" who has mastered the environment while portraying Africans as little more than baggage carriers and human mules. In reality, AFRICANS – who have survived in Africa for thousands of years without the guidance of a single white man – taught the Europeans how to survive and safely navigate the continent...

...the same way American Indians taught European invaders how to survive in North America and how to establish a government. It is interesting that the African's and the American Indian's kindness toward European invaders was repaid with death, disease, destruction, colonization, and genocide.

The "white savior" is a central figure at every African relief concert where white celebrities raise money for sick and impoverished Africans. To add to the myth of the backward African, every TV documentary about Africa only shows the most primitive parts of Africa, ignoring the African cities, universities, and business communities. Africans are NEVER shown helping themselves or each other – ***when in fact, AFRICANS are doing the lion's share of humanitarian work in Africa.***

A troubling new trend is the "white savior" entertainer who adopts (buys) African babies the same way one would acquire the latest fashion accessory. It is beyond comprehension how it benefits an African child to be removed from his or her family, language, and culture, and injected into an alien white culture that is hostile toward American blacks ***who were born there,*** to be raised by a series of white nannies (because the mothers are career-driven) – and call that a "blessing."

If these white Hollywood parents do not have close ties with the African or the black community, it is an absolute certainty that these (purchased) African children will have a horrific identity crisis once they realize they are black (in a black-hating society), instead of white like their adoptive parents.

Instead of adopting African children, uprooting them from a culture where it is ***normal to be black,*** and depositing them in a culture where to be black is abnormal, inferior, and despised, it would be more beneficial to help an entire village *save their own children*. Unfortunately, these "adoptions" are seen as a blessing because the assumption (in a white supremacy society) is that a black child is always better off with (superior) whites.

Suspect #4 -- White Savior Themes In Movies And TV

Movies like "Tarzan" perpetuated the myth that blacks (Africans) were less civilized than a savage, illiterate white man in a loincloth who communicated with grunts, head nods, and chest thumps. In "race" films, like *"Mississippi Burning,"* and *"To Kill a Mockingbird,"* the white male rescues the defenseless black person (or persons) who are being victimized by (white) racists. TV shows like ABC's "Home Improvement" with their all-white casts giving needy blacks (and whites) the homes of their dreams, also serve to create the illusion that whites are the sole benefactors of blacks.

There is nothing wrong with whites helping blacks, or with blacks helping whites. What is dangerous is the ***lack of balance***, and the missing images and stories of black people (and Africans) helping themselves AND each other.

The pitiful blacks/benevolent whites images foster the (false) perception that blacks are ***incapable*** of helping themselves and are ***unwilling*** to help each other. It is easy to understand why so many blacks think we cannot function without the goodwill of whites, and why so many whites believe they have done enough for those "ungrateful blacks" who have no right to complain about anything, let alone racism.

The truth is MOST of the time MOST black people are helped (or rescued) by other black people (family, friends, teachers, etc) NOT by black or white strangers.

These false messages are especially dangerous for black youth. As they enter the adult workplace for the first time, they will be forced to interact with strange, and sometimes, hostile or racist whites. If they are taught to worship the white hand that will one day slap them down, they will not have the will, or the self-respect to defend or protect themselves.

"A few years ago, I was working for a telemarketing company and this white sales manager said we'd have to wear Aunt Jemima scarves if we didn't make our sales quotas. Now, mind you, most of us were black, so we knew it was a race thing. All the black women and older black men refused to do it, but the younger black males put those head rags on. I don't think they really understood how racist it was." Alecia, 39, sales rep

It is only a matter of time before young blacks run head-on into racism at school or at work. Whether they resist the message of black inferiority, or embrace it, depends on how well we prepared them for a black-hating society.

AXIOM #11: IT IS PSYCHOLOGICAL SUICIDE TO KISS THE SAME HAND THAT SLAPS YOU DOWN, AND PSYCHOLOGICAL INSANITY TO BE GRATEFUL TO SOMEONE FOR PUTTING YOU IN A POSITION WHERE YOU NEED THEIR HELP.

Most black youth are not prepared to deal with racism because WE did not prepare them. A few will weather the storm and emerge victorious; some will stumble and get up; and others will simply drop out of the race altogether.

The Myth Of Black Dependency/Black Inferiority

The stereotype of the hapless, helpless, and hopeless black (African) still prevails in Western culture. However, the FACTS paint an entirely different picture. All human life and civilization began in Africa. Archaeologists have discovered Negroid human remains in Southern China, all of which point to a significant African influence on Chinese culture.

The Moors (Africans) excelled in architecture, medicine, science, culture, astronomy, engineering, philosophy, art, and politics; and had a significant influence on European culture after conquering much of Europe.

During and after chattel slavery, blacks greatly valued their family units and had a strong sense of community; and in some areas, blacks geographically, socially, and economically surpassed whites. During Reconstruction, newly freed slaves successfully ran for office, and owned businesses that rivaled those owned by whites, drawing white customers as well as black.

Without black creativity and ingenuity in the areas of science, medicine, music, architecture, art, fashion, business, politics, and 400 years of free labor, America would NOT be the super power it is today. Nor would the rest of the industrialized and so-called "civilized" world.

We did not come from nothing.
Don't fall for the hype.

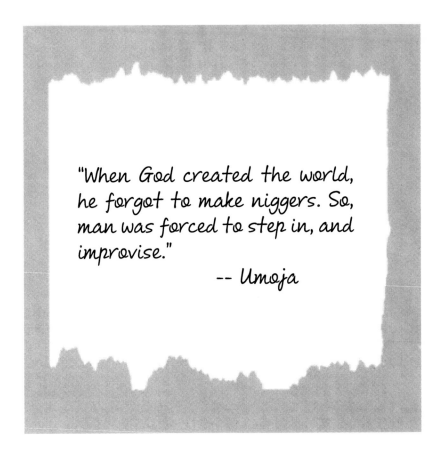

"When God created the world, he forgot to make niggers. So, man was forced to step in, and improvise."

-- Umoja

WEAPON #12

SHOWCASE BLACKS (DECEIVE)

"Harvard has ruined more Negroes than bad whiskey."

-- Adam Clayton Powell, Jr.,
the first African-American
elected to Congress (1908-1972)

CHAPTER 42

SHOWCASE BLACKS

"After all, if Americans vote for a black man to lead the nation, it will be hard to continue labeling the country as prone to racism." – Bill O'Reilly, conservative host of the "O'Reilly Factor". (2008)

The term "Showcase Blacks," coined by Mr. Neely Fuller, Jr., author of *The United Independent Compensatory Code/System/Concept,* refers to the high-profile blacks that are constantly paraded before the public. They may be political dignitaries, pro athletes, entertainers, educators, business people, Supreme Court justices, and even US Secretary of States.

However, their real purpose is to mask the REALITY of being black in America. These anointed black leaders and role models give license to the voices of exaggeration and deception via the media, and all the conservative right-wing talk show hosts, agitators, columnists, and pundits who cry:

"Look at all these successful blacks on C-Span, NBC, ABC, CNN, and ESPN! Blacks are sitting at the table in executive boardrooms and city halls all across the nation! They're in the NBA, MLB, and NFL! Two blacks even won an Academy Award the same year!

"If America was as racist as these (ungrateful) blacks say it is, would a black woman be the queen of the talk shows? Would a black man and a black woman have been the Secretary of State, or a black man have won the 2008 Democratic Presidential Iowa Caucus?"

Absolutely – If The Goal Was To Fool The Population

"I don't understand why those blacks are so upset when Obama tells them to shape up. Look how many are in jail. They don't have any fathers to teach them how to behave." – white female caller to a radio talk show after Jesse Jackson accused the black Democratic Presidential candidate Barack Obama of "talking down to black people."

Showcasing Prominent Blacks Accomplishes Several Things:

- It deceives the black collective about the realities of racism.
- It neutralizes the legitimate claims of racism by blacks.
- It offers a pressure relief valve for the explosive build-up of frustration and rage within the black collective. If blacks believed they had nothing to gain, the nation would be at risk from millions of blacks ***who had nothing to lose***.

In reality, the high visibility of Showcase Blacks actually confirms just the opposite. The more prominent the Showcase Blacks -- who are just a tiny percentage of the black population -- the worse things are getting for the black masses. In other words, ***the need to increase deception should serve as a warning to the black collective.***

When The Holy White Grail Has A Black Stand-In

A Showcase Black can "stand-in" for a Holy White Grail if he or she has the support of the mainstream media and the political system. The white validation of the Black Stand-In" creates the MYTH that blacks NEED white validation to be "legitimate." This explains why many blacks wait for a "cue" from the white mainstream before giving the Black Stand-In their approval and support.

The Black Stand-In deceives the black collective and allows whites to (falsely) reassure themselves that they can't be racist if they support a black candidate. The flaw in this argument is the kind of blacks they support. With a few exceptions, the Black Stand-In falls into one or more categories. He or she must:

- be seen as the exception to the inferior black rule (majority)
- be light-skinned or bi-racial (with a few exceptions)
- be endorsed by powerful, influential whites
- show favoritism toward whites
- surround him or herself with whites professionally
- not show any allegiance to blacks or talk honestly about racism
- not display any anger or resentment toward whites or blame them for racism
- validate negative black stereotypes either in public or as an author
- be willing to work against the interests of the black collective (for example, oppose affirmative action or boycott a UN Racism Conference)
- defend the interests of the white elite or whites in general

Using Showcase Blacks as Political Scapegoats

Showcase Blacks are used to put a "black face" on unpopular government and corporate policies. Whenever a white politician appears before the cameras, Showcase Blacks are standing in the background to give the impression that blacks are conspiring with white officials to deceive and defraud the public. In reality, these black bobbing heads have no power to agree or disagree with anything.

Showcase Blacks are also used to redirect citizens' anger over unpopular government or corporate policies from white policy makers to a black spokesman or woman. For example, a black female is "promoted" to the president of a utility company shortly before gas prices are hiked.

In the *Jena Six* case, six black boys were charged with felonies for a high school fight. The Louisiana District Attorney's office assigned a black attorney to handle the case -- and take the blame and absorb the wrath of the black collective to protect his white bosses from charges of racism.

Showcase Blacks Increase White Resentment

The popularity of a black stand-in among the white collective does NOT increase acceptance of blacks in general, any more than Michael Jordan and Michael Jackson's popularity with their white fans caused a reduction of racism. A black stand-in will be always be the exception to the inferior black rule as long as he or she serves a need for the white collective, such as entertainment.

In reality, Showcase Blacks actually increase envy and resentment among whites NOT acceptance. By promoting blacks to high-profile positions, this creates the (false) illusion that blacks have more opportunities than whites. TV specials about Black America create even more resentment from the white collective, because they feel they are not getting the same attention that blacks are getting -- when, in reality, neither group is getting the help they need.

Showcase Blacks are the perfect scapegoats (and lightning rods) for white frustration and rage. Since Showcase Blacks are rarely accessible to the public, this resentment and anger is often directed at everyday blacks in the form of increased racism, discrimination, and violence.

Professional Provocateurs & Civil Rights Pimps

The Professional Provocateurs and Civil Rights Pimps are a special breed of Showcase Blacks who operate as "double agents" between the black community and their white elite (bosses). These (so-called) black leaders:

1. Pacify the black collective by serving as a relief valve on the pressure cooker of racism, poverty, and injustice. By making it appear that someone (the Professional Provocateurs & Civil Rights Pimps) are fighting on their behalf, the black collective is LESS likely to take action themselves (a tactical mistake). However, the antics of these Civil Rights Pimps (never) create any permanent positive change -- ***which is why they are so useful.***

2. Distract (control) the black collective by turning minor issues into major issues. In other words, by constantly crying "wolf," blacks will be too emotionally exhausted to deal with more legitimate issues, and whites will be more inclined to dismiss all claims of racism.

   In January 2009, after Acme Markets ran an advertising special during Black History month for cornbread, collard greens, and grape soda, the Delaware NAACP called the ads *"racist, insensitive, and not culturally correct,"* and demanded a full-page apology in all Delaware newspapers.

   Now, try to imagine Acme Markets running an advertising special on buffalo mozzarella and balsamic vinegar during the annual St. Anthony's Italian-American Festival in Wilmington, Delaware. It is highly unlikely that Italian-Americans would have found the ads *"racist, insensitive, and not culturally correct."* When the black collective's attention is focused on non-issues, we are being distracted from addressing our REAL issues.

3. Incite racial tensions between whites and blacks by giving the impression that blacks are non-stop complainers who want special privileges, blame everything on racism, and expect whites to conform to our "double standards." For example, the black collective demanded action when a white man (Don Imus) called the black girls on the Rutgers team "nappy-headed hos," but largely remained silent whenever black male entertainers make millions calling black women much worse.

4. Deliberately alienate whites from blacks to keep both groups from uniting against the white elite. This "divide and conquer" strategy keeps the black and white collective working against their mutual interests.

The Showcase Black As Political Pacifier

Imagine a young African mother in Ethiopia holding a crying baby. The mother has no food; only a pacifier left behind by a UN Peacekeeper. The baby boy is starving, dehydrated, and in severe pain, so the helpless mother sticks the pacifier in his mouth.

The baby sucks desperately, only temporarily appeased, because he does not understand that it is impossible to get any nutrition from a piece of rubber and plastic. Without real food, the baby will eventually starve to death.

Showcase Blacks function the same way for the black collective. They are used to distract the black masses, who are suffering from monumental job losses, unemployment, foreclosures, predatory loans, homelessness, inferior schools, crime, rising high school dropout rates, police brutality and murder, and record rates of incarceration for non-violent offenses.

The Showcase Black is shoved into our eager mouths as a pacifier of hope that we will get the justice and the help that we need and deserve. Like the starving Ethiopian baby, the black collective is temporarily appeased until we realize we will NEVER get any justice from a black plastic human being who was created by the same system that created the injustices in the first place.

Unfortunately, by the time the black collective realizes we have been bamboozled, ***we will have starved to death.*** We must become more sophisticated in our thinking. If a showcase black is praised and rewarded by the white status quo then he or she is ***working for the white status quo***.

The Showcase Black (or Black Stand-In) is the ideal Trojan Horse to disguise racism. Because the Showcase Black is usually held in high regard by blacks, the black collective will not see danger coming and will stay in denial about what is actually happening -- ***right in front of our eyes.***

Increasing numbers of highly visible showcase blacks are NOT signs of black progress, BUT should serve as a warning that the black collective is under attack, and that we need to be distracted from what is really happening to us.

We are too easily pacified (and impressed) by Showcase Blacks, which is exactly why they are so effective in DECEIVING us.

Some Basic Truths About Showcase Blacks

1. Showcase Blacks will never trade their good jobs, careers, tenured university positions, salaries, awards, talk shows, movie star status, luxury foreign cars, bank accounts, stock portfolios, positions, titles, and non-black spouses in exchange for justice for black people. They will defend the white status quo to their and our detriment because they are terrified of losing everything (material) they have worked so hard to obtain.
2. Some Showcase Blacks are in deep denial, while others could care less about their true role in the scheme of things. A significant number of Showcase Blacks actually despise blacks who have not assimilated into the materialistic, white supremacist culture because they see them as a threat and an embarrassment.
3. On those rare occasions when a Showcase Black addresses the plight of Black America, he or she will spend most of their (mainstream media) time reassuring the white collective that racism, injustice, and black poverty is the fault of black people -- not the system of white supremacy.
4. Out of a sense of guilt (from selling out their community), some Showcase Blacks may write checks or start foundations for disadvantaged black youth, expressing concern for poor black folks, as they bask in the infra-red glow of TV cameras and photographers. Since there is no real involvement on their part and so little truth-telling, there are never any real consequences.
5. Some Showcase Blacks are Poverty Pimps (who pimp the black masses). They are masters at getting media attention, positive or negative. Because their actions benefit their real "masters," not the black masses, they are rewarded with corporate board appointments, financial donations (both on and under the table), distributorships from white corporations and foundations, and regular appearances on major networks and cable television.

What Do All Showcase Blacks, Professional Provocateurs, and Civil Rights Pimps Have In Common?

They (secretly) believe that the (unwashed) black masses lack the intelligence and the will to overcome their circumstances. If they did, they would be a member of the black elite "club," pimping the black masses, instead of being pimped for profit.

Showcase Blacks who openly or secretly hold the black masses in contempt CANNOT inspire real social change or justice for the black masses. Their hearts, minds, bodies, and souls have already been co-opted (bought and paid for) by the same white supremacist system that has so amply rewarded them.

The only real, constructive change must come from the black masses: those who are rewarded the least and penalized the most.

"Children have never been very good at listening to their elders, but they have never failed to imitate them."

James A. Baldwin

CHAPTER 43

THE RISE OF THE ANTI-ROLE MODEL

"I'm not a role model. Just because I dunk a basketball doesn't mean I should raise your kids." -- Charles Barkley

An Anti-Role Model Success Story

Pop-Eyes, aka Charles Taylor, a 34-year-old black comic, couldn't believe he was sitting in a Hollywood restaurant, celebrating his first acting role in a major motion picture. He felt like pinching himself as his agent, his lawyer, and a studio rep discussed the terms of his contract over medium-rare, 20-ounce T-bones.

Charles was thrilled but still had his doubts about his part in the James Bond-type thriller, playing the cowardly manservant of an escaped Nazi war criminal. Throughout the movie, his Nazi boss constantly threatened to fire up the gas ovens and turn him as *"black as a piece of charcoal."*

Charles knew why he had been cast in the role, and it damn sure wasn't his nonexistent acting skills. It was his trademark ability to pop his eyes out of their sockets, hence his stage name: *Pop Eyes*. He hadn't bothered reading the script because he completely trusted his new agent, a sharp Jew with the right Hollywood connections.

Dropping his old agent, Pat, had been the best decision of his career even though she had been with him from the beginning. Too bad nobody respected black agents in Tinsel town.

The studio rep predicted the new movie would make Pop-Eyes a household name. "Eddie M. better watch his ass," the rep added with a sly wink at Charles. They laughed at that, but the words sent a tingle all the way down to Charles' toes.

He was a little afraid of these fast-talking, arrogant, and expensively dressed white men. "You don't think the gas oven jokes are over the top?" Charles asked. The last thing he wanted was to be involved with anything that even hinted at anti-Semitism.

"I'm Jewish and I'm not offended," the agent and the lawyer said at the same time. Everybody laughed. The men dug into their bloody steaks, rattling off terms like options, box office grosses, and percentages. They said the studio might turn the movie into a weekly TV series.

If that happened, Pop-Eyes would have a regular role, playing the homosexual manservant of a Nazi war criminal, while a James Bond-type hero chased them from one end of the globe to the other. Charles hardly listened to the details, the words to the O'Jays song, *"Money, money, money! Money!"* ringing in his head. He sliced off a tiny portion of the steak, ignoring the pinkish-red juices, and shoved the fork into his mouth. He preferred his steak well-done, but he was determined to fit into the Hollywood bloody-meat-eating crowd.

To his surprise, Charles discovered Tinsel Town's power brokers loved seeing rich and famous black men sporting white women – especially blondes -- on their arms. That meant he would have to change his whole image, and stop partying with niggas. When they told him he would have to wear a dress in the movie and cut his hair, Charles almost rebelled. Not because of the dress, but it had taken him two years to grow his locks!

His old agent, Pat, called a few days ago. She said she'd heard about the script and begged him not to take the role. Said it would come back to haunt him for playing such a demeaning character. Charles told Pat he didn't give a damn what some broke-ass niggas thought about his movie and hung up on her with a quickness. Pat was just bitter because he dumped her after his career took off.

Still, Charles had to admit his new movie did remind him of the cowardly black dude, Birmingham Brown, in the old Charlie Chan movies, who was scared of his own shadow. Then it dawned on him: *his character's name in the movie was Birmingham Brown.* Charles could almost hear the black bloggers going berserk because he was playing the cowardly, pop-eyed, Steppin Fetchit, transvestite servant of a white Nazi war criminal.

Charles wondered if naming his character after Charlie Chan's sidekick was a coincidence, just like he wondered if the studio rep's shoe pressing against his under the table was an accident. He recalled all the rumors he'd heard about the famous black actor who had jumpstarted his career by giving his best performances on his knees before the studio bosses.

Charles was relieved when the meal and the meeting finally ended. The men shook hands with Charles and said they'd be in touch. He kept the smile plastered on his face even after the studio rep offered to give Charles a ride to his hotel "to make sure he was settled in."

Eyes burning, Charles tried to focus on his new movie instead of the hand that was resting on his thigh in the darkness of the back seat of the chauffeur-driven Lincoln Town Car. He gritted his teeth as the hand crept higher, swearing to himself he'd do whatever it took to become a big star, even bigger than Eddie, Will, and Denzel put together.

He'd make a ton of money, live in a big ass mansion, and throw parties with lots of beautiful females. Black ones, too. And, he'd give back to the community. Maybe, he'd start a scholarship fund for inner city youth – in his name, of course. Then everybody would be kissing his ass and saying what a great role model he was for the kids.

THE END

The broke-ass "niggas" Charles "Pop-Eyes" Taylor now holds in contempt are the same "niggas" who supported his career from the first time he stepped on the stage. Charles deludes himself into thinking a few scholarships for black youth will reverse the curse on the money he'll make by degrading black people.

Popeye's "contribution" to the mountain of negative black stereotypes makes life harder for every black man and black woman who applies for a loan, apartment, job, or equal justice under the law.

Rich And Famous: A Prerequisite For Role Model Status

In accordance with America's true religion – MATERIALISM -- blacks have learned to religiously elevate rich black entertainers and pro-ballplayers to role model status without knowing what OR if they stand for anything but themselves.

Whenever black celebrities are attacked for any reason -- justifiable or not -- even if they're accused of rape, domestic abuse, molesting teenage girls, or murdering an ex-wife, the black collective circles its wagons around them, with heartfelt war cries of "racism!"

We never notice that our blind support of black celebrities is always a one-way street going NOWHERE or that our black celebrities are the main ones poisoning black children with their "entertainment crack."

The forgiving attitudes we display toward black celebrities are rarely extended to the real people who have offended us. We will carry grudges against friends, family, and coworkers to the grave, while boasting how much we "love" this or that black movie star, singer, or athlete (stranger).

We defend these rich, black strangers even though we have never met them face-to-face but won't speak up or defend the real people in our lives. We salivate over the magazine photos that show off 25-room mansions and 10-car garages packed four-deep with cars that will never be driven, and hold them up as role models for our children.

What is it about rich blacks that provokes such blind loyalty and admiration? Is it their talent OR their money? Is it the vicarious thrill of linking their rich black skins with our poorer ones? If Michael Jordan only made $100,000 a year playing basketball but still possessed the same superstar skills on the court, would we pay $400 for a pair of sneakers with his name on them?

If we are worshipping their bling-bling and benjamins, we need to tell the truth and admit it has nothing to do with role models for our children.

After the Cameras Stop Rolling

What demons drive so many celebrity "role-models" to lead such destructive lifestyles? And why would we allow them to be our children's role models if they are engaged in sexual promiscuity, perversion, drug and alcohol addictions, broken marriages, abandoned children, financial irresponsibility, and excessive materialism? How can they be black "role models" if they never stand up for black issues -- or black people?

Will The Real Role Models Please Stand?

At the age of 16, Clancy was rated one of the best basketball players in his city. When his high school team made All-City in his junior year, he was offered a full basketball scholarship to a top Ivy League university. Once he arrived at the campus, he was constantly hounded by competing NBA scouts who offered him free sports cars, signing bonuses, cash (under the table), and all the white girls he could ball.

To his teammates' and his coach's surprise, Clancy rejected all their offers, and all the white girls who were eager to hook up with a future NBA player. He had a different dream. One that began when he was a 15-year-old gang member. His father was an ex-offender and former member of the same gang that recruited Clancy. One evening, as his father was coming home from work, a rival gang shot up his block. Clancy's father was one of the casualties.

Devastated by his father's murder, Clancy vowed to get revenge. He borrowed a stolen gun from a gangmember and hid it in the pocket of his winter jacket. Tonight was the night he would avenge the death of his father even though he had no idea who had killed him.

When Clancy opened his front door, he was surprised to find a stranger standing on the front porch. Without introducing himself, the man said he had a message -- from Clancy's father. Clancy was struck silent by the strangely familiar brown eyes. The man said Clancy's father wanted the killing to stop then held out his hand. Without hesitation, Clancy turned over the gun. He knew he didn't have the stomach or the desire to be a cold-blooded killer. The man squeezed Clancy's shoulder with a heavy hand before disappearing into the cold, dark night.

After Clancy's blood thawed, he collapsed on the porch steps, and cried for the first time since his father's death. His father used to squeeze his shoulder to show affection. Clancy never saw or heard from the stranger again but it was enough to convince him to make a life-changing decision.

Clancy quit the gang and threw all his energy into graduating from high school. He decided he was going to spend his life helping other boys who had lost their way, the way he had almost lost his. After he graduated with a masters degree in social work, he was hired by a non-profit foundation that worked with at-risk black youth. He started a basketball league, and managed to recruit a dozen hard-core members from his old gang. After breaking from the gang, a few returned to high school to get their diplomas or their GEDs.

Sometimes, Clancy regretted not pursuing an NBA career, like the times he donated part of his modest paycheck to a needy family to have their lights or heat turned back on. He could have turned pro but basketball had never been his passion. It had been a means to an end. A gift that God had given him to allow him to do the real work God wanted him to do.

During a highly publicized fundraiser for the foundation, the basketball superstar Jordan made an appearance. After Jordan heard Clancy had been an NBA prospect in college, he invited Clancy to join him in an exhibition game.

Clancy jumped at the chance of a lifetime, and to everyone's shock, he kept up with Jordan, dunking balls, passing effortlessly, almost scoring as many points as Jordan did for their team. When the game ended, the kids and adults formed a long line to get Jordan's autograph. No one asked for Clancy's.

After Jordan's entourage departed, some of the parents confronted Clancy and told him he was a fool for not turning pro. *"What a great role model you would have been for the kids,"* they said, *"If you had become rich and famous."*

Clancy almost said he already *was* a role model, because he was giving back what was needed most to those who needed it the most. He had just brokered a truce between two warring gangs and had saved God knows how many innocent lives. He wanted to tell them that black kids needed role models at eye-level that they could see, touch, and talk to, not superstars who might as well live a million miles from the ghetto.

Clancy's biggest role model had been his father – the man he saw every morning and every night. His father had been a gang member and an ex-offender, and that was the road Clancy had almost chosen, in spite of all the high-profile black "role models" he'd seen growing up.

Clancy finally cut them off by saying he was *"doing the work God wants me to do."* The parents walked away, shaking their heads at his answer. Sadly, Clancy was not the least bit surprised.

THE END

An Endless Celebration Of "First Blacks"

We must stop teaching our children to look OUTSIDE themselves, and encourage them to mine the diamonds that are already INSIDE. Black adults ***must become the role models*** for our black children and stop passing the buck to strangers whose TRUE characters are unknown.

Our children need REAL role models who will help them with homework, teach them how to be disciplined and moral, and show them ***by example*** how to live a good, decent life.

No superstar or politician can replace a living, breathing, role model who can help a struggling third-grader with their math lessons, teach them how to tie their shoes, or any of a thousand of things kids need to know.

When we encourage our children to look outside themselves, we are telling them to turn their eyes AWAY from us, because we cannot be their role models. If black "role models" and black "firsts" were the answer for our children, why are more black children dying, dropping out of school, and going to prison?

What We Will Choose? Showcasing Or Substance?

When six black teens in Jena, Louisiana were charged with felony assault after a schoolyard fight, over 20,000 protestors rallied for justice. Thousands of blacks from all over the country missed school and work to lend their support to six black boys who were being railroaded by a racist justice system.

Black rappers Mos Def, and Bun B, Reverend Jesse Jackson, Martin Luther King III, and Al Sharpton were among the tiny number of black celebrities who came to Jena to lend their support. Mos Def commented on the absence of prominent blacks:

> *"Shame on everybody who's not here. I'm fuckin' mad. I'm disappointed to always be coming to these things and it's only one or two people [from the industry here]. If you ain't gonna use your voice, then be quiet. I'm disappointed and ashamed."*

The next time we're tempted to put a rich black celebrity or public figure on a pedestal we need to remember that there ***wasn't a single black movie star, talk show host, politician, singer, dancer, motivational speaker, comedian, poet, scholar, educator, tenured professor, author, or athlete at the rally for six poor black boys from Jena, Louisiana.***

The Real Definition Of Black Progress

It doesn't matter how many rich or successful Showcase Blacks are elected, or how many get prominent positions, or win Academy Awards (once every 50 years). ***What matters is what happens to the majority of black people.***

What matters is the day unarmed black people are not shot down in the street by rogue police officers who will not be held accountable. What matters is the day the "Voting Rights Act" becomes unnecessary and obsolete because our votes will always be counted -- even in states like Florida and Ohio.

What matters is the day black infants have same opportunity as white infants to celebrate their 2nd birthday, and black neighborhoods stop being drug havens for the crackheads from the nice, drug-and-violence-free suburbs.

What matters is the day non-violent black drug users are treated with the same compassion and leniency that white drug users receive, like a slap on the wrist, community service, drug treatment, or a suspended sentence.

What matters is the day black schools offer the SAME quality of education that white schools offer, instead of using "property taxes" as an excuse to discriminate and under-educate. What matters is the day the Dead White Woman's Club (DWWC) goes out of business; because on that day ALL CRIME VICTIMS, regardless of color, sex, income, religion, or sexual preference, are EQUALLY IMPORTANT in the eyes of the law and the media.

THAT IS THE DEFINITION OF PROGRESS

Until that day comes, it is pointless to keep celebrating another "Showcase Black" as though he or she represents progress for ALL black people. That being said, this is not a blanket condemnation of all black celebrities, politicians, or public figures. We are simply calling a spade a spade, even if he or she is a high-profile one. It is up to the readers to decide for themselves if the high-profile black is all ***show*** or if he or she has any ***substance***.

CHAPTER 44

THE PET NEGRO SYNDROME

"Now it says here, and every white man should be allowed to get himself a Negro. Yea, he shall take a black man unto himself to pet and to cherish and this same Negro shall be perfect in his sight." -- The 'Pet' Negro System by Zora Neale Hurston (May, 1943)

The 'Pet negro' Syndrome (Updated For The 21st Century)

The owner of a **pet negro** loves to pet his negro, dress it up, brush its coat, give it fancy treats, tasty chew toys, and teach it to do tricks for the owner and his friends: *"Look! Isn't it cute? And it so articulate, too!"*

If the owner is very, very lucky, he has a very special **pet negro** he can proudly trot across a stage to get an award (or two). Regardless of how well a **pet negro** is treated; a pet is still a pet, which means it is an animal, NOT a human being. A pet will NEVER be human like its owner. A pet is the property of its owner and under the owner's complete control – if the pet wants to keep getting those juicy scraps of sirloin steak under the table.

The affection an owner has for his **pet negro** has nothing to do with negroes in general NOR does it guarantee the owner will treat other negroes with the same consideration that he treats his pet. In all likelihood, he won't, because his pet is special; not some stray negro he tries to run over in the street.

10 Ways To Tell If A 'Pet negro Adoption' Has Taken Place:

1. The **pet negro** is treated better (differently) than non-negro members.
2. The **pet negro** is treated better than all other negroes.
3. The **pet negro** is put on a pedestal and viewed as "exotic" and "special."
4. The **pet negro** is led to believe it is different (better) than other negroes.
5. The **pet negro** is told it is "not like other negroes". Translation: *"You're the exception to the inferior negro rule."*
6. The **pet negro** is discouraged from associating with other negroes who have NOT been pre-approved by the owner, for fear the **pet** will pick up bad habits and a few fleas.
7. The **pet negro** may be asked to publicly throw another negro "under the bus" in order to please its owner.
8. Whatever the **pet negro** achieves, its owner will take full credit for properly training his **pet negro**.
9. People often say: *"Wow, he treats his pet just like a person!"*
10. Only one (token) **pet negro** is allowed per household.

Petting A negro Is Not The Same As Respecting A negro

The **pet negro** may be genuinely liked and occasionally admired. However, liking a **negro** is not the same as respecting a **negro.** Being fond of a **pet negro** is not the same as believing that negro is the equal of the pet owner or any other human being.

House-Trained Pet negroes

House-trained **pet negroes** seldom come into contact with stray negroes. Because the **pet negro** is isolated from other negroes, the pet will begin to believe it is human just like its owner. Subsequently, the **pet negro** views other negroes as (inferior) aliens because it cannot relate to them.

This breed is a loyal and fiercely protective pet because it knows it cannot survive without its owner; therefore, it will not even attempt to establish any independence. Loyalty and obedience are the most desirable traits in a **pet negro,** with intelligence coming in a close third.

The most popular house-trained negroes today are the mixed breeds. While previously regarded as "mongrels," many owners now prefer the mixed breeds, and perceive them as more intelligent, attractive, and trustworthy. The demand for purebred negroes – especially the female – has dropped sharply over the last decade. Some **pet negro** breeders predict that the purebred negro species will become extinct if this trend continues over the next several decades.

How To Train A Pet negro

Training is more effective if it is started when the negro is still a young pup. Some form of Ivy League obedience school is ideal where the pup learns when and where to sit, speak, stand, beg, kneel down, whine, bark, heel, roll over, and lay down when told to do so by its owner or any authorized substitute with a big stick.

While a domesticated negro is a valuable addition to every owner's animal collection and provides many hours of amusement, all is not sweetness and light with the house-trained **pet negro**.

The house-trained **negro**, like all coddled pets, is spoiled, extremely territorial, and will jealously attack any stray negroes the owner brings home. The **pet negro** regards other negroes as a threat and a blatant owner-violation of **Rule #10: Only one (token) pet negro allowed per household (or organization).**

For this reason, the owner must maintain dominance over his **pet negro,** lest the negro think it is in charge. If properly trained, the right words and an occasional swat on the rear with a rolled newspaper is generally enough to reassert authority. There have been extreme circumstances where an out-of-control pet negro requires euthanization (put to death), but this is rare. Usually, the threat of taking the doggy bowl and its favorite foreign import toys is enough to strike fear in the heart of most house-trained **pet negroes**.

Pet negro Leash Laws

Some **pet negroes** are allowed to roam and associate freely with other negroes. However, to ensure that the pet does not wander too far or stray too long, an electronically monitored leash (much like an ankle bracelet) is attached to the pet's diamond-studded collar, in accordance with strict leash laws for pet negroes.

The leash laws allow law enforcement and animal control to identify which negroes are pets and which are strays so the wrong negroes will not be picked up, accidentally shot, or euthanized (killed).

The leash law mandates that all **pet negroes** have all their shots, licenses, and are under the control of their owners so the negroes can travel safely even when they are not accompanied by their owners.

Pet negroes In Media/Entertainment

This is one field where **pet negroes** are extremely popular. They can be found in most white prime-time dramas, TV commercials, and on the afternoon and evening news. The tip-off is there is always one smiling, grinning **negro** completely surrounded by owners – and there isn't another negro in sight for miles.

The owners avoid mixing male and female pet negroes to avoid increasing the numbers of unwanted strays. This explains why, in most TV shows and major studio films, a male **pet negro** is seldom paired with a female **pet negro** AND why so many **pet negro** males are neutered before they are allowed to mix with females of any kind.

If male **pet negroes** are not spayed, their instinctual sex drive may drive them to rubbing their hind parts against table legs and sofa backs, and howling at stray females, risking embarrassment for the pet and the owner.

Pet negroes In Politics

Pet negroes are often found center-stage in the political arena – literally speaking. It is common to see a **pet negro** standing behind its owner/ candidate, either to the left if the owner is female; to the right if the candidate is male. On cue, the **pet negro** may bark or lick the owner's cheek, depending on what is required of it at the time.

In those rare cases where the **pet negro** is the candidate, the owner and his team will proudly take all the credit for whatever success the negro achieves. This may seem unfair but it is necessary in order to validate a negro as a viable candidate.

The **pet negro** must be careful not to show any favoritism (or concern) for the plight of stray negroes, lest its owners think their negro is disloyal, ungrateful, and untrustworthy – thus, kicking that negro to the curb.

The Pet negro And Interracial Relationships

There are thousands of **pet negroes** involved in interracial relationships where their owners shun all other negroes in favor of their special "pet."

Contrary to what most **pet negroes** believe, the owner is always the one who does the choosing; not the other way around. There is no way a pet can force an owner to choose the little "negroette" in the pet store window if the owner decides to take a pass.

Occasionally, a down-and-out **negro** will show up at a prospective owner's back door, whining, barking, and looking for a hot meal, and a warm place to sleep. This is a very common scenario when the **pet negro** is a male and owner is a female. She may have a soft spot for stray negroes, or she may simply enjoy her superior position in regard to controlling a negro who is down and out on its luck.

This may be the first time the female owner has been able to call the shots, feel superior, and get a male of any kind to jump through her hoops. Unfortunately, once the owner discovers a **pet negro** is more trouble than it's worth and has outlived its usefulness, that unlucky negro will bite the proverbial dust.

"There was two kinds of slaves ... the house Negro and the field Negro. The house Negroes - they lived in the house with master, they dressed pretty good, they ate good 'cause they ate his food -- what he left.

They lived in the attic or the basement, but still they lived near the master; and they loved their master more than the master loved himself.

If the master's house caught on fire, the house Negro would fight harder to put the blaze out than the master would. If the master got sick, the house Negro would say, "What's the matter, boss, we sick?"

He identified himself with his master more than his master identified with himself. In those days he was called a 'house nigger." And...we've still got some house niggers running around here."

-- Malcolm X

WEÂPON #13

POLITICS (CONTROL)

"The two parties have combined against us to nullify our power by a 'gentleman's agreement' of non-recognition, no matter how we vote ...

May God write us down as asses if ever again we are found putting our trust in either the Republican or Democratic Parties."

W.E.B. Dubois (1868-1963)

Chapter 45

ARE BLACK LEADERS OBSOLETE?

"The man in the street does not notice the devil even when the devil is holding him by the throat." -- Johann Wolfgang von Goethe

These Are Different Times From The Days Of Martin And Malcolm

In their day, no one anointed or appointed black leaders. They stepped forward and led. They followed their own convictions, not the carrot-and-stick of financial or professional rewards from our oppressors.

Martin and Malcolm were real flesh-and-blood leaders, not the media-created, larger-than-life "icons" paraded before the public. Martin and Malcolm didn't live in gated communities, wear $1500 suits, or drive Mercedes-Benzes.

Malcolm and Martin were common, everyday black folks, just like the folks they represented. That's why their message rang so authentic; why they *moved* people; why they were so dangerous; and ***why they had to be destroyed.***

That's Why It's Important We Ask:

1. Who picks today's black leaders?
2. Who foots the bill for our so-called "civil-rights" organizations and finances the lifestyles of today's "black leaders?" If the black collective does not pay the cost, someone else is certainly the boss.
3. If a black leader truly opposed racism and injustice, would they be embraced, supported, and legitimized by the white status quo? Or would they be attacked?
4. Why would a legitimate black leader continuing using the same old civil rights strategies that haven't worked? (If they had, we would NOT be using them ***four decades later).***

Black Folks Are Still Marching, Protesting, And Back (And Buttock) Sliding Four Decades Later...

> *"Let me say just a word about the Jew and the black man. The Jew is always anxious to advise the black man. But they never advise him how to solve the problem the way the Jew solved their problem. The Jew never went sitting in and crawling in, and sliding in, and freedom-riding, like he teaches and helps Negroes to do. The Jews stood up, and stood together, and they used their ultimate power: the economic weapon." -- Malcolm X*

Jews Had The Correct Response To Bigotry

Malcolm X's statement was not anti-Jewish; it was an ***acknowledgement*** that the Jews had the most ***correct and constructive response*** to bigotry. Regardless, no time will be wasted here being politically correct. If the truth offends, then let it offend as long as we are attempting to tell the truth.

Had we followed the examples of Jews and other immigrant groups, and focused on ECONOMIC POWER instead of SOCIAL INTEGRATION (aka white validation), we would not be in this sad condition. Had the black collective focused LESS on eating IN restaurants with whites, and MORE on OWNING our OWN restaurants, we wouldn't be in this sad condition.

Had we realized that giving whites the power to VALIDATE US was the same as giving them the power to DEVASTATE US, we wouldn't be in this sad condition.

The day we stop caring about being socially accepted by those who reject us because we are black -- is the day we get our self-respect, sanity, and power back.

The Definition Of Insanity

Blacks marched, protested, and died for the right to vote -- yet we still require a "Voting Rights Act," and four decades later, a million black voters in Ohio, Illinois, and Florida are denied the right to vote in the 2000 Presidential election.

Blacks marched, picketed, and protested against employment discrimination, yet the black unemployment rate is triple that of the white unemployment rate - regardless of our education and experience -- and that number is climbing.

Blacks marched, picketed, and protested for equal education, yet our schools are the most substandard, and the black high school dropout rate is the highest in the nation. We marched against violence in the black community, yet the violence in our communities has reached epidemic levels. We marched against police brutality, yet unarmed black men and women are still being murdered by the police with no recourse for their loved ones.

Blacks marched for equal justice, yet the nation's prisons have become holding pens and modern day concentration camps for over one million black men, women, and children, whose collective misery has been farmed out for profit to Wall Street investors and the prison-industrial complex.

Blacks marched against racism in the media, yet Don Imus returned to the airwaves a richer, more popular personality for an audience that relishes white shock jocks attacking (our) black women for the nation's contemptuous amusement. And in 2008, during the US fashion industry's biggest yearly event, "Fashion Week," not a single black model graced the runway.

The definition of "insanity" is doing the same things and expecting different results. Either we have mass racial amnesia, we are insane, or both.

If marching, picketing, and protesting was an effective strategy to achieve justice -- why are we still marching, picketing, and protesting FOUR DECADES later? Why is there MORE violence, MORE drugs, MORE guns in our communities, MORE black men and women in prison, MORE black children at risk, MORE family instability, MORE out-of-wedlock births, MORE single mothers, and MORE black children dropping out of high school now than before the civil rights era?

If marching, picketing, and protesting was an effective strategy, why aren't other minority ethnic groups marching, picketing, and protesting their problems away?

Because they are too busy running businesses and making money in our communities.

The black community is a rite of passage (and a goldmine) for non-white immigrant entrepreneurs who cut their first business teeth with the black customer. The black community is the ideal market to unload low quality and substandard products, food, and clothing. There are few regulations and inspections, fewer discriminating customers, and ***no competition*** from their black customers.

Instead of imitating their success, we grumble about their foreign presence in our communities while we hand over our hard-earned cash. Instead of resenting these enterprising immigrants, we should be asking them - begging them -- to show us how to do it.

Instead of encouraging the black collective to march, picket, and protest, our so-called black leaders and civil rights organizations should be vigorously promoting economic independence and business development in the black community. Again, the question must be asked: who do our so-called "black leaders" really represent if they keep encouraging us to stay on our knees?

Some blacks passionately defend the old guard civil-rights organizations, even though these organizations are controlled by non-black outsiders. Some blacks justify that totally unacceptable control by saying without the financial support of these powerful non-blacks, our organizations would go bankrupt.

THEN LET THEM GO BANKRUPT

It is better to be financially bankrupt than morally bankrupt. If any black civil rights organization works in secret to fulfill the agenda(s) of their NON-BLACK financial backers, they should be SHUNNED by the black collective. If ANY black civil rights organization is NOT supported by the people it serves, the people do not deserve that representation. If any black civil rights organization does NOT serve the best interests of the black collective, then it is NOT WORTH SAVING.

Somebody got it wrong. We do not owe "black leaders" our loyalty, our votes, or anything else. They owe us -- because without us, they would not be where they are. We have the right (and the obligation) to ask them: who do you really represent?

The Litmus Test For TRUE Black Leaders And Leadership

1. Are they embraced and rewarded by the white elite via distributorships, book deals, corporate donations, political appointments, and appearances on major network or cable stations?
2. Do they publicly chastise or criticize black people, or appear to blame racism and poverty in the black community on black people?
3. Do they avoid hot racial issues, like Katrina, the Jena Six, the UN Conference on Racism, or the Sean Bell police shooting (murder), and prefer to be "race-neutral?"
4. Do they get mainstream media exposure on a regular basis?
5. Are they praised by the mainstream media instead of being demonized?

If the answers to ANY of the above questions is "yes" – these so-called black leaders DO NOT REPRESENT THE INTERESTS OF BLACK PEOPLE. We must become more sophisticated in our thinking. Our own history has taught us (or should have taught us) that ANY black leader who TRULY opposes the white status quo will be **punished NOT rewarded**.

A true leader cannot be bribed by money or (the appearance of) power. A true leader sacrifices whatever is necessary -- even his or her life -- for the cause they believe in.

Black liberation will not come from the black elites who have been bribed, wooed, coaxed, and stroked by the very system they only pretend to oppose. Black liberation will not come from the black elite who often view the black masses with as much contempt as their white masters do.

Black liberation will not come from the black elites who depend on the white status quo for their paychecks, tenure, donations, grants, book deals, endowments, endorsements, media exposure, distributorships, talk shows, and other symbols of success and self-importance.

The only time the black elite challenges the status quo is through politically correct channels; writing politically correct nonfiction; making fancy speeches at fancy dinners; or by politely expressing outrage as a guest on CNN or MSNBC.

The black elite are terrified of losing what they have worked for. They are smart enough to know there will be life-changing consequences if they step too far out of line or become too "politically incorrect" by telling the whole truth. They know the only safety in being a rich or educated black is to be a good black, too.

Sadly -- in spite of all the brilliance in the black elite -- no real solutions will ever come from their esteemed ranks. They are too addicted to their creature comforts, titles, degrees, awards, status, white validation, and non-black spouses.

If history ever blesses the black collective with another Martin or Malcolm X-caliber black liberator, there is no doubt that he or she will come hard from the streets -- NOT from the hallowed Ivy League or corporate boardroom.

This is not intended to demean all the brilliant and successful blacks among us. Some are deeply devoted to black causes; however, they have a very difficult balancing act, standing with a foot in both worlds.

Leanita McClain, the first black editorial board member for the Chicago Tribune newspaper, wrote about the dangers of being precariously balanced in two diverse worlds -- the black one and the white one:

"I have a foot in each world," she wrote, "but I cannot fool myself about either. I can see the transparent deceptions of some whites and the bitter hopelessness of some blacks. I know how tenuous my grip on one way of life is, and how strangling the grip of the other way of life can be." (A Foot in Each World' by Leanita McClain).

Tragically, Leanita McClain lost the will to continue her struggle. At the age of 32, this gifted writer committed suicide.

We Must Face Some Cold, Hard Facts:

1. There Is No Equality Without Equal Power

If you have to beg for equality, you'll never get it. If you have to ask for it, you're not in a position to get it for yourself. If you demand it, you better get ready to fight for it. If you're not willing to fight for it, you don't deserve it. And if you only think you have it, you definitely don't.

2. White America Has Hardened Its Heart Against Us

White America is in a moral, spiritual, and financial crisis of its own. It believes it done enough for Black America, and feels it is time for Black America to stand on our own two feet. We should heed their advice and stop begging, pleading, rioting, marching, protesting, and demanding that white people "do something" and start doing that something OURSELVES.

3. It Is Our Responsibility To Solve Our Own Problems

If we don't find a way to solve them, we are condemning our children, grandchildren, and great grandchildren to a permanent second-class, or worse, existence. The system of racial and economic oppression is more sophisticated and deceptive than ever before. The iron fist in the velvet glove pummels our conscious and unconscious minds with a barrage of mixed signals. We are so dizzy; we are literally hanging from the ropes. If we do not shake off our false sense of security, one good knockout punch will put us down for the count.

4. We Must Get Rid Of Our Racial Amnesia

If we have to keep asking ourselves, "Are blacks are making progress," then the answer should be obvious. Real progress is self-evident -- NOT fighting the SAME battles over and over. **We know the truth.** Now, we must have the courage and determination to FACE IT.

5. If Black Youth Are Screwed Up, We Screwed Them Over

We didn't teach our children about the sacrifices their elders made so they could walk in the front door instead of shuffling through the back. We didn't share our collective humiliations -- and the lessons we learned from them -- with our children. Instead, our fear, false pride, and shaky egos sealed our mouths shut and deprived them of our wisdom.

We did not teach our black children how to navigate a white supremacy society - OR even that it *was (*and still is) a white supremacy society. We did not create another path so they would not have to demean themselves just to make a living. We taught them by example that success could be measured in dollars, diamonds, and Mercedes-Benzes, instead of the qualities they possessed inside.

Instead of wrapping our collective arms around our children, we sent them out unprepared into a racist society that despised their beautiful skin. Instead of arming them with the truth, we avoided the subject of racism, sex, and money because those topics made US uncomfortable.

We made a million excuses NOT to talk about racism because we didn't know what to tell them, so we told ourselves that we were going to "let them make up their own minds" about it.

LET THEM?

Would we let them make up their minds about graduating from high school? Or let them drive our brand new car without a driver's license? Or let them stick a fork into an electrical outlet? Or let them do any number of things that would put them in harm's way, or jeopardize their futures?

Are the Jews teaching hate when they teach their children about anti-Semitism? Then why are we teaching hate when we tell our children the truth about racism, or that there are people in the world who would cheat, mistreat, imprison, or kill them simply because they are black? No wonder so many of our young black people are so angry, disrespectful, and disappointed in us.

6. We Refuse To Learn From Our History

Instead of using our collective experiences to benefit us, our enemies are using them against us. They study what makes us tick; what we react to; how to pacify and/or deceive us; how to control and manipulate us. They know where our "hot" buttons are, how hard to push them, and what we'll do in response. We are a predictable people, if nothing else.

One thing is painfully clear. We cannot afford our racial amnesia/idealism one day longer. The ship called denial has already sailed, and in many cases, is sinking to the bottom of the educational, political, and economic ocean. America is in a state of transformation that does not bode well for Black America. We cannot wait for another Malcolm X or Martin Luther King. We cannot wait for someone else to do something. ***WE must do what we can where we can.***

Are Black Leaders A Luxury We Can No Longer Afford?

The assassinations of Malcolm and Martin should have taught us the dangers of putting all our eggs (or faith) in one basket because baskets BREAK. So do movements, once the "leader" is eliminated. Whenever a black person -- especially a black man -- has the vision, charisma, and leadership skills to move black people toward REAL self-respecting and constructive action, he or she will suffer one of the following fates:

1. They will be bought off with flattery, awards, lofty positions, status, and material things (bribed).
2. They will be discredited by revealing (or creating) situations that destroy their reputations (humiliated).
3. They will be falsely imprisoned to derail their ability to influence others (neutralized).
4. They will collapse under the tremendous pressure of being gifted, conscious, and conflicted, like Leanita McClain (demoralized).
5. Or they will be killed -- instantly with a bullet to the brain, OR slowly, with a "fatal" disease (destroyed).

The strategy of marching, protesting, and begging (for attention and acceptance) has outlived its usefulness. It is time for the most adaptable people in the known universe to stop begging and take our destiny into OUR OWN CAPABLE HANDS.

Africans existed and thrived on planet earth for thousands of years, long before they were enslaved by Europeans. It is time to continue the struggle of our African ancestors who survived the worst global Holocaust in human history: ***The African Holocaust.***

Each One Of Us Has The Power To Become A Leader Of One

> *"We are all born with the seeds of greatness within us. We made America what it is today. We have all the power we need -- within ourselves - to become our own LEADER OF ONE. We must become a LEADER OF ONE -- for ourselves, our families, our children, and our communities." -- Anon*

Being a leader does not require TV cameras, talk shows, marches, a huge organization, a big war chest, fancy speeches, ego trips, or the approval of the status quo. Leaders do what they can, where they can. A leader knows that the smallest (good) deed has a positive rippling effect that can spread from person to person, neighbor to neighbor, and community to community, until it is felt around the world.

Become a Leader of ONE.
Each ONE; teach ONE.
Do what you can; where you can.
Become your own Leader of ONE.

The last word on leadership goes to the great South African freedom fighter and leader: Nelson Mandela

"Our deepest fear is not that we are inadequate. Our deepest fear is that we are powerful beyond measure. It is our light, not our darkness that most frightens us.

We ask ourselves, 'Who am I to be brilliant, gorgeous, talented, fabulous?' Actually, who are you not to be? You are a child of God. Your playing small does not serve the world.

There is nothing enlightened about shrinking so that other people won't feel insecure around you. We are all meant to shine, as children do. We were born to make manifest the glory of God that is within us.

It is not just in some of us; it is in everyone. And as we let our own light shine, we unconsciously give other people permission to do the same. As we are liberated from our own fear, our presence automatically liberates others."

*** * ***

Chapter 46

Commentary

Our Children Are Watching

Segregated water fountains in the South (1940)

(The event below was reported in the New York Times on-line edition (May 24, 2009) a few days before this book went to press. The lesson in this article was too important not to include it -- so we did. -- the Authors)

69 YEARS LATER...

Two Proms: One Black, One White

In May 2009, in Montgomery County, Georgia, an "integrated" high school continued a 38-year tradition of hosting two racially segregated proms. The black prom was open to all students. The white prom had strict "rules" that excluded certain (all the black) students.

Despite claims from black and white students that interracial friendships are common at their high school, the blatant racism of the white students, school administrators, and parents tells the real story.

A Surprising (and Disappointing) Turn of Events

On the evening of the white prom (held the night before the black prom), a small group of black male and female students stood among a crowd of white parents and onlookers outside the community center.

The black students snapped photos and cheered as their white classmates strutted into the building in their high-school finery. One of black students admitted they got some stares, but claimed it *"wasn't too bad."* (Their white friends didn't return the favor by cheering their black friends at the black prom).

Afterwards, over a bucket of KFC, the black students joked about how "lame" the white prom was but their hurt (and confusion) over being excluded was obvious. One girl, who stated her "best friend" was white, didn't understand why they couldn't attend the same prom with their white friends.

One black girl predicted that *"half of those (white) girls, when they get home, they're gonna text a black boy."* Another girl seemed disappointed that she hadn't received a single text message from her white friends as they partied at their whites-only prom.

It's Not About Race (Or Racism), It's About "Tradition"

In contrast, the reaction of (many) white students ranged from awkwardness to justification to pride. One white male senior -- who claimed he had as many black friends as white friends -- didn't see his whites-only senior prom as racist. *"It's how it's always been. It's just a tradition,"* he said.

"It's not about being racist," added the white mother of a senior girl attending the whites-only high school prom. *"It's what we've always done."*

Colored Waiting Rooms (1940) -- Another "Fine Tradition"

"It's not really about being racist, or having all white friends, or black friends," insisted one white female student. *"We all hang out together, we're all in the same classes, we all eat lunch together at the same tables. It's not about what color you are, it's not about if you're black or white..."*

Yes, yes, we know, it's all about "tradition," like the fine traditions of America's Jim Crow past, with its "Colored Waiting Rooms," separate water fountains, separate schools, and separate black and white restaurant entrances...

Separate Black and White Entrances

"This community and this school system is fine like it is," the white parent of a senior student agreed. "Why change something that works? It's not broken. The kids are perfectly fine with it."

She's only half-right. The white half may be perfectly fine with segregated proms, but, apparently, the black kids are not:

"I want to have my senior prom with the people I'm graduating with."

"I don't understand. If they can be in there, why can't everybody else?"

"If my best friend is white, why can't we attend the same prom?"

A Different Kind Of Educational Genocide

Do not misunderstand our point. The tragedy of this story is NOT a segregated prom. It is the ***LACK of self-respect (and self-esteem)*** that would drive those bright, caring black students to DEMEAN themselves by showing up, armed with cameras and smiles, to cheer the racist participants of a "whites-only" high school prom.

The real tragedy is young black people who want to be accepted so badly by their white peers that they are willing to disrespect themselves, without understanding that surrendering their dignity gains them NOTHING. The real tragedy is black boys who think it's a "compliment" to be the sexual playthings and "negro pets" of the same white girls who can't be seen with them in public, or even at the same prom.

One can only imagine that race relations at any high school that insists on segregated proms is far from rosy or ideal. One would rather NOT imagine what other indignities, insults, slights, and self-esteem damage these black students are experiencing on a daily basis.

This is not a condemnation of those black students from Montgomery County. On the contrary, they appear to be sensitive, loving, (and forgiving) young people. It is NOT their fault they do not understand. They are simply playing the roles taught them from birth in a white superiority/black inferiority system.

Our children are also imitating what black adults do every day. They SEE us smile and pretend not to notice when we are being disrespected. They are WATCHING as we grovel for crumbs from the economic table, and beg for acceptance from whites even while we are being rejected. They are LISTENING as we praise whites for the smallest things, and elevate those blacks who are the closest in appearance to whites, while degrading our own black features, hair, skin color, and humanity.

NO WONDER SO MANY OF OUR CHILDREN FEEL SO INFERIOR

It is undeniable that WE -- black adults and parents -- have dropped the collective ball when it comes to our black children. We have NOT taught them about the system of white supremacy because we have NOT educated ourselves.

We have NOT built up their self-esteem so they WON'T NEED TO BE VALIDATED BY SOMEONE JUST BECAUSE THAT SOMEONE IS WHITE. Most of all, we have NOT taught our children what a true "friend" is NOT.

1. Anyone who condones your mistreatment is NOT your friend.
2. Anyone who condones your mistreatment should NEVER be your friend.
3. Anyone who condones your mistreatment CANNOT be trusted.
4. By accepting their bad behavior, you are TEACHING others to mistreat you.

Those who insist, *"it's not the kids', it's the parents' fault,"* or who (falsely) believe that the next (white) generation will be "different" (less racist) than their parents, should heed the words of the mother of the 2009 black prom queen, who attended her own segregated prom three decades ago:

"It's hard to see my girl in the same situation I was in 30 years ago."

The More Things Change; The More They Stay The Same

The odds are (great) that the 2009 white graduates of Montgomery High School -- who claim their racist traditions are their "parents' fault" -- will pass along the same "traditions" to their children 20 years from now.

40 years ago, blacks believed that the Civil Rights movement, integration, interracial marriages, and the anti-establishment white hippies who preached "flower power" and "peace and love" in the 1960s, would lead to the elimination of racism, because these young whites would be "different" than their racially-intolerant parents. Our own experiences as blacks in America -- if we are honest -- has proven this was NOT the case.

By the time these white 17 and 18-year-old 2009 graduates from Montgomery High School have to compete for a coveted seat at a university, a college scholarship, a job, a promotion, or a spouse, it's a sure bet that the vast majority of their interracial "friendships" will have already bitten the dust.

The segregated proms in Montgomery County, Georgia are stark reminders of the *Montgomery, Alabama bus boycott of 1955*, and the kinds of conversations that could have taken place between black domestics and their white employers, whose houses they cleaned, dinners they cooked, and children they raised:

> *"Now, Mabel, you know you're just like one of the family, but I just don't understand for the life of me, why it's so important for you coloreds to sit in the front of the bus when the back seat rides just fine."*

It is time to tell our children the TRUTH for sanity's sake

PART TWO

COUNTER WARFARE

"In a time of universal deceit, telling the truth is a revolutionary act."

George Orwell (1903-1950)

CHAPTER 47

IT'S TIME FOR A (PSYCHOLOGICAL) REVOLUTION

The word "revolution" evokes horrific images of bloodshed and violence but that is not the kind of revolution being proposed here. The most important revolution will NOT be fought with guns and bullets. The most powerful revolution is the one that takes place **inside our minds.** If we learned one thing from our long, bloody history in America, it should be this:

POWERFUL PEOPLE NEVER GIVE UP POWER VOLUNTARILY

Until the PENALTIES of practicing racism/white supremacy outweigh the BENEFITS, racism/white supremacy will continue to devastate us. We cannot beg, buy, borrow, plead, march, cry, protest, boycott, integrate, assimilate, sex, marry, or shame racism/white supremacy out of existence. We cannot wait for whites to end racism/white supremacy if they believe it is necessary for their economic and genetic survival. **What we must do is correct our RESPONSES to it.**

We are not proposing hatred or revenge. While hate is an understandable (and emotional) response to injustice, it is not a solution to correcting it. Hate is counterproductive and clouds judgment at a time when sound judgment is needed the most. Hate also transforms the victims of injustice into potential perpetrators of injustice. If we want to defeat white injustice, we cannot replace it with a system of injustice against whites.

The FOUR Most Powerful Responses To Racism/White Supremacy

1. EDUCATE ourselves about the system of racism/white supremacy. We cannot defeat what we do not understand.
2. FACE the hard facts about our collective condition as blacks in America, and ACCEPT that it is our responsibility to fix our problems.
3. USE this knowledge to CHANGE OUR BEHAVIOR.
4. STOP lying to ourselves that we are smarter than whites (who function as white supremacists) because...

...if we were smarter than the people who are function as white supremacists, we would not be in this terrible condition.

This truthful statement is not intended to insult blacks, or to compliment whites. However, it is foolish and vain to believe the oppressed are smarter than their oppressors. This does not mean blacks are less intelligent because we are black; it means we do not understand what is being done to us, because we do not understand the system of white supremacy.

Being Ruthless And Cunning Is Not The Same As Being Wise

A man or woman who is truly wise is humble and compassionate; not mean-spirited, greedy, and arrogant. They understand that there is nothing more powerful than universal karma and nothing more deadly than the UNIVERSAL BOOMERANG.

AXIOM #12: THE UNIVERSAL BOOMERANG: WHAT WE PUT OUT INTO THE UNIVERSE – FOR GOOD OR FOR EVIL – IS WHAT WE WILL GET IN RETURN.

Do not confuse more "justice" with more material things or more money. Do not confuse the wealth of the white elite with having more freedom and more happiness. They have neither.

Whites – collectively -- are enslaved by the fear of losing privileges they have not earned, and the fear of losing things that do not belong to them. They are driven (enslaved) by a desperate need to control everything and everyone on the planet -- an impossible goal because only the CREATOR has that power.

Whenever anyone benefits from victimizing people, there is no joy; only the illusion of joy. To feed this illusion, the victimizer must acquire more things, more money, and more power. When this fails to satisfy (because it can't), this deadly cycle leads to more dissatisfaction and even more greed.

AXIOM #13: NEVER ENVY ANYONE WHO HAS THE WEALTH OF THE WORLD AT THEIR FEET AND IS STILL DISCONTENT. THEY DO NOT UNDERSTAND WHAT IS HAPPENING. USE THEIR IGNORANCE AS A LESSON.

13 Fundamental Truths About Racism/White Supremacy

1. Racism/white-supremacy guarantees "inequality" and "injustice" for ALL non-white people.
2. There can be no "racial equality" when blacks are NOT equal economically, educationally, or politically to whites, and do not have equal access, equal resources, or equal power.
3. There can be no "racial equality" when whites control everything and blacks control little or nothing.
4. Blacks and whites sitting in the same airplanes, classrooms, theaters, and restaurants, will not eliminate racism/white supremacy.
5. Being a good, law-abiding black will not eliminate racism/white supremacy.
6. Proving our "patriotism" by fighting in every war America has ever fought has not and will not eliminate racism/white supremacy.

7. Interracial sex, dating, marriage, and bi-racial children will not eliminate racism/white supremacy.
8. Having a few good jobs in white corporations we will never own will not eliminate racism/white supremacy.
9. Being a successful black entertainer, news anchor, athlete, or talk show host when we do not own the TV networks, movie studios, and distribution companies will not eliminate racism/white supremacy.
10. The "browning" of America, where it is estimated that people of color will become the majority in America by 2025, will not eliminate racism/white supremacy. This myth is illogical and anti-historical. The minority ALWAYS rules the majority. In South Africa, the black African majority was ruled (and is still ruled) by the white minority. In America, a few hundred elites rule hundreds of millions of people.
11. Everything that happens, happens for a reason, and ANYTHING that happens over and over to the same people, in all places, at all times, IS NOT an accident or a coincidence.
12. Racism/white supremacy is an economic, political, and social system; a behavioral necessity (genetic survival); and a psychological addiction (mental illness). As long as racism/white supremacy benefits or is perceived to benefit those who practice it, they will continue doing it.
13. Until we understand how the system of racism/white supremacy works and correct our responses to it, we will continue to be its victims -- **and the biggest co-conspirators**.

Truth Is Stranger Than Fiction: Non-Whites Are The Biggest Supporters (and Co-Conspirators) Of White Supremacy

- If non-whites did not COOPERATE with white supremacy, it would not exist.
- If non-whites did not betray, degrade, or mistreat non-whites because they are NOT white, white supremacy would not exist.
- If non-whites did not teach their children that white is superior by their words and deeds, white supremacy would not exist.
- If non-whites did not place whites on a pedestal economically, socially, intellectually, sexually, or romantically, white supremacy would not exist.
- If non-whites did not believe they were inferior, white supremacy could not exist.
- White supremacy is first and foremost, **a MIND GAME**....

...because there is no way TEN PERCENT of the world's population can physically overpower the other ninety percent without their cooperation.

White Supremacy is a MIND GAME that we continue to play without understanding the game at all.

Don't Buy Where You Can't Work

"...the gas, electric, and bus companies, and the city subways. Black people support them, yet are refused employment in all of them.

60 percent of all Harlemites are unemployed. The remedy lies within our grasp. We must simply stop spending our money where we cannot work."

"The Don't Buy Where You Can't Work" Campaign (1933)

CHAPTER 48

COUNTER WARFARE SOLUTIONS & SUGGESTIONS

What Is Counter-Warfare?

Counter-Warfare is a strategy of ***non-violent resistance*** to the system of racism/white supremacy, the most SOPHISTICATED MIND GAME ever designed. In self-defense, non-whites must develop an equally powerful counter-intelligence to neutralize the "mind games" by:

1. **CHANGING THE WAY WE THINK (EDUCATION).**
2. **CHANGING OUR BEHAVIOR (CONSTRUCTIVE ACTIONS)**

Three Counter Warfare Strategies

1. The Theory of Non-Participation
2. 33 Rules of Disengagement
3. Become a Leader of One

These strategies put the focus where it belongs: on black people NOT white people. We did not get in this terrible condition overnight, and we will NOT solve our problems overnight. We cannot afford to waste any more time talking about what white people should do for us -- and find a way to ***do for self***. If we need better schools for our children, we must POOL our resources and CREATE better schools. If we need more jobs, we must POOL our resources and CREATE our own jobs.

We cannot afford to wait one second longer for "someone else" to end racism. We have already waited 400 YEARS. It is time to STOP begging, marching, and protesting. It is time to STOP expecting the white elite to eliminate the white supremacy system that was designed for their sole benefit.

All we will get is what we have always gotten: **the false appearance of real change**. As we watch the civil rights clock spinning backwards, it should be clear that despite all our "progress" black people still control nothing in America, including the ability to rescue a single black person off a single rooftop after Katrina.

The Real Revolution Takes Place In The Space Between Our Ears

Once we become empowered (illuminated) with knowledge of self, and knowledge of how the system of racism/white supremacy works, we will attract other empowered individuals who seek real change – not the kind of "change" that is seen on television under the banner of a "National Convention."

We must stop deluding ourselves that such FALSE displays offer any real change. THEY DO NOT. They are simply updated dog-and-pony shows to pacify, deceive, and exploit the masses. We know from history that black leaders who TRULY advocate real change are NEVER rewarded, promoted, or given airtime by the same powerful elites who created the system of injustice.

Real change is not glamorous or pleasant. It has nothing to do with being popular, articulate, or presenting an attractive image. It does not happen while we sit in front of a television set, or walk into a voting booth and push a button. ***Real change is hard, dirty, and dangerous work.***

Fortunately, none of the suggestions in this book are hard, dirty, or dangerous. They do not require money, special skills, talents, bravery, or bloodshed. In fact, most suggestions involve NOT doing something that wastes our precious time and money, or that harms us individually or collectively.

These recommendations (as well as the contents of this book) are a FRAMEWORK that the reader can adapt as he or she sees fit, and decide what is beneficial, constructive, and useful, and what is not. No one, including the authors of this book, represent the voice (or voices) of authority.

STRATEGY #1: THE THEORY OF NON-VIOLENT, NON-PARTICIPATION

NON-PARTICIPATION is the most powerful weapon we possess. We have the freedom to NOT PARTICIPATE in those things that demean or short-change black people. This includes NOT spending our hard-earned dollars where they are not respected. For example, from 2007 to 2009 at the biggest fashion events in New York City, Paris, and Italy, top American and European designers, like Jil Sander, Burberry, Bottega Veneta, Roberto Cavalli, and Prada had no black runway models.

> *"I am virtually never allowed to photograph black models for the magazines, fashion houses, cosmetic brands, perfume companies, and advertising clients I work for. Whenever I ask to use a black model I am given excuses such as, '...black models do not reflect the brands values.'"*
>
> *-- Fashion photographer, Nick Knight.*

Despite the lack of black representation on the runways, in high-fashion advertising, and behind the scenes of the fashion industry, blacks have plenty of representation at the cash registers when we collectively spend billions on designer clothing, accessories, shoes, and apparel.

Utilizing the POWER of NON-PARTICIPATION, we would STOP begging (or demanding) to be included, and STOP BUYING WHERE WE CAN'T WORK. No dialogue would be necessary. Our CONSTRUCTIVE ACTIONS would speak for themselves. A constructive (and self-respecting) response to the racism in the fashion industry would be:

> *"They don't have to hire blacks for their fashion shows. They have the right to hire (or not hire) whoever they see fit. They can do their thing, we'll do our thing. Just understand this "thing" cuts both ways.* ***We don't have to include them in our shows OR spend our money with them, either.****"*

The black collective would then spend our fashion dollars with our black designers and turn their wonderful creations into OUR fashion status symbols. To take a page out of the white economic book, non-black designers could participate ONLY ***if they hire blacks and advertise in black-owned media.*** We would REFUSE to PARTICIPATE or SUPPORT ANY people, places, and things that do not respect our dollars, and START CIRCULATING those precious dollars in our own communities.

STRATEGY #2: 33 RULES OF DISENGAGEMENT

Stop Showing Off, Bragging, And Talking Too Much

1. STOP styling, profiling, bragging, and boasting about who you are, what you look like, or what you have. It matters more WHO you are when no one is looking.
2. STOP showing off or trying to impress white people. *They don't care.*
3. ALL opposition to racism should be constructive and promote justice and correction; not avenge racial wrongs. If the offending parties refuse to stop practicing racism, replace dialogue with constructive self-help strategies.

Sex & Relationships

4. STOP HAVING SEX WITH STRANGERS, acquaintances, and people we are not committed to. Sex is SPIRITUAL as well as PHYSICAL. Every time we have sex with another person, we absorb the spiritual nature (good or bad) of our sexual partner, and this becomes part of OUR spiritual nature.
5. STOP HAVING UNPROTECTED SEX outside of marriage. This will limit the spread of venereal diseases, manmade viruses, the number of unplanned pregnancies, and at-risk, neglected children.
6. STOP HAVING SEX FOR MONEY and material things. You do not have to stand on a street corner to be a PROSTITUTE. If you are selling your precious body for a promotion, favors, money, or things, *you are PROSTITUTING yourself.* This is true for males and females.
7. STOP MAKING BABIES if you are not in a committed marriage with a committed partner. We must break the generational curse of the dysfunctional black family and at-risk black children.
8. STOP HAVING CHILDREN YOU ARE NOT WILLING OR ABLE TO RAISE, love, nurture, provide for, and protect. This will break the generational curse of the dysfunctional black family and at-risk black children.
9. STOP HAVING BABIES to hang on to a man or a woman. If they don't want you, why do you want them? ***Above ALL else -- respect yourself.***

Stop Worshipping Money And Material Things

10. STOP CHOOSING ROLE MODELS for our children because they are rich. Stop looking to strangers to be "role models" and become your own children's role models. Children need role models at eye-level: parents, adults, teachers, police officers, firefighters, and the business people in their communities.

11. STOP TEACHING OUR CHILDREN TO LOOK OUTSIDE THEMSELVES and teach them to VALUE what is already inside. If we help build them their self-respect and self-esteem from the gifts GOD gave them, our children won't need black role models, superstars, showcase blacks, false prophets, political pimps, Holy White Grails, OR white validation.

Self-Respect/Self-Reliance

12. STOP DEMANDING RESPECT from other people. You do not have a social contract with everyone you meet. The only person who is obligated to respect you is YOU. Unless someone's behavior harms you (other than hurting your feelings), the most POWERFUL RESPONSE is to put them on IGNORE. Worry MORE about respecting yourself.
13. WE DO NOT CONTROL ANYTHING in a white supremacy system but OURSELVES. We cannot out-police the police; outspend the super-rich; out-fight the military; or out-televise the networks, BUT we do have control over the most important possession we own: OURSELVES. We can refuse to participate in anything that degrade, demean, and destroys black people.
14. STOP DOING THOSE THINGS THAT REQUIRE FREE WILL and work against our individual and collective interests. For example, no one can make us buy, listen to, or watch a CD, movie, or DVD that degrades black people.
15. STOP PRAISING BLACK PEOPLE because they are bi-racial or their skin color, hair, skin, and eyes makes them look more white than black. What does that say about YOU (and your self-esteem) if you look more "black?"
16. STOP SUPPORTING BLACK ENTERTAINERS, artists, politicians, poets, filmmakers, scholars, and activists who degrade black people by promoting negative stereotypes.
17. STOP DISRESPECTING BLACK PEOPLE. No one can make us disrespect black people or call black people foul names. No one can make us turn against our mothers and fathers, wives and husbands, sons and daughters, or neighbors. No one can make us replace love with hate. No one can make us place a white woman or white man on a sexual pedestal, or knock a black man or black woman off one.
18. STOP PARTICIPATING IN ACTIVITIES THAT DESTROY THE BLACK COMMUNITY. For example, if we stopped using drugs, the drug dealers would be forced to find another profession. If we refused to buy stolen merchandise, the burglars, robbers, and thieves would be forced to find a legitimate source of income instead of victimizing their communities and filling up the nation's prisons. If we refused to buy or watch degrading movies, TV shows, and music videos, ***they would stop making them***.
19. STOP EXPECTING WHITE PEOPLE TO SOLVE OUR PROBLEMS. It is OUR responsibility to solve our own problems because we have the most to lose if we don't.

20. BECOME YOUR OWN AUTHORITY on the things that affect your life and and family. We must become our own authority (educate ourselves) so we cannot be deceived OR intimidated by those who practice racism.
21. STOP WORKING AGAINST THE INTERESTS OF BLACK PEOPLE. In other words, the system of white supremacy requires our COOPERATION and PARTICIPATION in harming other black people.

Save The Children & The Black Family

22. TAKE CONTROL OF THE EDUCATION OF OUR BLACK CHILDREN so their intellectual potential will not be destroyed by the anti-black educational system. We must start our own independent school systems so we can empower our children with the TRUTH, instead of allowing them to be poisoned by LIES -- and an inadequate education.
23. STOP LETTING THE RADIO, TELEVISION, VIDEO, AND DVDS RAISE YOUR CHILDREN. Spend more FAMILY TIME talking, at the bookstore, the playground, and the library.
24. TURN OFF THE TELEVISION AND STEREOS (once in a while) and read a book (like this one) in front of your children. Our children imitate what they see us do -- NOT what we tell them to do.
25. TEACH OUR CHILDREN TO LOVE THE WRITTEN WORD. If our children are taught to love the written word, they will always be in the LEARNING MODE. Blacks adults must educate themselves by reading books (like this one), and encourage the massive intellectual power of our children.
26. TEACH YOUR CHILDREN TO LOVE THE WRITTEN WORD. The reason slaves were punished for reading is the slavemasters knew READING led to THINKING. The same thing is true today. The average black public school deliberately makes LEARNING boring, humiliating, and painful. If our children hate to read (or learn), they will be forced to rely on their enemies for information -- and everything else they need.
27. DO NOT CONDUCT ILLEGAL AND DISHONEST ACTIVITIES IN FRONT OF YOUR CHILDREN or accept the reality that your children will not respect you even while they IMITATE you.
28. STOP FUSSING AND FIGHTING WITH YOUR CHILDREN'S MOTHER OR FATHER. Our children must take priority over our own selfish ego interests. We made the decision to have them (or didn't make the right decision to NOT have them). Our children did not ask to be born. We must NOT make them pay for our foolishness.

Politics

29. HOLD BLACK POLITICIANS TO THE HIGHEST POSSIBLE STANDARDS. Demand to know WHAT they are going to do for us, not what they think we should be doing for ourselves. Demand that all black politicians treat black voters with the same respect they give non-black voters.

30. UNDERSTAND THAT A POLITICIAN IS A POLITICIAN IS A POLITICIAN. A POLITICIAN IS NOT A PREACHER. We do not need them to preach at us, we need to know what they are GOING TO DO FOR US IF WE VOTE THEM INTO OFFICE. If, after ONE term, they cannot prove they are working in the black collective's best interests -- VOTE THEM OUT OF OFFICE.
31. BLACK CIVIL RIGHTS ORGANIZATIONS THAT ARE FUNDED BY OUTSIDERS (non-blacks) should be automatically suspect. Everyone has an agenda. Until we know what their agenda is, they should not be trusted.
32. DO NOT TRUST the "Showcase Blacks" who are used to wow and amaze us. Their "success" has NOTHING to do with progress for the black masses. Black progress can only be measured by what happens to the black masses, not to a few handpicked blacks. Even the cruelest master must throw his starving dog an occasional bone to keep it loyal AND to keep the dog from attacking its tormentor. (Yes, we are the starving dogs, not the masters).

MINIMIZE CONFLICT

33. MINIMIZE conflict at home, at work, in public, and at all places. The powers-that-be use conflict to divide and conquer non-white races. We must stop falling for their attempts to divide the black male from the black female.

Strategy #3: BECOME A LEADER OF ONE

1. **BECOME A LEADER OF ONE**. Once the INDIVIDUAL is empowered, they do not depend on other people to do the right thing.
2. The empowered individual raises EMPOWERED CHILDREN. This also ensures that a "movement" does not rest on the shoulders of one man or one woman. An empowered individual is spiritually CONTAGIOUS – if their actions are just, constructive, and righteous. The empowered individual can spread the gospel in a way a so-called national leader cannot.
3. The empowered individual leads by example; the national leaders CANNOT because most have already been purchased, bribed, or threatened into cooperating with our enemies. They are the wily foxes in sheep's clothing and the false prophets who will lead the (black) sheep to slaughter.
4. Most civil rights organizations are like sprinters. They start off running at full speed and are out of steam – and ideas -- before the end of the race for justice. The empowered individual is a marathon runner; in the race for the duration. The empowered individual is a LEADER OF ONE and does not get frustrated as easily as those whose power comes from a group, because he (or she) is NOT totally dependent on what a GROUP does OR does not do, and is not disabled because a so-called "leader" is disabled.
5. By choosing NOT to participate in those things that demean or degrade black people, we increase our PERSONAL POWER and SELF-RESPECT.
6. You cannot control anyone but yourself. By making more self-respecting decisions, you will influence others around you – even those that try to

make you look or feel foolish.

7. BECOMING A LEADER OF ONE means you are making a powerful change from low to HIGH SELF-RESPECT. This may frighten and intimidate those who are still locked into self-disrespecting behavior. Do not let them discourage you. Before you know it, they will be singing your praises.
8. If you have children, teach by example. When your children hear you say you refuse to do X or Y because it is disrespectful or harmful to black people – ***they are listening to you.*** We must plant the right seeds in our children if we want to grow flower gardens instead of weeds.
9. **STUDY THE SYSTEM OF RACISM/WHITE SUPREMACY** so you will understand how it works. You cannot defeat racism if you do not understand how racism/white supremacy works.
10. STOP ASKING (BEGGING) for inclusion into a club (the White Supremacy system) that does NOT want you as a member. If you become a "token member," you become part of the problem, NOT the solution.
11. POOL OUR SKILLS, RESOURCES, MONEY, AND TALENT to benefit and enrich the black collective instead of making other communities stronger and richer with our dollars.
12. STOP TRUSTING SHOWCASE BLACKS simply because they are black. Being a black "first" does not mean they will work on our behalf. Pay MORE attention to what they DO (or don't do) and LESS on what they say.

The Power Of Universal Karma = The Universal Boomerang

The **Universal Boomerang** is the most powerful force in the world. It is GOD-FORCE. Karmic. Universal. What good we put out into the universe will be returned to us. If we are just and morally correct, what our enemies put out into the universe against us will be turned ***against*** them.

We Will Attract The Kind Of Justice We Deserve

We must not make the mistake of imitating those who abuse their power. Once the black collective regains our sanity and self-respect, only then should we seek unity with the non-black masses to fight for a more peaceful, and God-loving planet ruled by *Universal Man, Universal Woman, and the Law of Universal Justice.*

Each ONE, teach ONE
Do what YOU can, where you can
Become your own LEADER OF ONE
Pass this book along

EPILOGUE

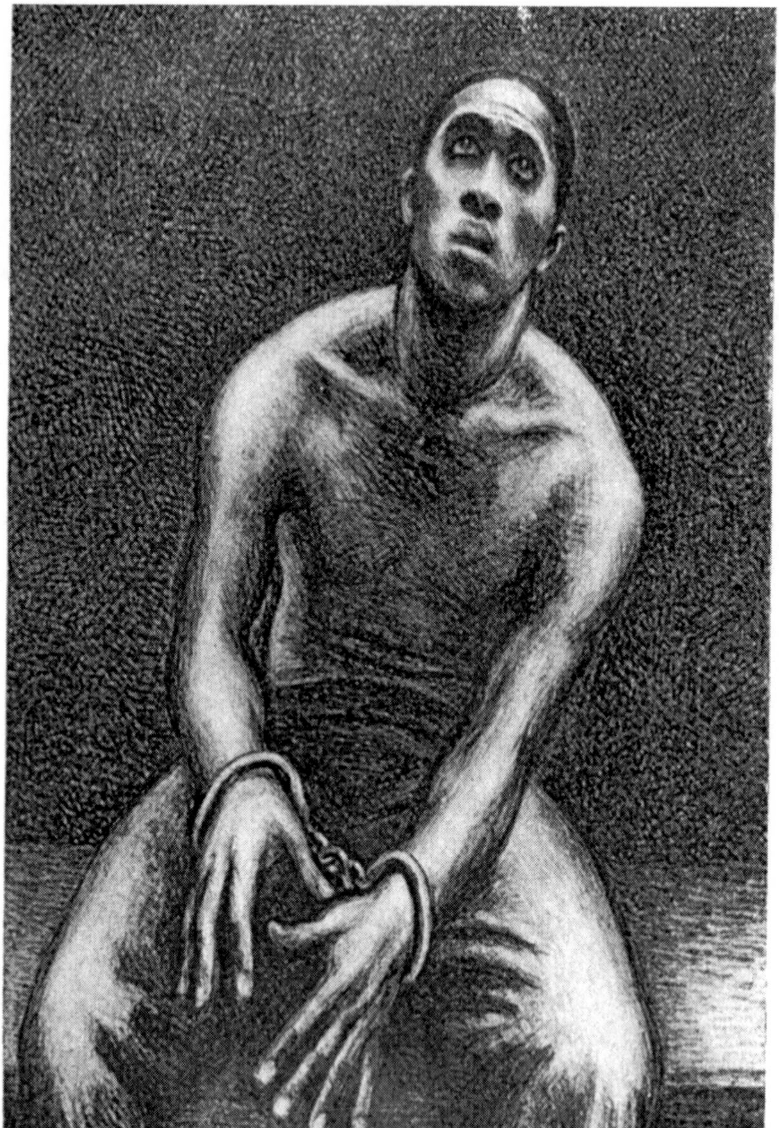

None are more hopelessly enslaved than those who falsely believe they are free. - Goethe

CHAPTER 49

MAN IN THE MIRROR: CONFESSIONS OF A RECOVERING WHITE SUPREMACY ADDICT

It was one in the morning. I had to be showered, dressed, and out the door in a few hours, but I couldn't sleep. By anyone's standards, I was living the American Dream. I had a great job with all the high-status perks: a corner office with the requisite window; a company-leased black BMW 760i; and a generous six-figure salary. All this belied the letter of resignation secreted in a pocket of my Italian leather briefcase.

After six years of working for one of the largest investment firms in New York City, I was cashing in my chips. By this time tomorrow, I would join the ranks of the undistinguished and the unemployed.

I walked into my gray and black bedroom of my high-rise condo and stripped down to my silk shorts. Standing in front of the full-length mirror, I stared into familiar eyes. My gaze traveled down the smooth black skin stretched taut over my lean six-foot frame, thanks to Tai Chi, racquetball, and a largely vegetarian diet. In my business of creating the illusion of wealth where none existed, appearances were everything.

My features were proportional, undeniably African, with full, defined lips, clear black eyes and a wide-bridged nose. It was a face I'd once thought was the absolute definition of ugliness. With the passing years, it was a face I'd grown comfortable with and had eventually learned to cherish.

My face was the undiluted face of history. The face of my ancestors who had survived the world's first global holocaust. Over 100 million Africans died in mid-passage. It was a mind-blowing number; impossible to digest. My ancestors had survived the worst that man could conceive and yet we were still *here*.

I stood a little straighter now, studying my somber reflection. A black woman I'd dated briefly once asked if I had ever hated being so dark. I admitted that I had. I didn't try to deny it. It was a natural reaction to growing up black in a black-hating culture.

Like thousands of black children, I was teased about my dark skin, nappy hair, and big lips; often by children as dark as I was. Even then, I instinctively sensed that something more sinister than childhood cruelty was taking place. In self-defense, I used the only weapon I had: my brain. By the time I entered high school I was certain of only two things: I was the smartest kid in my school, and the way I looked didn't matter once people discovered the first.

I let nothing get in the way of my studies – except my deep, passionate love for the vanilla-crème and high-yellow black girls that every black boy at my school wanted. It didn't matter if they were pretty or not — many times they weren't — but they had the kind of status my young, starving ego required to compensate for my dark-skin complex.

My academic performance, extra-circular activities, and a perfect SAT score won me a full scholarship to a prestigious Ivy League university. My senior year I spent two years of savings working weekends and summers, at the high-end clothing stores frequented by college-bound white boys of substantial means. Now that I was getting out of the ghetto, I was determined to fit in.

Most of the new friends I made in my dorm were the white boys who were at the top of their classes, too. My new Abercrombie & Fitch crewnecks, ripped jeans, and perfect diction attracted the attention of certain well-to-do white girls who were fascinated by the unlikely combination of dark skin and extreme intellect.

Since I could count on one finger the number of times I had gone all the way, I was pleasantly surprised by the ease at which these pretty girls from the best homes shed their clothing and their inhibitions. I was suddenly thrust into sexual heaven. The black girls I'd wanted in high school had been too worried about their reputations to let me fully satisfy my teenage lust. I didn't understand then, that the white co-eds who allowed me into their beds knew a poor black boy, who wasn't their racial or social equal, was in no position to judge them.

With my stellar academic record and a growing list of sexual conquests, I could do no wrong—at least in my small circle of white friends. Even the disdain of black students, especially the black co-eds who resented my "white-only" dating policy, failed to dim my rising star and expanding ego.

Midway through my sophomore year, I discovered the black students weren't the only ones who held me in low regard. That year I had my first black professor, Dr. Charles, who taught political science. Throughout the semester, I would catch Dr. Charles giving me distinctly disapproving looks. This annoyed me tremendously. I was the top student in the class but instead of praising me for being a credit to my race, Dr. Charles was giving me the evil eye. As far as I was concerned, the semester wouldn't end soon enough.

On the last day of class before Christmas break, Dr. Charles told me to wait until the others had left. I didn't know a tactful way to say being alone with him was the last thing I wanted so I did as he asked. After the last student filed out of the classroom, Dr. Charles locked the door. Anxiety moistened the underarms of my neatly pressed Polo shirt. I affected a look of nonchalance I didn't feel, throwing impatient glances at my watch to signal that the professor was keeping me from an urgently important destination.

Ignoring my theatrics, Dr Charles retrieved a package wrapped in plain brown paper from his desk drawer and handed it to me. In a somewhat ominous tone, he warned me not to open it until I was alone. I was confused and suspicious. Why was he giving me – his least favorite student -- a present? And why all the secrecy? Was it an exploding bomb?

I didn't ask and Dr. Charles didn't volunteer any additional information. As we shook hands and said our good-byes, Dr. Charles gave me a smile that was more like a grimace, and said, "Mr. Legend, those who fail to learn from the past are doomed to repeat it."

I dismissed the comment. It wasn't an original quote. All the strange encounter did was confirm what I had suspected all along: Dr. Charles was a real-life "Nutty Professor." Still, I did as I was told and waited for Scott, my white roommate, to leave for the airport before I tore off the brown wrapping. Inside I found two books, the covers worn and discolored.

I flipped through the first book, *Destruction of Black Civilization* by Chancellor Williams and put it to the side. I stretched out on my neatly made bed and began to read the second book, *Enemies: The Clash of Races* by Haki Madhubuti.

Around three that morning, only halfway through *"Enemies"*, I dozed off. I dreamed hard that night and awakened several hours later, irritable, and mentally exhausted. I felt like I'd just eaten a huge meal and was unable to digest it. After I showered and dressed, I took the book to the deserted dorm cafeteria and ate three bowls of cold cereal while I whipped through the pages.

Midway through, I started over at page one to be sure I hadn't missed a word. By the time I stepped off the plane in Chicago that evening, I had finished the entire book. As I closed the book, I spotted something scrawled in red ink on the last page:

If you got this far, you still have time to redeem your manhood.

There was a phone number written below the cryptic message. I later discovered that it was Dr. Charles' private number. I called him several times during the Christmas break. There were so many questions I wanted to ask that the book had only begun to answer. Like, why were black people in the terrible condition they were in America and in much of the world? Why did we look so different? How important were the physical differences, and were they proof that blacks were inferior to whites? Was it possible for blacks and whites to share this planet without one oppressing the other?

As I listened to the masterful prose of Dr. Charles flowing through the receiver, I felt like a drowning man in the stormy seas of self-doubt who had spotted land in the not so far distance. After our conversation ended, I immediately tackled the second book. I was certain my salvation lay between those well-worn covers and I was determined to discover it.

Each phone call was a reminder of how dangerously close I'd come to becoming another over-educated, self-hating black man. I'd seen them around the university, that certain breed of black men who affected a patronizing manner with other, less-educated blacks, but seemed to grovel before whites. These men, who I once looked up to as my role models, I now viewed with a mixture of curiosity and contempt. Did I really want to be the kind of black man who would do anything or be anybody other than the person in his mirror?

I made excuses to my family that I had to study for a test and returned to school the day after Christmas. I had to be alone to reflect on my newfound wisdom. But was I truly wiser, or had I fallen victim to the desperate ranting of desperate black men attempting to resurrect themselves by shifting all the blame to the white world? What if blacks were in this condition because we really were inferior?

According to Dr. Charles, the black man--the African man -- had once ruled the earth. I couldn't wait to see him after the Christmas break and view all the promised photos, documents, and books that Dr. Charles said were absolute proof that all human life and all civilization began in Africa, and that Africans – who he called "Moors" -- had been the world's first architects, astronomers, scientists, builders, doctors, and the designers of modern civilization thousands of years before Europeans crawled out of caves.

Dr. Charles told me not to take his word as gospel, but to seek out the historical treasures in every corner of the world that confirmed what he told me. He said, every man had an obligation to discover his own truth and back that truth with his own hard-earned knowledge. Once I saw the truth with my own eyes, no man on earth would ever be able to sell me the lie of black inferiority again.

I remembered all the despair and dysfunction I had witnessed growing up. The premature demise of so many brilliant young black men and women who never made it out of believing the lie into knowing the truth. It seemed obvious that once you convinced people that they were inferior, you had programmed them to fail. So many black youth with all the potential in the world, yet it hadn't mattered because they didn't believe they could overcome their circumstances. Now, it all made sense.

Centuries of systematic racism had created a self-perpetuating cycle of rage, inadequacy, and despair that was passed from generation to generation. The real question was how did one break that cycle permanently?

One evening, after studying for an exam, I retrieved a notepad and pen from my desk and wrote:

It is not a lack of intelligence; but a lack of belief in SELF.

I stared at the words for a long time before I broke. I was helpless against a flood of emotions. Alone, in my tiny dorm room where no one could see or hear me, I sobbed like my heart was breaking. I had been so ignorant, so vain, to think I was better than the people who hadn't been as lucky as I had been. Afterwards, I rolled over on my back and stared through swollen eyes at the beige popcorned ceiling. The pain in my gut was the implosion of all the stereotypes I'd learned about black and white people for the first 18 years of my life.

It occurred to me that I had seen little at my prestigious university that demonstrated any racial superiority on the part of blacks or whites. Most of the academic excellence I'd witnessed had clearly been a result of economic superiority, access, and exposure — not genetic or intellectual superiority. Even the so-called brainaics I associated with were so severely limited in other areas, it was impossible to see them as "superior" in anything but academics.

If a person had a certain talent or skill, did that make them superior to someone who didn't? Was a trained opera singer superior to everyone who couldn't carry a tune? If a race of people had controlled a nation's educational and financial resources for 400 years, wasn't it logical that they would be ahead of a race that had been denied the same opportunities during the same period of time?

It was so basic, even to my immature mind, that it was hard to understand how Dr. Shockley, and all the "Bell Curve" theorists who claimed blacks were intellectually inferior, weren't smart enough to distinguish nature from nurture. Obviously, they didn't want to understand the difference. My hand whipped across the page until every line was filled:

In order to prove one race is superior to another race, systems and institutions must be created to perpetuate the lie. In reality, the need to create such systems actually disproves any racial superiority. A superior race would not need to discriminate against any so-called inferior peoples. Without interference, nature would simply take its course.

What had happened – and was still happening – to black people were the same tactics Hitler used against the Jews in Germany. If Aryan people had been truly superior -- as Hitler had claimed -- he could have dominated the Jews and other non-Aryans without spilling a single drop of blood. Instead, to perpetuate his mad, desperate vision of a "superior race," Hitler built a war machine, concentration camps, and gas ovens so his lie would become "truth."

I paused, chewing on the rubber tip of my pen. What I observed in the white students, even the esteemed faculty, had been above average at best. I had rarely seen any instances of outright brilliance in the year and a half I had been on this campus.

In college, I met dozens of students; black and white, that excelled at academics but lacked common sense. In contrast, the most profound thinkers I'd ever known had lacked formal education but were well-read, and had street and common sense along with a deep intellect.

The most shocking discovery was the sheer number of students who used their affluence to buy term papers and the answers to midterm and final exams. Had I not run with that crowd, I would have never known how widespread cheating was on my college campus. I often wondered why the university administrators turned a blind eye to the obvious shenanigans that were common knowledge among the student population.

The fear that I would be thrust into the same category as the other supposedly inferior black students stopped me from following their example. I could pass my courses without cheating, and the irony is, so could my white friends had they made the effort. Most had come from the best school systems that money could buy. Even in my city, some of the white high schools resembled college campuses while the black schools were substandard, with outdated books and leaking roofs.

I came from one of the most poorly performing schools in my city, yet I consistently outperformed the other students—white and black--in my college classes. I refused to believe I was a fluke, a freak, or some abnormality in a vast sea of black inferiority. Had I not been so confident in my abilities, I would have succumbed to defeat like so many black freshmen who dropped out by their sophomore year.

Almost two decades later, I could still recall the many moments of private humiliation among my peers. I was often the only black in a classroom where most of the white students and professors made it abundantly clear they thought blacks lacked the intellectual equipment to attend an elite Ivy League university. Because I outperformed most of the people in my class, I was often viewed with shock, deep disappointment, and barely disguised outrage.

Despite my confident exterior, at times I felt more like a kinky-haired, big lipped, dark-skinned alien than a human being. Like the time my white chemistry lab partner asked if it was hard for people with big lips to eat – then proceeded to touch mine!

Rather than confront his ignorance, I had chosen the path of least resistance by pretending to ignore it. Then, it had been more important to be accepted than to examine my willingness to be disrespected.

I would never forget my first day in freshman calculus. After introducing himself, Professor Schmidt talked about students who enrolled in his class and couldn't perform the work. Without looking in my direction, he declared that the poor academic performances of students from inner city schools had nothing to do with a lack of money; it was due to poor parenting by too many single mothers.

I felt exposed; singled out. I was the product of a single parent home and an inner-city school. I stared down at my paper; too humiliated to meet the eyes of my white classmates who I was certain were focused in my direction.

Like most grade-school boys, I hated sitting still for long periods of time, and was easily bored. My first-grade teacher labeled my restlessness as a "learning disability" and said I would be better off in a "special education" class. Thank God, my fiercely determined mother refused.

That entire summer she made us turn off the TV and took us to the library while she studied for her nursing exam. My mother made a game out of reading the books we brought home. We'd take turns acting out the parts and she would be the audience, applauding and cheering as we took our bows. By the time school resumed that fall, I was hooked on books, and would read everything I could get my hands on, including the backs of cereal boxes.

My sweet mother worked two jobs then came home to cook and clean. I know she must have been exhausted when she dragged us to Sunday school because she wasn't *"raising no heathens."* She went without the things she wanted so my three siblings and I would have what we needed.

To hear this white man dismiss my mother's Herculean efforts to raise four children alone -- all of whom graduated from college -- in such a callous, cold-hearted manner brought furious tears to my eyes.

The same words that condemned my mother also condemned me. I wanted to ask this insensitive white man if money didn't matter when it came to a quality education, why did white people spend so much money on their own schools? But, I kept silent for fear of drawing more negative attention.

When Professor Schmidt turned back to the blackboard, I raised my head and locked eyes with the gray ones of the girl sitting to my right. The look she gave me was so kind, it was almost apologetic.

Rather than feel grateful, her gesture only deepened my shame. That was the moment when I swore that I would not only do my work; I would become the best student in that class. To the astonished chagrin of Mr. Schmidt, I kept that promise.

When that fateful Christmas break in my sophomore year ended, before my classes resumed, I spent the remaining afternoons and evenings talking to Dr. Charles. He lived alone in a small bungalow after his wife passed away three years ago. I sensed he was as lonely as I was desperate for knowledge. I learned more from my new mentor about the world and myself in five days, than I had after 14 years in the American education system.

I understood that my bigoted calculus professor was a simple-minded cog in the machinery of lies that masqueraded as American "history." I understood that lies and logic had become interchangeable. That in order to justify one lie, it was necessary to continually create new ones.

When the next semester resumed in January, I set out on a self-prescribed course of redemption. I distanced myself from my white friends and attended my first black student union meeting. I refused to be discouraged or intimidated by the chilly reception I received.

I volunteered for all the tasks no one else wanted to do and never once explained what had caused my change of heart. Eventually, the black students' distrust thawed into lukewarm acceptance, then sincere friendships; some of which I maintain to this day. Dr. Charles had been right. I still had time to redeem my manhood.

With the assistance of Professor Charles, who I now met for coffee on a regular basis, I applied to his old alma matter for my junior year. On the day I received my acceptance letter in the mail from Howard, a historically black college, I ran into Melissa, the pretty, blue-eyed daughter of a judge I had dated for a few months in my freshman year. As we passed within a few feet of each other, her eyes held the blank look of a stranger.

Instead of being angry, I burned with shame. It wasn't Melissa's snub that hurt; it was remembering the comment she'd made on our first date. "You're not like other blacks," she told me, as we sipped steamy cups of cappuccino in a quaint campus cafe. When I asked her what other blacks were like, she flashed a radiant smile that would have made her orthodontist proud, and said, *"You're not ignorant."*

I could tell Melissa thought she was paying me a compliment. What made me feel ashamed later, was that I hadn't called her on it. I had let the comment slide so I would be able to slide into her later that night.

As I stood there watching Melissa and her friends shrink in the distance, relief washed over me. She was right. I was a stranger. The person who had once viewed her whiteness as a prize was dead because I had killed him. And I had the blood on my hands to prove it.

In my junior year, I had changed my major from psychology to mathematics. Contrary to the theories of Sigmund Freud, I never met one black woman with penis envy or one black man who wanted to sleep with his mother.

I never read one word in all my half-dozen psychology textbooks that dealt with the psychological effects of racism on its victims, or how to cope with anything I had experienced on that elitist Ivy League campus. I didn't understand how I, in good conscience, could help others when I wasn't able to help myself.

Once I graduated and found a job on Wall Street, I spent my vacations traveling to Europe, Asia, Africa, and the Caribbean. I traveled alone so I wouldn't be pressured to waste time at the usual tourist spots. I was seeking answers in the ravaged faces of history that aren't shown in glossy travel brochures.

Now I understood how those who had profited from 400 years of African slave labor still owed the descendants of those slaves, and how 400 years of brutality and degradation was responsible for the condition of black people today.

Once an Addict; always an Addict

My story doesn't have a happy ending, nor does it end here. I am an addict in recovery; and like all addicts, I live one day at a time. The monkey is always sniffing at my door, radiating from a television set, emanating from my car radio, or perched on the movie theater seat next to mine. I see the monkey's face in every advertisement and media message that floods my conscious and subconscious mind.

I am still addicted to white supremacy, and suspect I always will be. No one completely kicks an addiction that took 35 years to develop. After that much time, the addiction is permanently implanted on the cerebral cortex.

I'm particular about the kind of entertainment I expose my mind to, so I seldom watch television. I know the moment I let my guard down, the monkey will bare its sharp, gleaming teeth in my direction. It's the same monkey that is running wild and creating devastation in my community.

I hear the monkey's screams in the ugly words black people use against each other and in the drug-crazed violence that plagues our communities. I hear its voice in the degrading music that is piped into our homes, cars, and brain cells. The monkey leers as we sit transfixed in front of the glowing television and movie screens, licking blood from its greedy lips as it consumes thousands of new souls in one sitting.

The monkey sits on our shoulders as it whispers in our ears that we came from nothing. That everything of value was created by anyone and everyone but us, to make us feel so inadequate we won't have the strength or the will to defend ourselves, let alone love each other.

I call it "SOUL MURDER"

There's an old African proverb that says it takes a village to raise a child. It also takes a village to keep black people sane and emotionally healthy in a sick, black-hating society. No one can do it alone, or on their own. I know because I tried – and failed. That's why I called on my sweet, departed mother's God to guide me through the most perilous journey of my life.

My soon-to-be-former employers have no idea that I'm about to testify against them. Before it's over, millions of Americans will lose their homes, because unscrupulous firms like mine sucked the financial lifeblood from the trusting, unsuspecting public.

A comment my managing director made years ago still haunts me to this day: *"The little people are like pigs feeding at the trough, too stupid and greedy to see the ax coming."* I remembered feeling offended at the time. It hadn't been that long ago, that I had been one of the "little people" he referred to with such casual contempt.

Still, I'm in no position to be self-righteous. I was no innocent bystander. I was part of the largest Ponzi scheme in world history, and I made an unconscionable amount of money helping the "big" people at the expense of the little people -- who my colleagues privately referred to as the "dumb money." Had the government not convinced me it was in my best interest to turn states' evidence against my employers, I doubt I would have ever come forward.

When the Feds first approached me, I was scared, then outraged. If I cooperated with them, I stood to lose everything I'd worked for: my income, high-status job, and privileged lifestyle. Now, looking back months later, I realize it was a blessing. It was more important to be able to look into the eyes of the man in my mirror without flinching, than it was to profit off the misery of others.

I stood at the window and stared out at the glittering view of the city. I could almost imagine the ghost of my mother in the window's reflection, standing behind me, and nodding in approval. It reminds me of something Dr. Charles -- the father I never had -- said shortly before he passed away four years ago:

> *"Son, always live your life like an open book, because you will pay for everything you get, and double for everything you took that did not belong to you."*

I am telling my story so others might see their own reflection in my tarnished mirror before it is too late. Hence, the genesis of the book you now hold in your hands. Call this an intervention from the black canary that almost choked to death in the depths of the coalmine. Better yet, think of this book as an opportunity to see the world through this black man's ***now authentically black eyes.***

Regards,
TL Legend
P.S. Pass this book along!

RESOURCES

RICHARDS & PRINGLE'S
FAMOUS
GEORGIA MINSTRELS
DOG CAKE
Russell-Morgan Print
6542
"IT'S A SHAME TO WASTE DAT ON A DOG."

The Four Stages of Niggerization

Stage 1: Niggerization

When the original (natural) cultural values of a group are replaced with a false belief system that degrades, dehumanizes, and programs that group to believe they are inferior to another group, the process of "niggerization" is taking place.

Stage 2: Self-Niggerization

When a group acts out of those false beliefs, and begins to degrade themselves, the process of "self-niggerization" is occurring. An example would be black male rappers referring to black females as "bitches and "hos," and black females supporting those black male rap "artists" by buying their music, singing their lyrics, and "affectionately" calling other black females "bitch" and "ho". This is proof that the process of "self-niggerization" for black males and black females has taken place.

Other example of "self-niggerization" are: (1) a "niggerized" black employee who snitches on other black coworkers to gain favor with whites, and (2) a "niggerized" black male or female who deliberately chooses white lovers over potential black lovers because he or she is convinced (on a conscious or subconscious level) that whites have (superior) qualities that blacks (like themselves) do not possess. Self-niggerization is common among all "niggerized" people, regardless of education, title, income, skin color, ethnicity, or social standing.

Stage 3: De-Niggerization

"De-niggerization" takes place when a "niggerized" person begins the process of neutralizing (rejecting) his or her inferiority programming by educating themselves about the white supremacy system. Warning: this is a slow and painful process. *Potential side effects:* anger, sadness, increased irritation, nausea (while viewing obvious racism/white supremacy in person, on TV, and in movies), shortness of breath (after screaming at the TV), and the inability to enjoy the same things and people they now know are false, deceptive, and/or degrading to non-white people.

Stage 4: Emancipation

Once the "de-niggerization" process is complete, the formerly "niggerized" person sees the world differently, through more authentic eyes. He or she understands that, politically speaking, they are still "niggers" in a white supremacy system, which means he or she is a victim of white supremacy. However, when referring to themselves, they fully embrace their own humanity because they know when God created the world, he didn't make "niggers" on the first, third, or seventh day; therefore, "niggers" are not born, "niggers" are always created by a system of injustice.

13 Axioms of Racism/White Supremacy

1. You cannot oppose something and knowingly benefit from it at the same time. (pg 11)
2. Black Supremacy can exist only in the total absence of White Supremacy. White Supremacy can exist only in the total absence of Black Supremacy. The textbook definition of "supremacy" is: *the highest rank or authority.* This means only one thing can be "supreme" or occupy the "highest rank" at a time. (pg 12)
3. In a system of White Supremacy, skin color always triumphs over cash (green supremacy). (pg 17)
4. In a system of White Supremacy, it is natural for black people collectively to fear and resent white people collectively. (pg 34)
5. It is impossible to love yourself when you are mistreating others. (pg 43)
6. The "Black Victim = A Victimless Crime" Theory. A black person in a conflict with a white person (or white system) cannot BE the victim in a White Supremacy society. The black individual is ALWAYS at fault, regardless of who initiated the conflict or what facts or evidence are present. (pp 82,229,245)
7. Any group (or race) whose collective actions penalizes their own group (and rewards another group) is self-genocidal and self-destructive. (pg 136)
8. Black normalcy cannot exist in a system of White Supremacy. (pg 137)
9. A non-white person cannot be equal to OR the same as a white person in a White Supremacy system. (pg 140)
10. A black eyewitness in a white supremacy system cannot be credible if his or her testimony contradicts the official (or desired) version of events. (pg 240)
11. It is psychological suicide to kiss the same hand that slaps you down, and psychological insanity to be grateful to someone for putting you in a position where you need their help. (pg 254)
12. The Universal Boomerang: what we put out into the universe – for good or for evil – is what we will get in return. (pg 296)
13. Never envy anyone who has the wealth of the world at their feet and is still discontent. They do not understand what is happening. Use their ignorance as a lesson. (pg 296)

Recommended Reading

BOOKS

Black Love Is A Revolutionary Act by Umoja

Enemies: The Clash of Races by Haki R. Madhubuti

The Isis Papers by Dr. Frances Cress Welsing

The United-Independent Compensatory Code/System/Concept A textbook/workbook for victims of racism (white supremacy) by Neely Fuller, Jr.

The Destruction of Black Civilization by Chancellor Williams

How Capitalism Underdeveloped Black America by Manning Marable

The Conspiracy to Destroy Black Boys by Jawanza Kunjufu

What They Never Told you in History Class by Indus Khamit-Kush

Africans at the Crossroads: African World Revolution by John Henrik Clarke

The Spook who sat by the Door by Sam Greenlee (a novel)

The Golden Age of the Moor by Ivan Van Sertima

Your History J.A. Rogers by J.A. Rogers

The Secret Books of Egyptian Gnostics by Jean Doresse

Message to the Blackman in America by Elijah Muhhamad

Return to Glory: The Powerful Stirring of the Black Race by Joel A. Freeman, PhD, and Don B. Griffin

Black Man of the Nile and His Family by Yosef Ben-Jochannan

No Disrespect by Sister Souljah

Books can be purchased from:

- www.trojanhorse1.com
- www.azizibooks.com
- www.thirdworldpress.com
- www.counter-racism.com
- www.houseofnubian.com
- www.freemaninstitute.com
- www.africanwithin.com

AUDIO CDS

Racism & Counter Racism by Dr. Frances Cress Welsing

Maximum Development of Black Male Children by Dr. Frances C. Welsing

The Psychopathic Racial Personality by Dr. Bobby E. Wright, PhD

(above available at: www.houseofnubian.com)

No Sex Between White and Non-White People by Neely Fuller, Jr.
Racism and Counter Racism by Neely Fuller, Jr.

Racism and Counter Racism by Neely Fuller, Jr.

(available: www.counter-racism.com)

Return to Glory: The Powerful Stirring of the Black Race
by Joel A. Freeman, PhD, and Don B. Griffin

(available at www.freemaninstitute.com)

DVDS

Dr. Frances Cress Welsing on Phil Donahue Show

Dr. Frances Cress Welsing Debates Dr. William Shockley & The Analysis of The Bell Curve

The Isis Papers by Dr. Frances Cress Welsing

Racism and Mental Health by Dr. Frances Cress Welsing

Worship of the African Woman as Creator by Dr. Yosef Ben Jochannan

(above DVDs available at: www.houseofnubian.com)

A White Man's Journey Into Black History
by Joel A. Freeman, PhD

(available at www.freemaninstitute.com)

Index

Lightning Source UK Ltd.
Milton Keynes UK
UKOW04f1106261015

261404UK00001B/265/P

9 780982 206102